Best of Rebelle Society, Volume I
Celebrating the Art of Being Alive

Curated by
Andréa Balt & Tanya Lee Markul

Edited by
Andréa Balt, Tanya Lee Markul, Christian Ryd Hoegsberg & Soumyajeet Chattaraj

Cover design by
Andréa Balt & Tanya Lee Markul

This is a production of RebelleSociety.com.

"Rebelle Society is the scene of a major car accident of writers, caused when 'creative peculiarity' went careening off into the lane of 'erudition.' But seriously, its cast of characters are trending social media to good things. They are an impassioned co-op of literary farmers out harvesting the global corpus of creativity; showing us that the best and most creative solutions for the seeker-of-inspiration can be found in the composing-masses-of-inspirers.

Rebelle proves there can be no last beautiful idea...because just when you think you've read (or written) the pièce de résistance in one of its many rich literary parlors, something amazing lights up your screen. It truly is a book written by its readers; one in which the content of each page is inspired by that of another.

For me, it's where bees go to get their bumble; where verdant goes to get green; and where pirates bury their imagined bounty. Indeed, if writers were fruits and vegetables, Rebelle Society would be the consummate literary juice press. Deeeeee-ah—licious!"

~ Skip Maselli | Writer, Rebelle Columnist

A Love Letter from the Editors.

Dear Creator,

Thank you for being a part of this compilation in any way, creative shape or form.

A tad over a year ago, we embarked on one of the most risk-taking, life-changing and rewarding adventures of our lives: creating an online platform where writers, troublemakers, creativists, artists, dreamers, healers and all kinds of Renaissance people could come together to share their passion and wisdom with the world through daily articles focusing on every aspect of the human experience – with creativity as our modus operandi and life as our greatest work of art.

Over the course of this extraordinary journey, we have witnessed an unprecedented creative power work miracles in our own lives and in those who've shared this journey with us; our missions have magically aligned, intertwined and expanded; our international community has grown beyond our wildest expectations and our little virtual country has been occupied by the highest expression of all: the Art of Being Alive.

Upon multiple requests from those touched by our authors' words around the world, we have put together this golden first volume with a delicately selected and plucked compilation of the articles that we've had the exquisite pleasure and honor to publish on RebelleSociety.com during our first year of life.

Although the selection process was difficult due to the caliber of creative mojo we've attracted to Rebelle Society, we hand-picked pieces that we felt were truly authentic, healing and creative – narrations of a hero's journey that either brought us to our knees, threw us off our chairs or made us clap out loud, and inspired us to re-create ourselves from the inside out.

This collection in many ways, took our breath away, made us feel whole, real and it gave us permission to be, as we are, a living work of art.

This collection has truly inspired a lot of us to rekindle a creative and proactive relationship with our beating hearts and to share our innermost expression with the world or, to say the least, to soften the barricade around our imagination.

We dedicate this volume to all rebels with a cause – that of connecting all of our human bits and pieces together into a more mindful, freeing, creative, inclusive, life-giving collage.

We hope it inspires you to look beyond the surface, reactivate your imagination, share your story, and to celebrate and practice the Art of Being Alive.

Creativity is our pencil. Beauty is the ink. We are innate designers of reality. Rebelling against a divided, unquestionable status quo with the power of our voice is our first step into wholeness.

Rebelle with us!

Yours in Creative Rebellion,

Andréa Balt / Tanya Lee Markul
Co-Founders / Editors in Chief

Christian Ryd Hoegsberg
Rebelle CFO / Business Manager

In Deep Gratitude, We Bow.

To our passionate, spirited, hopeful and relentlessly believing team of Les Rebelles: Your open minds, talented hands and creative hearts have brought a strong pulse not only to Rebelle Society but to all our contributing artists, writers and creativists. You have been an honest reflection and a constant map toward the light. We love you.

Soumyajeet Chattaraj – Lead Editor and Volunteer Coordinator
Tracy Wisneski – Managing Editor
Kristi Stout – In-House Designer & Social Media Editor
Shanna Shaffer – Head of Creative Recruiting
Tabatha Kirke – Editor
Chantelle Theroux – Editor

To our growing, extended and beloved family of Rebelle Society Supporters. Thank you for believing in our mission and participating in the creative rebellion. We heart and appreciate your constant care and support.

To the spirited, talented and brave writers included in this collection: Never doubt your call. Never give up on your dream. You are worth every bit of it.

And to all the Rebelle Society authors all over the world, who took the first creative step and shared their stories and passion with us. We art you, always.

"The saving of our world from pending doom will come, not through the complacent adjustment of the conforming majority, but through the creative maladjustment of a nonconforming minority."

~ Martin Luther King Jr.

Table of Contents

Rebelle Society's Creative Manifesto.

By Les Rebelles

"The world without spirit is a wasteland. People have the notion of saving the world by shifting things around, changing the rules, and who's on top, and so forth. No, no! Any world is a valid world if it's alive. The thing to do is to bring life to it, and the only way to do that is to find in your own case where the life is and become alive yourself."

~ Joseph Campbell

1. We are editors of life.

We cut and paste its daily beauty and pain with the sharp scissors of our minds on the canvas of humanity.

As human beings we can only assimilate the world through selective perception. The more we train our perception, the more aware we become of the world around us, in its light and darkness. We turn into what we digest on a daily basis. Due to our spongy nature, we must absorb carefully.

2. We regard Art as a dynamic matter of Now.

Art is not just a museum affair. Objects are less than people and no work of art is ever finished. We are our own living collage of images, memories, experiences, relationships, thoughts and feelings.

As such, we must constantly make Art that is synonymous with Life, in order for it (for us) to keep on being art. By existing to our fullest potential we become our own greatest works of art. Whatever comes out of us is secondary to what's already in us.

3. Life is short and it is running through our fingers.

Our hour won't come in some kind of imagined, distant or near future, our hour is happening this very moment. Wherever we are – or are at, we'd like to make it count.

Be here now. And now. And now. And now. And now…

4. The only censorship we apply to ourselves is the kind that will censor other people's genuine right to be whole.

Love the way you want to be loved and recognize a piece of you in every piece of life. There are no strangers in this room. It's just a bunch of Us. There are no tribes or constellations. Only lonely stars with a light of their own.

5. Life is homemade, painful, intelligent and beautiful. We avoid nothing, we want it all.

As creators, healers and journalists it is our duty to curate reality and communicate it in our own, unique words. We don't want the shortcut, we want to walk on water and walk on burning ashes.

Give us the whole package, even if it takes longer and it demands more. If we're going to jump anyway off of life's inevitable cliffs, we might as well pick the highest one and use our own heart as the only parachute.

6. We long and steer toward the light but we don't hide or get rid of the darkness.

It's only by accepting, integrating and finally reusing every bit of ourselves that we are able to meet and face life for what it is, in all its brightness and all the shadows it casts.

Fear is biodegradable fuel. We will never get rid of it, but we can recycle it into a more human-friendly version.

7. There is no time for apathy or mindless distraction.

We are natural, organic, living tissue. We are the skin of a broken world and as living metaphors, we must reflect it in both its greatness and its desperation.

There's so much good to do, much to be mended and healed. One lifetime isn't enough and less than our everything is too little.

8. We regard the human experience as an indivisible whole that includes all aspects of the human experience: physical, intellectual, relational, emotional and spiritual.

We also recognize both, beauty and pain, as the two common threads running through all of our life scripts. For most of history, our different human elements have been divided, segregated, hidden, punished, misunderstood and ultimately, separated from the whole.

We want brains and beauty to make peace with each other, we want heart and mind to be friends, we want body and spirit to be a home to each other. All our parts are created equal.

9. Our virtuality is just the tip of our iceberg of humanity. We are so much more than our words and the speed of our fingers.

The internet is, perhaps, the only truly democratic medium left, which allows us to reach freely across countries and oceans, intolerance and preconceptions and dive straight into each other's hearts.

Thanks to our online connection, we're now reuniting with each other and, in a strange way, with ourselves. We're just one click away, so close we almost hear each other breathing.

Beyond this screen we're also flesh and bones, with broken hearts and sweaty hands. We must never mistake our frames for the whole picture, but use this virtual frame to better understand our real pictures: the real, complex, breathing You and Me and Everyone we know.

10. Hey Frodo, it's a lonely battle, and we need help taking the ring to Mordor.

In this lifehouse, we collaborate, we share and e-hug daily. We can't do this (or anything) alone. We need each other badly.

The only possible form of existence is co-existence. Beyond our own, unscripted individual stories, we're part of a bigger, universal story, to which we add every day with our thoughts and actions. We are responsible for the course of events and desperate status of our world.

When it comes to technology and communication, we're at a place of synergy and synchronicity like never before. It is imperative that we make a mindful, heartfelt use of it. *Please hold my pixel hand, I promise you, the skin is there, even if you can't touch it.*

11. We know enough, we have enough, we are enough and we care enough to make it wonderful.

Now.

A Self-Made 12-Step Program for Living an Authentic Life.

By Tanya Lee Markul

Let us commence with a few wise words from Mr. Timothy Leary:

> *"Admit it. You aren't like them. You're not even close. You may occasionally dress yourself up as one of them, watch the same mindless television shows as they do, maybe even eat the same fast food sometimes. But it seems that the more you try to fit in, the more you feel like an outsider, watching the "normal people" as they go about their automatic existences. For every time you say club passwords like "Have a nice day" and "Weather's awful today, eh?" you yearn inside to say forbidden things like "Tell me something that makes you cry" or "What do you think deja vu is for?" Face it, you even want to talk to that girl in the elevator. But what if that girl in the elevator (and the balding man who walks past your cubicle at work) are thinking the same thing? Who knows what you might learn from taking a chance on conversation with a stranger? Everyone carries a piece of the puzzle. Nobody comes into your life by mere coincidence. Trust your instincts. Do the unexpected. Find the others..."*

Scary beginnings, sad endings and all the meaningful stuff in between.

I'm thinking about getting out. I'm antsy and have itchy feet. I'm gonna do it. But it takes time, right? I mean, I can't just up and go, change or do or can I? Can you? May I?

For me it's not really about getting away or going on some worldly exploration, at least not right now. I just want to go deeper into the experience of an authentic life right now in these shoes or better yet in bare feet.

So, what's the formula and how I do I put this secret into practice?

I'm up for anything. A new dance step, a more confident voice. I'll even brush my teeth with my less dominant hand while sending sentiments of love to all the lefties of the world. I'm ready to detoxify, love-ify, sanctify, practice, apply and fulfill with a conscientious and diligent attitude of the padawan's ageless steps for living an authentic life.

Are you with me?

(A few more ponders, question marks and little corporate digs: How do we get real, step out of the matrix, the simulation, the computer programming? How do we escape The Truman Show? How can I be sure my values are my own? How do we leave our mundane routines yet still survive? How do we stop Dow, Exxon Mobil, Wal-Mart or The Coca-Cola Company from dictating our lives? By the way, do people still believe that Hershey's is actually chocolate?)

I recognize the loop – I've just been going round and round and round. I'm sure you've heard someone else's broken record declaration of he said this, she said that, that's the reason why I'm doing this or why I can't do that, but I've realized that the real question is: can you hear your own broken-record-speech?

How do I turn it off? It's hurting my ears!

Once I heard my own quadrupled platinum recorded compilation of what ifs, buts, ands, and incessant blame that frighteningly keeps on playing even without batteries or electricity, I found that all signs lead back to one place. Yes, it all circles back just like a boomerang to Me.

I've also recognized that this self-depleting album comes with a range of multiple-choice reactions: A) Secret denial B) Find it repulsive and resort to self-deprecating behavior in order to bury it and not admit to it and C) Don't know what to do about it so procrastinate and do nothing... then enters: mind-numbing self-medication.

Who's in charge of the life preservers?

The good news is, there's actually an option D) but you have to really, really want it. It is: Figure It Out.

R.I.P. Old Self. You Served a Great Purpose.

As much as I love original recipes, formulas and programs, I often find that along the way, and after much experimentation, failures, tantrums and tears, I have to write my own. I feel that in a way, all of these books, teachers, scholars, gurus and Universal Principles want us to do just that. Through their own sharing of wisdom, experience, and love, they want you to discover your own... dance with me? So, here are mine in random order and by chance, I hit the number 12.

Step 1 – Do You.

Have no apologies for who you are. If you fit in, great. Perhaps you found your tribe. If you don't fit in, don't beat yourself up about it. If you feel like the people around you aren't speaking your language, perhaps it's time to explore new flocks. Be brave and true to who you are. Wearing unnecessary masks just to fit in or avoid facing the reality of you can make life feel hopeless and imprisoning! Even in a crowd of faces, it's easy to feel lonely if we aren't being ourselves and if the people around us don't appreciate who we are.

Take back your right to be you in front of everyone and in every situation. When you are yourself, you not only invite others to do the same, but you become a bright watchtower for the people you'd wish would find you.

"The clearest way into the Universe is through a forest wilderness."

~ John Muir

Step 2 – Let Wildness In.

Stepping into the wilderness does wonders to the vibrational energy of our bodies and our nervous systems. There's a subtle reassurance that everything you need to know, you already contain and everything you don't know may eventually be revealed in time without struggle and without desperation.

The wilderness strips us of competition and comparison and invites us into a state of peaceful awe. It also offers a reflection of our individual relationship with life versus being just a mere part of the human race. Who

14

are you without people? You may just find this answer in the wild. It's powerful medicine.

> *"When you get the blanket thing you can relax because everything you could ever want or be you already have and are."*
>
> ~ Bernard Jaffe, I Heart Huckabees

Step 3 – Hear the Voices.

Open up to your life's purpose and your heart's deepest desires by listening to the voices inside of you. There's a lot of dialogue going on some incessant, some nonsensical but if we learn to listen more sincerely, we'll discover that a deeper, all-knowing conversation is happening. It takes practice to hear this guidance as it takes practice to hear your heart's desire, to trust your gut and to listen to your intuition.

Pay attention to the whisper and the serendipitous moments that remind you of what's important to you. Keep listening and keep following the signs. You have the ability to live a life that's true to who you are and a life that you really want.

Listen like your life depends on it.

> *"Creativity comes from trust. Trust your instincts."*
>
> ~ Rita Mae Brown

Step 4 – Take the damn risk already.

Make choices that put yourself first above everything and everyone else, even those you love and cherish the most. If you don't take care of yourself, if you don't do what is best for you, your relationships will eventually suffer. Trust in the fact that doing what is best for you is best for everyone even if it doesn't feel like it at first. Sometimes sacrifices have to made. People will get hurt and there will be losses, but the rewards gained from following your heart are absolutely everything in comparison.

Do something difficult for no other reason than that you like to do it.

Step 5 – Believe.

The secret formula: Believe in yourself and people will believe in you. Don't give up due to predefined perceptions and limitations of yourself. Don't give up because of the perceived effort. Millions of people give up before they even get started. They fail to realize their potential and give up as soon as they reach the first hurdle. Why? They don't believe in themselves.

If you don't believe in yourself you will end up throwing away your creativity and ideas. On the other hand, if you believe in yourself, you will no matter the outcome, find success even in what you perceive as the greatest of losses.

> *"And the day came when the risk to remain tight in a bud was more painful than the risk it took to blossom."*
>
> *~ Anais Nin*

Step 6 – Use your body and love who and what you are.

It's never been about the symmetry of your face or your body. It's about the light that shines from within.

Have you ever witnessed a person that has been in a tragic, body deforming accident who has come out stronger, more compassionate and yes, even more beautiful? Their light shines so bright that after just a few minutes, you don't see their asymmetry anymore, you simply feel and connect with their light.

If you see yourself as mere looks, if you believe your worth is merely skin deep, others will see you and judge you the same. Aren't you more than that? Remember, no matter what you do, your looks will eventually fade. What will remain is the fire that burns within. Stop smothering it with delusional judgments and superficial shape chasing. Stop holding yourself back from life because you don't believe you look good enough.

Self-love exercise: go look in the mirror and tell yourself: You never ever were more beautiful than you are right now. Believe it.

Use your body in every way that you know how. Allow the intelligence of your vessel to reveal and share with you the secrets of the Universe the secrets of You.

Step 7 – Defy your genetics.

Evolve from the base point you've been born into. Don't allow the limitations of your parents or their parents deter you from your path. See it all as potential to evolve your bloodline, your genetic makeup, your life to a place where neither you, nor your ancestors, have ever gone before. You hold the torch.

If you are the black sheep of the family, be grateful. The path can be lonely, but know that you broke free. Celebrate this freedom.

You are the architect of your existence.

Step 8 – Integrate into wholeness.

Accept all parts of your life. All parts. This is one of the deepest healing elixirs you can ever offer yourself. Allow it all to integrate your mind with body, your body with spirit and your entire being with all of the experiences of your life. Accept your irrevocable wholeness. When you accept what has been, what you thought was and what is, you loosen your grip on delusions, limitations and stale beliefs that hold you back. What's left? Space. Space and room to expand into the shape you are naturally, wholly and fully with a deeper sense of truth, wisdom and compassion.

Step 9 – Paint a spectrum of love for all.

Serve and be accepting of others of what they want to create, what they want to be and what they envision. Remind them to do everything it takes not to fail. Remind them that the bad that comes along with the good is the journey and the most beautiful, most fulfilling experience anyone could ever have. Offer and support a new way of living, thinking, creating, even working listen and be open to the ways of others.

Have conversations that make you smile and ponder. Offer solutions that bring us closer together versus farther apart.

Step 10 – Take the time to do nothing.

Clear the slate. Erase the chalkboard. Wash it all clean. Don't do anything. Just let everything be as it is. No matter how it is, no matter what your mind is screaming or what confusion you have in your life, for a few moments or as long as you can each day, let it be. Doing nothing and sitting still, helps us recognize all the ways in which we don't let go. Explore the profound, beautiful simplicity and subtlety of doing nothing... and all the challenges it endures.

In the simplest instruction from Andrew Cohen: take a seat, be still and don't do anything. In the words of The Beatles: Let it be.

Step 11 – Seek connection versus perfection.

Living an authentic life stems from your ability to be self-aware and genuine in the ways in which you express, react, dance, share, create, listen, etc. in other words, how you connect with yourself and the world around you. Authenticity also heightens from your ability to be aware of when you are being and/or reacting non-authentically. Being authentic develops a connection with who you truly are, your real essence, and liberates you from the superficial pressures and expectations of always trying to be perfect.

Step 12 – Recognize that you already have everything you need to be you.

Clear away the small minded and limiting ideas of who you are that keep you bound and feeling small, hopeless, even unworthy. You already have everything, *everything* you need to be you. In the present moment, you have very clear goals. There is much to be done as you are right now.

Discover the clearing, discover the openness and the deepest part of your own Universe. Tap into your unlimited energy and passion to follow-through.

Living a life of authenticity is a path of personal evolution – and as with any journey, it's up to you.

Thank you and I love you.

7 Myths About Creativity.

By Andréa Balt.

> *"The truly creative mind in any field is no more than this: A human creature born abnormally, inhumanely sensitive. To them... a touch is a blow, a sound is a noise, a misfortune is a tragedy, a joy is an ecstasy, a friend is a lover, a lover is a god, and failure is death. Add to this cruelly delicate organism the overpowering necessity to create, create, create – so that without the creating of music or poetry or books or buildings or something of meaning, their very breath is cut off... They must create, must pour out creation. By some strange, unknown, inward urgency they are not really alive unless they are creating."*
>
> *~ Pearl Buck*

For a while now, I've been trying to exercise my creative muscle daily in order to learn to approach creativity in its purest essence – as a lifetime practice, modus operandi and a way of life, and as such, not only a quality reserved for those "born abnormally, inhumanely sensitive" (though that's been quite a journey), but an intrinsic power and essential right of all people – and other living creatures.

Through this renewed creative awareness, one of the aspects that struck me the most is how hard it is on most days to consciously practice the art of being alive.

Anyone can get inspired when the muse is in the house. But the bitch doesn't show up every day – ask any serious creator, she's capricious and unreliable. Most days are unedited, raw, moody, and they have messy hair, puffy eyes and almost no time to do the dishes, let alone do them "creatively."

On those days, I would rather learn Esperanto, pick a fight with any inanimate object that hurts my toe, memorize all prime numbers, clean my house (and the neighbors') – anything but have to open my tired eyes to the vibrant wonder all around me.

How do animals look at flowers, or at the rest of nature? – I wonder. How do they enjoy life?

Without a purpose, beauty for beauty's sake. They drink it in, absorb the joy like a sponge and once it's in their system, they can't help but spread it everywhere they meow or bark.

Whenever I try to imitate them, I become suddenly (and dangerously) aware that there is so much beauty around me, it could kill me: things and people and plants and sky and wind and rocks and sun and animals and even objects and buildings and the breath of life aligned with this or that... Everything is illuminated.

Beauty has this way of hurting. A human chest can't hold it in. Where was it all hiding all these years? Where was I?

With an increase in beauty comes an increase in possibilities. When you expand, all life expands.

You'd think it's innate – this ability to transcend the mundane and discover a second, more magnificent world within the one you've been taught to argue with. And it is true you come to Earth with superpowers, but you lose them as your mind painfully conquers your heart, over time.

As you grow older, you change your name to Clark Kent and you truly believe you work at the Daily Planet, and maybe it's a good job and a decent life. But damnit, you look so alive in tights and cape.

So why should we turn creativity into a habit, a modus operandi, a daily practice?

Why can't we just get visited from time to time by inspiration, by the muse, the genie, our higher unicorn selves vomiting rainbows in the pretty sky? Why won't you just leave me (the fuck) alone?

Because... (let me get a sip of water).

The status quo consists precisely in believing that there is one – that's the big lie, the trick – that there is a given reality, an unmovable existing order of things and beliefs about life, and that's that, and you're free to argue, free to preach, free to pledge allegiance or not, free to raise your fist and call yourself a revolutionary – yet deep down, you're not free to question, deconstruct and dismantle the very perception that makes you adopt the status quo as friend or enemy in the first place.

So I disagree with death. I disagree with everything that hinders you and me from being the gods we deep down know we are. I reject any notion that rejects abundant life. Not true. Who said it and why should we believe it?

Life is rooted in habit. Even your aloneness, your mediocrity, your shit-holes, your lack of inspiration, everything you consider "normal" is, at its root, a habit. Your dear life is nothing but a series of repetitive actions. You are a process, not a unit or a thing, but a compilation of hundreds of processes taking place right here and now. You are happening now, and now, and now... and until you leave this form of life. So whatever your repetitive thoughts are, they direct the course of your life.

Since all palpable reality is an extension of an impalpable yet powerful thought, the habits that rule our entire existence begin to develop in the subconscious headquarters of our mind.

Here is where it gets complicated. It is estimated that we have around 60,000 thoughts a day. Approximately 95% of our thoughts are the same as the day before and 85% of these thoughts are negative. Good morning, Doomsday, I didn't know you lived inside my chest.

Negativity doesn't have to be about mood. In fact, the most destructive negativity is the type that pollutes the root of your deepest thoughts. A stagnant idea about life will suck your creativity dry and get you stuck in ways you won't even be aware of – other than the fact that something is missing and that nothing (or no one) ever feels quite right.

You can put on any smileys you want. But if you're dried up inside, your life will bear no fruit.

So here are seven myths and truths about Creativity, to support your middle finger to the Lying Bastard Status Quo in the face of all the people, circumstances, limiting beliefs – that keep you from turning it into your official life extension, heart plug-in, mind companion and official superpower.

1. It's not reserved to certain people or not even specifically human – but one of nature's original forces, present in every living organism.

Look around you. Life will survive no matter what. If that's not creativity, I don't know what is. Our whole structure – as an ecosystem as well as our most basic individual level – operates by this principle. Our body finds a way as long as it can, and so does our mind.

Where there's a will, there is life. And where there is life, there is Creativity.

2. It isn't inspiration or a state of mind.

It's a muscle. Like any other habit, Creativity also grows with practice. Think of it like the invisible half of your heart. It can shrink or expand, get stronger or weaker. All life is muscle.

> *"This is the other secret that real artists know and wannabe writers don't. When we sit down each day and do our work, power concentrates around us. The Muse takes note of our dedication. She approves. We have earned favor in her sight. When we sit down and work, we become like a magnetized rod that attracts iron filings. Ideas come. Insights accrete."*
>
> *~ Steven Pressfield (The War of Art)*

3. It has nothing to do with talent or ability.

Some people are incredibly talented. Others haven't had a chance to develop half of all their latent talents. Some may not even know what they're capable of, until they're faced with it. There are over 6 billions of us. Nature understands and thrives on variety. Forget about what you have, what you don't, what you could have or who has more or less than you. The only thing that matters now is what you do with what you know. That's where creativity comes in.

I have a bucket filled with yellow paint (and snakes) ready to throw at people when they say: "Oh, but I'm not creative." It's like rejecting air because you think you haven't been "blessed" with the ability to breathe. You don't need this blessing because it's already installed in your hard-drive. You just didn't know it. Nobody told you and you didn't ask. And living creatively is ultimately just a matter of what version of this story you choose to believe.

4. It doesn't have a time or a place. You give it that time and place.

Does your blood only flow on Tuesdays or past 5 p.m.? Do you only breathe at night? Well, if creativity is a modus operandi – a way vs. a thing – it is always present within you and it permeates through everything you think and do.

It's not an event. You are the event. Let's get our grammar straight. You are the subject in your life, before you become its object. You are the director of your movie, before you become the actor.

This is not to say you don't need specific times set aside for creative work. But beyond that, your very breath is an act of creativity (and rebellion). You can always reach for it, grab it, use it, it's yours for the taking and it never ends.

5. It isn't Art. We are Art. You and me and a cup of herbal tea.

All other works of art you can make or admire are secondary. Art is a result – an expression, manifestation and interpretation of life – from its highest, most magnificent form (You) to its lowest, most inanimate state: your objects.

Creativity, on the other hand, is what fuels all Art (make that Life). It is a verb, not a noun, and a basic human need, which automatically turns it into an essential human right. Hey, UN, did you forget something in your Declaration?

6. It isn't comfortable. It will ruin your one small and cozy life.

Think of it as traveling to a country you've only dreamed of. At first, you won't feel at home – not until you become fluent in the language you were born speaking but forgot along the way. It will make you shed old skin, expose your nakedness, shiver in the cold like an embarrassed reptilian until you grow new, thicker skin.

Creativity will force you to do the work and get your hands dirty. There's no way out but through the fire.

7. It isn't stagnant. It will change your perspective, open your eyes, renew, re-create and restore you.

Life is constant change. When lived to its fullest – that is, creatively, you will stop resisting change and start embracing it, because every day is a new day, and every song is still being written and you're not set in stone.

Creativity will turn you into a river. And you'll be filled with fish and creatures. And people will have picnics right by you and some will swim in you and others drink out of you. And that's the meaning of life.

And you will take off your shoes in awe, because when regaining your Creative sensitivity, every ground you step on is holy ground.

> *"'You,' he said, 'are a terribly real thing in a terribly false world, and that, I believe, is why you are in so much pain.'"*
>
> *~ Emily Autumn*

And so are you, I said.

So let's take that pain (and sister beauty) and turn them into art, that is, into our messy everyday extraordinary Life. Let's reclaim Creativity as our innate superpower, our royal right by birth, and add it to both, our dreaming and our doing. Let's just experiment with truth and see what happens.

For Zeus' sake, aren't you hungry?

To get it started, I wrote William Hutchison Murray's famous reminder, with lipstick on the mirror. It looks good on any face:

"Until one is committed, there is hesitancy, the chance to draw back, always ineffectiveness. Concerning all acts of initiative (and creation), there is one elementary truth the ignorance of which kills countless ideas and splendid plans: that the moment one definitely commits oneself, then providence moves too.

A whole stream of events issues from the decision, raising in one's favor all manner of unforeseen incidents, meetings and material assistance, which no man could have dreamt would have come his way.

I learned a deep respect for one of Goethe's couplets:

'Whatever you can do or dream you can, begin it.
Boldness has genius, power and magic in it. Begin it now!'"

Let Your Demons Guide You.

By Anjana Love-Dixon

> *"Well, I looked my demons in the eyes, laid bare my chest, said 'Do your best, destroy me. You see, I've been to hell and back so many times, I must admit you kind of bore me.'"*

> ~ Ray Lamontagne

Entertaining the audience of your demons is a rite of passage – a birthright of your humanity. It is the necessary introspection that will frighten you to the core and liberate you from judgment, both at the same time.

We are not talking about those skeletons in the closet that our defense mechanisms attempt to say are our deepest secrets. No, the lies that we tell ourselves are only the tip of the iceberg. They are merely the bastard children of the demons that prevent us from waking up and taking control of our reality.

It is time to take control of reality and clasp hands with aspects of ourselves that we fear the most. Becoming a better person does not mean you must hide away character flaws or what you perceive to be your worst.

You have stood along the sidelines long enough, wishing to taste the freedom you witness other people seem to effortlessly express in their own procession of truth. You know it's going to hurt, you know it is going to be difficult to break out of that suffocating film of judgment, but you know it is time to be reborn. It is time to reevaluate what is keeping you from living your life without such abandon.

It isn't your parents' fault, it isn't your current circumstances, and it isn't even the way you were treated by your peers. It is you and your choice to remain in the imprisonment of comfort, which you have named *normalcy*, so you can hide the little troublemaker inside. This way of life has become so familiar to you that a normal happy day is the scariest event of your life.

Yes, you must have courage to get past the shadowy haze of comfort and experience a little hell. Each and every time we dip our toes into the lake of fire, while staring our demons in our face, we are heroes. We are triumphant in truth and fearlessness.

One of those times, you will realize that the burn of the lake doesn't actually have the power to destroy you, and you will feel the heat of courage that is the only true transformative burn. Look at your mistakes and actualize this newfound courage by forgiving yourself and moving on to bigger and better moments.

In the thick of the fire, you may be bloodied, bruised, burned, scorned, and impaled by the truth that is your darker side.

Stop hiding from your darkness.

Commune with it and you will no longer wage a war, but have an ally to help you stand your ground when the moments count. Your expectation of how your personality should be, things that are appropriate to say or not say, feelings appropriate to feel or not feel do not come from you. They come from sources that do not have the responsibility of bearing the weight of your soul when you look in the mirror and have no authority on the subject of you.

Be you, for you. Make no other compromises and care nothing about what other people think and their judgments. They are not there to help you, they are there to be fascinated by your dirty laundry and lack of conformity.

Your demons are the truest teachers of courage. When the last battle has been fought, expect more, and let them help you grow.

Sweep away the remains of who you think you are and welcome the depth of your inner light. This is a divinity that has proof of life in the path you have created all around you. Aren't you awesome? You are a hero! You are Shiva, the destroyer. You are Brigid, the transcendent fire goddess who has risen from the depths.

Hope is the only weapon you will need. It is the key that opens you to a world without hate or bitterness, free from the jaded edges of your heart. Hope is the sword that cuts through the thicket of defeat and shame. It is the healing salve that will make you invincible to the wounds of the ego. Hope takes courage to activate its transcendent powers.

Don't waste another moment of this gift by repressing any unexpressed feelings. Do not writhe in the pain of secrecy and internalizing. Own your life and face the greatest adventure you will ever experience.

Redefine your Crazy: 5 Declarations of Independence from the Norm.

By Alison Nappi

"You have to leave the city of your comfort and go into the wilderness of your intuition. What you'll discover will be wonderful. What you'll discover is yourself."

~ Alan Alda

Don't believe them, when they tell you something's wrong with you. The world is full of psychopaths, sociopaths, killers of revolutionary creativity. They're lying to you when they tell you you're a broken toy, so they can put you in a box with all the other broken toys, where you won't cause any trouble by asking questions, wearing hats or lighting the curtains on fire.

Insanity is a privilege when it's not aborted by the other more common forms it takes in the world. If you see your madness through to its end, you will realize that true insanity has been re-branded as normalcy. You will fall on your knees at the altar of your greater self as you come to realize what you really are. You will be appalled by the ordinary life. You will hear your own song for the first time since you left the spheres of heaven, and will worship no truth but your own.

"Some people never go crazy. What truly horrible lives they must lead."

~ Charles Bukowski

These people, who have been given status because they've gotten with the program, are not there to help you become free.

They will offer you a chemical straitjacket or some other kind of cage and promise you release from your pain but pain is just what you need to become your true self. It is an electrified fence, a vast virtual landscape that stands between you and all that is divine. It is designed to shock you awake. Don't let them take it from you.

Consider your depression, your bi-polar disorder, your DID, your ADD, your PTSD rites of passage. They may feel disorderly, but they are not without order. In fact, they are perfect road maps designed to bring you through your shadow valley and into the promised land.

And you orchestrated it. Aren't you clever? Aren't you brilliant? And of course, they'll tell you it's not real. They'll tell you you're too sensitive, that your brain malfunctions, that you don't know the difference between reality and non-reality.

When you are tempted to believe them, look out at the ordinary world. Does it seem sane to you? Does it seem sane to you to live in a world where chemical companies are making your food, putting frog genes in your tomatoes? Does it seem sane to you that when you look up at the sky the sun is a faint, fuzzy, globe struggling to be seen through layers of wispy silver clouds that emerge in long lines from the assholes of military aircrafts?

Does it seem sane to you to that a faceless corporation dictates – directly or indirectly – when you can eat, sleep, smoke, shit as you sit for two hours in traffic, heat rising in waves from cracking pavement on your way to the factory line where you put screws into the backs of barcode scanners all day long?

Who would want to be sane in a world like this? Who would want to be satisfied, compliant, accepted here in the nuthouse of now?

Your inner pain is the chaos of the world. The war is inside you. The enslavement is etched into your cells. The silver skies are your pain blocking your never-dimmed, bright and shining soul from view. The distance between who you think you are, and who you really are is a wasteland of lies.

Only you can create clear vision from blindness. Only you can pluck the diamonds from the singed earth. Only you can slash your way through a thousand miles of mazes: a techno-magical obstacle course filled with wizards and riddles, designed by you and for you to make your smallness feel real.

How else could you be a victim? How else could you show up to fold shirts at the Gap? How else could you know despair? How can the sun see itself but through the humble eyes of earth? How is value understood without contrast?

If you're not traumatized by the ordinary life, you are already dead; you are a goat about to be sacrificed to the lion, surrendered on your back, waiting for him to take his fatal mouthful. What have you left to be scared of? What can you risk that is not already at stake?

Here are some declarations to help you reclaim your brilliant and unique shine:

1. I am willing.

I am willing to stand on the precipice of the greatest adventure of my inner life, and liberate all that I am from the lonely, dark, forgotten places within me. I am willing to risk all that I am for all that I might become. At least then, I will know. I am willing to leap madly into my destiny, and meet myself where the worlds collide in celestial fields of glory and redemption.

Willingness is all that is necessary to begin. You don't need to pack anything else. You will become determined as you go, entranced by the infinite mystery of yourself. You will become invested as you find out what you're willing to fight for. Metaphorical blood will spill, resurrections will occur, immaculate conceptions will happen, and points of no return will be passed.

You will become increasingly pregnant with the light of yourself, and consumed with meeting the Christ-child in your belly. You are living the story that creates and dispels all myth, all religion, all the forces that bind heaven and hell to the sidewalks.

2. I am not the labels cast upon me.

They are like spells from small men with big hats waving sticks. I am greater than these. No spell within which I do not believe may hold power over me. I define who I am. I define what is right and what is wrong with me. I cannot be labeled. I transcend labels. There is no language that can hold me, no lie that can bind me.

"Care about what other people think and you will always be their prisoner."

~ Lao Tzu

The mind is shaped in large part by words. It is a meta-computer, referencing a lifetime of programming: tribal programming, cultural programming, national programming. It absorbs everything it sees and hears: on television, in church, at the flea market, in those little welcome packets you glance over when you take a job at the big box store, on the radio playing from a tinny speaker in the dressing room.

Your depression, your anxiety, your internal screaming is just a sign that the truth within you contradicts what you have been downloaded with, and the hospitals will tell you it's the blue screen of death. And they're right, it is. It's the death of the android self, the death of "Yes, Sir," the death of time cards.

3. The meaning of my experience is only that which I assign.

It is up to me whether I use my experiences to run towards or away from my true self. It is up to me whether my pain is a beautiful and ingenious means to sift for gold through many miles of river bed, or just a cruel prank played by sadistic gods who get off watching me cut myself and complain.

> *"To change, a person must face the dragon of his appetites with another dragon, the life-energy of the soul."*
>
> *~ Rumi*

If it benefits you to believe you're crazy, then by all means wear your tin foil hat to the grocery store. If you are comforted by having your personal responsibility stripped from you, shivering outside while the hard cold rain whips your naked flesh, then you have chosen to resign yourself to begging for crusts of bread and pennies from heaven while the vast riches of your true nature stay in a cave, guarded by a dragon that only you can slay.

As in every hero's journey, you will find the resources you need along the way, so don't worry if just yesterday you were a peasant sheering sheep. You'll remember where you left your dragon when the moment of truth is upon you. You will remember all kinds of magnificent things you've forgotten.

4. I am the expert of my experience, and the only authentic expression thereof.

There is no oracle with greater insight than I. No one knows this terrain better than me. I lead this expedition and only the loyal, the courageous, the compassionate bearers of lanterns and secret soul scrolls may accompany me. Everyone else, step aside; you would not survive here.

> *"If I had not created my own world, I would certainly have died in other people's."*
>
> ~ *Anais Nin*

Don't be afraid of the wreckage. Don't be scared of the dark. You are the dark, too, and in the beginning only the tiniest spark will light your way. It's in your belly.

You will see almost nothing but the tips of your shoes and you will straighten your ankle and sweep your foot out in front of you to be sure there is ground there, before you move: just one step. Sometimes, just a half step. And somewhere, in a world you can't yet perceive, your greater self will step toward you 10,000 times.

You will learn to become decisive as you come to realize what's at stake. You will find superpowers you didn't know you had. You will pick up rings of power and rubies and emeralds that you steal back from ogres and sorcerers and creatures your ancestors wrote myths about. You will use them later to pay back the gods of karma or to cross the River Styx with Charon. Stay long enough to be reborn.

You will bump into your selves again and again, and most of the time you won't recognize them: they will be great glowing angels, they will be raving red-eyed demons, they will be priests and will be star-dusted. You will fall out of time and space. You will tumble down rabbit holes inside of rabbit holes. You will do impossible things. You will summon your weapons from air so thin no flesh could survive it. You will make things disappear and reappear. You will scream, and topple cities. You will cry and the mothers of mercy will come to you when you are on your knees, begging. You will shape a new earth this way. You will write your plans here, so you can live them later.

5. The only way out is through, and I am predestined to win.

Even though it doesn't look that way, the game is fixed in my favor. The out-there is in here, and I am the Kali of this microcosmic universe. I destroy and create. I am creator and created. The resolution of opposites happens here, on these hallowed grounds within me.

"I am not afraid. I was born for this."

~ Joan of Arc

We think that it's normal to be five-sensory. Things are simpler that way. In five sensory reality, we participate in a shared illusion, and it comforts us. What we see makes us wretch, but when everyone is covered in vomit, it's *en vogue.*

When your spirit starts speaking to you, everything within you that is anything else feels it first, and in great chaos it will rush at you, and form a wall of fire through which you must pass.

You have been cryogenically frozen and you are thawing already. The bondage of your encasement in ice is melting away leaving you, perhaps for the first time, with a choice. To you, it may seem like many choices, but really there is only one. One glorious, blazing choice. One moment of unspeakable courage.

If you think there has to be more to it than labor and alcohol, then say yes. If you believe you are destined for something great, then say yes. If you know – and you don't know how you know – that somewhere inside you is something that has no master, then say yes.

Say a prayer. Write your will. Have an adventure. Bring an angel with you. Find God in the fire. Be changed, from soft and impressionable clay. Get reshaped on the way by the swords and the teeth and the claws of your inner enemies, and when you are perfect, you will emerge with a story to tell, and little left to fear. You will have discovered the wizard behind the curtain.

The world will still fear you because you will have found the eternal within yourself, and that which is eternal cannot be bullied, cannot be brutalized, cannot be stolen from and cannot be manipulated. This is not the state of the average or normal person, but by now, you've let go of normal in exchange for something of far greater value.

And you will know this. You won't think it, or intellectualize it or wish it so. You will know it, and your very existence will be an impossible rebellion to suppress.

"The privilege of a lifetime is being who you are."

~ *Joseph Campbell*

Fuck Balance, Try Alignment – the Beauty of Disequilibrium.

By Jeanette LeBlanc

I'm at the end of my rope. I can't keep all the balls in the air. I am overwhelmed and under-satisfied. How do I keep the love turned on with my partner while managing children and a home-based business and my creative passions? How do I find balance?

Short answer: You don't.

Long Answer: Sugar, you really absolutely, positively don't.

In fact, the quest for this ever-elusive equilibrium is pure crazy making. Balance is a fallacy. A giant conspiracy designed to make us all feel like we're continuously fucking up and falling short. It sells yoga videos and meditation retreats and time saving kitchen devices. We download productivity apps and make to-do lists and buy things that plug into our electrical outlets to make us feel like we live in the midst of an artificially scented rainforest. Serenity now. Please... And despite all of this we are wildly, continuously off kilter. Unbalanced. Crossing the universe on a tightrope with no safety net below. There is not enough time, or money, or passion or even interest to sustain it all perfectly all the time. And darling, of course something has got to give.

But here's the real truth. We're made for the ebb and flow. Just like the ocean. Just like the cycles of the moon. Just like the movement from dark to light to dark again. We were born to shift and be selfish and howl and get messy. We were made to create beauty and to make crazy love and to find the bliss right at the center of our raw, aching parts.

That's the heart of life, the center of the paradox. And it often says, to hell with balance, because balance keeps us safe.

What if we halt the chase for this impossibly esoteric notion of balance and give ourselves to something a lot more earthy and true and real? How about we let ourselves be seduced by the beauty of disequilibrium? What if we agreed to let it all go, with a wild, lusty abandon...

That's when we find that it's all about the moments – moments for pure creation, moments of uninhibited sex, moments of the sweetest mother-baby love and of pissed-the-fuck-off anger. And, of come-here-right-now lust, of falling head over heels in love with the world, of feeling like the ground is going to give way beneath our feet, of feeling free and wild and true, and of feeling chained and constrained and too heavy to get out of bed.

And yes, in the midst of all this, even moments where it all feels like it's sliding into the most exquisite alignment. And before, you might have been tempted to call that balance. To try subduing it and controlling it and keeping it at all costs. But now? No. You're too fierce, too elemental, to unabashedly you to be something as mild and tame as balanced. And that's fucking hot.

I'm pretty sure your partner would agree that you living in the fullness of your perfectly unbalanced self is a pretty good way to keep the love turned all the way on.

No balancing act required. So don't wait to fall off the tightrope. Take a flying leap. Trust your wings. And the unsteady ground that greets you will be perfect and exhilarating and true.

Just like you.

14 Tidbits to Stir in Your Coffee when the Sloth Visits.

By Carolyn Riker

I am not depressed, but I am selectively choosing not to engage in a dramatic affair with life. I call it my inner sloth.

Seasonal changes are like a giant toggle switch: I gather energy in spring and summer. By fall, I filter out the debris and prepare to slip into hibernation. I'm getting ready for winter.

I aim to seek balance though, as I dip a bit deeper into the long midnight blues. I choose to be quietly creative with myself. I cherish this space. I also crave copious amounts of dark chocolate that melodically dances with a cornucopia of words.

Meanwhile, my mind and body don't do well from constant inertia. Therefore I coax myself to do semi-accelerated sun salutations to chase the chilly cobwebs from the dark corners. I have to listen and push myself along the riverboat in my mind to stay afloat.

It's a lesson of self-love versus judging myself harshly; a perpetual cognitive awareness to balance my needs. I recently tapped into my tender sloth-like heart and she shared some inner truths to assist in this seasonal navigation.

14 tidbits to stir in your coffee (or tea) when the sloth visits…

1. Spread kindness and love whenever you can. Reach out your fingertips and feel the energy flow. As you start sparking kindness, it'll lift the cloak of darkness. Love really is the answer.

2. Projections, my dear, are viral. Replaying the past will drown you. Get the bolt cutters and cut the chains of heaviness. Turn the emotional fanfare off and stop twitching at every little leaf that moves. Ground your inner wildebeest. Watch without attachment and let your mind settle into the quietness of an observer. The lake is a mirror and you are the image.

"Be not the slave of your own past. Plunge into the sublime seas, dive deep and swim far, so you shall come back with self-respect, with new power, with an advanced experience that shall explain and overlook the old."

~ Ralph Waldo Emerson

3. Always seek real. Speak from your heart and walk around the steaming piles of bubbling bullshit. No one is going to save or rescue you from the demons you fight. Many are fighting to learn their own generous life lessons, which include Heaven and Hell. Be gentle. Be kind. Speak softly. It's often louder than a roar.

4. Be your own Sun and Moon. The Sun shines to keep you and every living thing alive. The Moon is the healing afterglow. You have both qualities within you. It's a powerful alchemy – one you can tap into. You have the capabilities to catapult through space. Believe in the trajectory of your heartfelt intentions.

5. Life isn't about cruise control. You are the driver and not the passenger. Get lost. Get found. There will be triggers. Lots of them. Watch. Look. Listen. Learn. But don't sit there stewing in the brew. Change lanes: Avoidance has a kinship with procrastination. The pile-up effect can be debilitating.

6. Pull out your inner GPS, it is guided by your intuition. Set your compass to the four corners. Going one-way is incredibly boring.

7. Declare a rapture of your senses and sip raindrops from your eyelashes. Walk your fingertips along each vertebra. Watch each hair follicle dance in the quiver of your aliveness.

She had to breathe in peace, for in peace she found the quiet solitude her heart had been aching for. In the moments between raindrops she let her focus dwell, and the sound of silence comforted her more than an avalanche of superficial banter.

8. Let it out. When you see the monstrous waves of anxiety pouring in, swim out further to sea and settle into the fear. The part where you panic and dread is exactly where you need to tread. It's the painful parts you try to stuff down an endless rabbit hole. If the road gets blurry, pull over. Take a few exquisite deep breaths. Breathe in freshness and flush the rest into a cosmic portal of silky white feathers.

9. Unstick yourself and dare to do what scares the hell out of you.

> *"And one has to understand that braveness is not the absence of fear but rather the strength to keep on going forward despite the fear."*
>
> *~ Paulo Coelho*

10. Letting go is continuous. It's not a one-time affair. It is a perpetual process of assimilation. Once one layer is shed, another one comes up. This is good because it means you are alive and well.

11. Quiet times are essential. It is necessary to step out of the drama of meaningless drivel, part the rain from the drops and melt into the puddles. Solitude is like water. Drink it, create it with no regret.

I dip gratefully into the sunshine and sip dew from the grass. I befriend nature and listen to the messages. I fly to the tops of branches and feel the hum of a hummer fluttering in my heart. In the speed of light, I see the patches of shade and dance lightly. I catch a wisp of a spider's web and dangle between the echo and the silence. It is here I find a moment to fill my heart with joy.

12. Create a fire and ignite your inner flame. Laugh and dance to the rhythm of your joy and resonate with the heat of your core creativity. Step outside of the normal and find your inner crazy. Reflect with gratitude the shifting kaleidoscope, it is a part of *you.*

> *"Creativity involves breaking out of established patterns in order to look at things in a different way."*
>
> *~ Terry Tempest Williams*

13. Life is like a metaphorical handstand. At times, it can feel upside down, inverted and confusing, until we kick up into the fear. Challenge yourself to balance the weight evenly by relaxing into the space of the unknown. And above all…

14. Choose to live life as a miracle, because it is.

"There are only two ways to live your life. One is as though nothing is a miracle. The other is as though everything is a miracle."

~ Albert Einstein

Normal or Abnormal: the Choice is Yours.

By Ramanjit Garewal

> *"Love said to me, 'You are not crazy enough, you do not fit this house.' I went and became crazy; crazy enough to be in chains."*
>
> *~ Rumi*

If you are abnormal, then read no further. You are in *The Happy Zone*, with no fear of living a dull and dreary life.

If you are normal, then you definitely need to read this – again and again – you are in danger of being moved from *The Happy Zone* to a dull and dreary life.

I say that normal is ugly, very ugly. There is beauty, great beauty, in being abnormal.

I ask you, was Shiva normal? Or Rama, or Krishna or Moses? And what of Buddha or Jesus, Nanak or Michelangelo? Who would call Leonardo da Vinci normal? Or Mahatma Gandhi, Picasso, even Steve Jobs? I say, no! They were *not* normal.

Did any one of them accept or propagate what was normal at that time? You know the answer.

So, I ask you, were they ugly? Of course not. They were all beautiful. You would never deny their beauty, yet you accept that being normal is beautiful, because you have been conditioned since childhood to believe it is so.

Do not be normal. Do not be ugly. Be abnormal. Be beautiful. Realize yourself, with Real Eyes. With Real Eyes comes *Real-I-zation*.

You are as unique and worthy as all of them. There is so much beauty in you, so much magic. You are great. Do not settle for anything less.

How were they abnormal? They all broke free from the shackles and fetters of the normalcy of their times, shattered the societal conditioning, and by doing so, freed and liberated not only themselves but millions over the millennia. I ask you, how many normal people can do this? Not even one.

Being normal means living within imposed boundaries, being enslaved and entrapped by the prison of societal conditioning. Being abnormal smashes those boundaries so that you may break free and liberate yourself from the prison of societal conditioning.

Normal is limited. Abnormal is unlimited. Normal is finite, while abnormal is infinite. So, I ask you, would you be limited and finite, or unlimited and infinite? Do you prefer to simply survive, or do you want to truly live?

The goalposts of normalcy are always still, always the same, never changing or evolving. Being abnormal means that the goalposts are never still. They are ever changing and evolving.

Parents pray for children who will break boundaries, but then they train their children to live within the prisons of conditioning. What an irony! What a paradox!

They do not want their children to be afraid, yet they instill fear – fear of the past and fear of the future. Systems, institutions and corporations select new recruits based on their ability to think out of the box, but once hired, their first experience is *orientation*. Orientation is just another way of drawing the lines and boundaries of the box. Absolutely ridiculous!

The systems, institutions and corporations are the ones that need to be boxed. And by "boxed," I mean literally boxed in and retrained! Why is abnormal always understood as being less than normal? Why can't we see abnormal as being ab(ove)normal and normal as less? A shift in perception is all that is required.

Is the Divine normal? Not even by the wildest stretch of imagination! Normal is predictable and the Divine is totally unpredictable. Would you rather be normal and non-divine or be abnormal and Divine?

Predictability is death. Isn't it death to know exactly what is going to happen and when? What could be more boring than certainty, predictability and normalcy? It is the uncertainty of what is or is not going to happen, the uncertainty and unpredictability of life, that makes life exciting and worth living! I say being normal is dying and being ab(ove)normal is living.

See the abnormal and the beauty in the other. Recognize it and celebrate it in your self. See this beauty in your self. Know that you are abnormal, unique, and therefore, beautiful. Repose in that. Revel in that. Rejoice in that.

See the ugliness in being normal. See the beauty in being abnormal. I say, do not be ugly, do not be normal. Be beautiful in your abnormal glory.

Yet, the normal is needed to throw up the abnormal. One is not possible without the other. Both are necessary as life is paradoxical.

What is being normal? Normal is living within boundaries, in neat little boxes. Normal is always being worried about what others will think and say and living life as per your imagination of others' expectations, without the courage to live beyond your fears. Normal is being afraid – afraid of what others will think, afraid of what lies beyond the imposed boundaries of conditioning, afraid of the known past, and also afraid of the unknown future. Oprah asked herself, "What would I do if I weren't afraid?" and then she went ahead and did just that. She went beyond her fears. What an inspiration!

"Forget safety. Live where you fear to live. Destroy your reputation. Be notorious."

~ Rumi

Abnormal is breaking barriers and smashing boundaries, throwing off the shackles of societal conditioning, rejecting and discarding the past. Abnormal is welcoming and embracing the unknown.

Paraphrasing Mahatma Gandhi, "When you are abnormal, first the normal ignore you, then they laugh at you, then they fight you, but then you win, and they follow you."

The result of being normal is like a black hole imploding, sucking everything from the circumference into its center of darkness and killing it. Being abnormal is like exploding from the center to the circumference, illuminating everything and giving it life, like the sun.

There are two primary choices in life: to accept conditions as they exist, and be normal; or to accept the responsibility for changing them, and be ab(ove)normal. What is it going to be? You have only today. Make it a great day, make the right choice – choose ab(ove)normal. You are so worth it!

Being normal is copying, imitating, conforming, accepting and limiting. Being abnormal is creating, innovating, non-conforming, rejecting and liberating. Being normal means living within the parameters of patterns. Being abnormal means smashing the parameters of patterns.

Normal is ordinary. Abnormal is extraordinary.

If you are wed to normal and you expect magic to birth in your life, it is like expecting coconut trees to spring forth from pea pods. If you want magic in your life, then you have to first divorce normal. The day you rip apart conditioning and divorce normal, it will be the first amazing day of your life. Go to bed with abnormal, shed inhibitions, have an orgy. Your life will be full of magic, and you will be the magician – day after day.

When you can throw off every form of fear, both known and unknown, you will have a mind without fear. A mind that has no fear is capable of great love.

Being normal means being full of fears, anger, greed, ambition, attachments, hatred and a clinging to life. Being abnormal means being full of love, love, and more love and a celebration of life.

Musicians, writers, artists, dancers, singers, musicians, playwrights, poets, philosophers and lovers have to be thanked – for they take you to places in your mind and in your heart that are not normal, that are ab(ove)normal and free you. They have always been and always will be the true liberators.

Abnormal is beauty, madness is genius. Abnormal is being alive. It is better to be absolutely insane and full of *joie de vivre* than to be normal and absolutely boring and dead.

Normal is an illusion – what is normal for the early bird is death for the early worm. What is normal for a bat – hanging upside and sleeping – is abnormal for others.

Normal ridicules love, and love smiles knowingly at the whole absurdity of normal. Abnormal embraces love.

Nobody has the right to judge anybody as normal or abnormal. These are the ways of dominating people. When you judge someone, you are trying to interfere in their life, which is none of your business.

A real, authentic Society simply allows people to be themselves, allows them to be abnormal. Societal conditioning has forced you to adjust to a normal and profoundly sick society. You have to rebel against societal conditioning. Stop walking the clumsy walk of the normal, sprout wings of the abnormal, and soar like a Butterfly on the wings of an Angel to your True Love – soar to the Divine. What type of sick, normal society is this?

The first thing people talk about when they meet is about their misery – what a bum deal life has given them and how miserable they are, and they are happy that they are miserable. They are happier if the other is also miserable. If everybody is miserable, then they fit and everything is okay. They are members, they belong – they belong to us. How wonderful!

If people become creative and ecstatic, then Society thinks they have gone berserk, insane, mad, crazy, and abnormal. They no longer fit in, they no longer belong – they no longer belong to us – and the green-eyed monster of jealousy raises its head in the collective mind of normal Society. Society condemns them out of jealousy. Driven by this jealousy, Society will try – in every way possible – to forcefully return them to their former state of misery. They – the Society – call that old miserable state 'normal'.

Psychoanalysts and psychiatrists will help to bring them back to a state of misery – the state of fitting in, the state of belonging to Society, the state of belonging to the State – the normal and miserable state.

Society has done a great job in transforming abnormal to normal by squeezing you into The Box, and then asking you to jump out of and think outside The Box, after maiming you with normalcy. The normalizing agencies of culture, tradition, education, parents, teachers, schools, colleges, corporations, politicians, police, priests, *pirs*, pundits, prelates, the State – they have done a great job of this. They have made normal miserable creatures out of abnormal ecstatic creators.

Every child is born ecstatic. Every child is born in Love. Every child is born Divine. And, every man dies a madman.

Nobody is going to get out of this madhouse alive. You have got nothing – absolutely nothing – to lose in breaking free from the chains of normalcy that are keeping you shackled in this madhouse of normal people, locked up in cells of societal conditioning.

Unless you recover, unless you reclaim your childhood, you will not be able to free yourself from this mad house. You have to regain your childhood, and become abnormal. If you succeed, then the cells of this madhouse of normal will magically open to liberate you, to spring you into the abnormal World of Love.

You have two choices in life. Be normal and travel in a tunnel which has light, but one that is tapering and getting darker with each passing moment or...

Be abnormal and travel in a tunnel which is dark, but one that is opening progressively as the light is increasing with each passing moment...

Travel from light to darkness, or from darkness to light...

Be normal or be abnormal – the choice is yours, the life is yours.

Love is the ultimate outlaw and totally abnormal. It just won't be normal or follow any rules. Join the Gang of Love and become an accomplice in spreading Love.

Bring in the Rule of Love – for where Love rules, there are no other rules except Love.

I have joined the Gang of Love and become Love's accomplice; what are you waiting for?

Join The Gang of Love.

Remember: no rules, only Love... Love Rulz...

Have an orgy of Love, being abnormal.

6 Sweet Survival Tips for Supersensitive Souls.

By Victoria Erickson

"I have sea foam in my veins, for I understand the language of waves."

~ Le Testament d'Orphee

Like most sensitive souls, you already know you are sensitive. You soak up others' moods and desires like a sponge. You absorb sensation the way a paintbrush grasps each color it touches on a palette. The ethereal beauty of a dandelion, the shift of a season, the climax of a song, or the scent of a certain fragrance can sometimes move you to tears.

Super sensitive souls like you and I have always been a part of the human landscape, and according to the *Highly Sensitive Person* pioneer Elaine Aron's research, we make up around 20 percent of the population.

It is important to note that all human beings are actually quite fragile, and Super Sensitive Souls are no more fragile than everyone else – we are just more easily stimulated due to our wiring.

This means that if you are sensitive, you have the ability to see colors and feel energy the way others hear jet planes. The world takes on a rich tapestry of immense gorgeousness at almost every turn, which then fuels your imagination and makes you spin with aliveness. And aliveness is a grand thing.

"Aliveness is energy. It's the juice, the vitality, and the passion that wakes up our cells every morning. It's what makes us want to dance. It's the energy that moves a relationship from the status quo to something grander and much more expansive, something that makes our hearts beat faster, our minds and our eyes open wider, than ever before. Everything is of interest to a person who is truly alive, whether it's a challenge, a loving moment, a bucket of grief, or a glimpse of beauty."

~ Daphne Rose Kingma

Yet, it also means that much like the spirited and hot-blooded Arabians in the horse world, your alertness and reactivity may easily cause you to shy away with fright at things that should not be so scary.

Since your nervous system responds so easily to stimuli, it can oftentimes be overwhelming and exhausting to be so flooded with sensation – which makes you prone to bolting from uncomfortable situations, relationships, and jobs.

And sometimes your sensitivity makes life extraordinarily painful, and you want to shut down and hide your raw self from the loud chaos that accompanies this earth's continual rotation.

Continually swimming in an endless sea of sensation can at times be exhausting, regardless if it is beautifully terrible or terribly beautiful, and this is why your deep-rooted need for peace and self-care is essential to support your superb sensitivity.

Here are a few things you can practice daily in order to both preserve your energy and keep your sanity:

1. Create. Sensitive types and creativity go hand and hand, because their rawness and innate ability to pick up on information and energy that others do not feel can easily be translated into art and passionate expression. So rescue that fleeting gorgeous moment, and then recycle it through your chosen medium.

Perhaps you can make your guitar cry, weave beautiful cloth into wearable clothing, bleed powerful words on a page, or capture that perfect light before you with a camera. Just create, create, and then create some more, so other people can see through your eyes.

2. Enjoy the company of animals. Sensitive souls tend to have a deep connection with animals due to their innate intuition, understanding of energy and compassionate nature.

Animals know and appreciate this, so give yourself permission to spend as much time as possible bonding with your particular animal, because the time spent with animals is never wasted.

3. Seek out water. Water is magical, and one of its many uses is as a tool to achieve peace, calm, and balance. Take a trip to the sea, a lake, a stream, or even your bathtub. Let the water invigorate and cleanse you for you to feel clear again.

4. Be aware of what is yours and what is not. When you take in other people's energy, you must learn to instantly let go of what I like to call *the yuck*, because if that energy, that was not yours to begin with, is negative or imbalanced, it can actually make you physically sick.

Learn to recognize what is only your energy and emotion, and place a protective invisible shield around yourself to block out anything that is not.

5. Surround yourself with people that understand your nature and nurture that connection. Pierre Teilhard de Chardin once said, "There is almost a sensual longing for communion with others that have a larger vision. The immense fulfillment of the friendships between those engaged in furthering the evolution of consciousness has a quality almost impossible to describe."

Find us, because firstly, we understand, and secondly, we can sit beside you and revel at the outstanding beauty and synchronicities all around. Perhaps we will share poetry or take hikes, or contemplate life, or geek out sharing our favorite photo-editing applications.

6. Retreat, replenish and rejuvenate. Take some time for yourself when your body and mind need it. When you are sensitive, you need to fiercely guard your serenity to protect your open heart and regroup.

Once you have these things in place, go and experience this mind-bendingly incredible world, you super-sensitive soul, you.

If the world is patiently waiting for everyone else's senses to grow sharper to reveal magical things, all you need to do is step outside and ride the energy of the earth, for there is always a brilliant sunrise, rolling fog, shifting seasons, and rising waters to experience, as well as new, inviting lands to step foot on.

And the view is glorious.

Self-Criticism: The Way You Break Your own Heart.

By Saran Kaur

Most of us would say that one of the most painful experiences in life is being criticized or judged by our loved ones.

Yes, it feels painful and yucky to feel rejection or "not feeling enough" in the eyes of those that we deeply care for and desire to be loved and accepted by, but there's something that is more painful than any rejection that we can receive from others. It's the rejection and criticism of ourselves.

Self-criticism and judgment is the way you break your own heart. Self-criticism and judgment stem from holding ourselves to an external measure of performance and/or being. It's striving for an unattainable goal of perfection that can never be reached.

Perfection is a tricky issue. First of all, it doesn't exist. There is no fixed place called "perfection" that we can hang out in if we work hard enough.

Life is an ongoing calibration process, and an ongoing learning game! But the concept of perfection serves us in subtle ways that we might not recognize at first. We often times use perfection both as a safety-zone as well as a way of punishing ourselves.

Perfection as an excuse and a safety zone… Where are you not showing up as you, not expressing your truth or not engaging because "you'll just wait until it feels a bit safer" or your expression/product/communication is a little better or until you "feel ready"?

This is you keeping yourself safe inside your comfort zone by putting up a goal of perfection. Your ego tells you that this is the safe way, you won't get laughed at or hurt if you wait just a bit longer, take another class, or abandon your truth altogether.

The concept of "being ready" does exist. But it is usually the Universe that decides when we're ready and propels us out into new circumstances. It's rarely the ego that ever feels ready! Life happens through us, whether we feel ready or not. And mostly it happens in that annoying place where we are definitely not completely ready because it's called the learning zone.

Learning means venturing outside of that which you already master and know, and exploring new territory. There's no way around it, so you might as well enjoy it!

Being at peace and content with ourselves and where we are gives a deep sense of coziness in our bodies and soul. It's a place of an open heart and an easy connection to other people and beings. The surest way to disrupt this coziness is through self-criticism. Judgment closes the heart chakra, the most powerful center of your being.

In order to start examining how you put yourself in this painful place, look at your self-communication. How do you talk to yourself? Would you talk like that to anyone else?

Would you tell a baby who's learning to walk that they're not good enough to walk and should never try doing it because they keep falling down in the process of learning? Yet this is often times the way we talk to ourselves as we're in our own process of learning to walk our dreams.

To take action means to regularly make mistakes. Mistakes are a recalibration and resetting of your course.

How do you want to look at your mistakes? Is it worth beating yourself up about them, or are you simply going to choose differently next time? Mistakes mean you're on your way, you're going somewhere, you're exploring and you're engaging with the light and the dark. You're exploring what feels good and what doesn't. "Never doing that again!" or "That's the way forward!" we learn through this polarity.

You don't look at a flower seed and say, "Oh, that'll never grow into a flower" because you know that the process of nature is for a flower seed to grow into a flower. It's time to understand that you have the flower seed within you. It is your consciousness, your Divine Soul that calls you to expand and evolve. And your life is the soil.

So where do you criticize your you-ness? And where did you learn to do that? Where are you guilt-tripping yourself about your being or actions? You know that guilt is present when you hear the word *should* echo inside you.

So, where's the *should* in your life? It *should* be like this. I *should* wear that. I *should* perform in a certain way… this is the highway to hell and your guilt is the driver.

Guilt is constructive only when it serves as a pointer of where you went off track and how you're going to handle the same issue in the future in a different way. Without a new solution present, guilt is useless. So every time there's a *should*, listen up and pay attention to it: are you feeling guilty about something – and is it constructive?

Where do you talk yourself out of going for your heart's desire? Where do you tell yourself the lie that you don't know, that you don't deserve? Holding ourselves to a standard of perfection is how we tear our budding dreams apart. It is how we break our own hearts.

Self-criticism and the creative process...

Criticism usually comes into the picture when we attempt to express ourselves in ways that are new to us. When we attempt to expand our expression of ourselves, be it cooking a new recipe or changing our job.

The critique sounds like this:

What's the point?
   ...of writing poetry
   ...of learning to meditate
   ...of starting a community
   ...of creating a blog
   ...of learning a new language
   ...of changing your diet
   ...of dreaming of a vacation in the Bahamas
   ...of wanting to change your job
   ...of {insert your dream of choice}

It's the voice that says: it won't make any difference. I don't see it. No one's going to want it. It's not possible for me. It's not going to work!

This is your ego trying to keep itself in control. (Remember, your ego is here to protect you from everything it sees as scary!) When these road signs pop up, you know you're on your way to expansion. Because these are the markers of your old limits and as you move beyond them, you grow beyond who you thought you were and begin to discover who you have the potential to be!

In reality, we know. We know what we desire. And since the creative process is just that, creative, it will create a flow of its own as soon as you allow it. You don't need a master plan. You don't need to know the result. You don't need to account for anything. You don't need to have a result, because there will be new results as you allow yourself to create and play!

The only thing that is required is that you start. Your voice needs to be heard. Someone needs to hear your unique message through your voice through your words.

Take out a pen and paper, and start. Take out your crayons and start. Sit down with your instrument and start. Go into your kitchen, pull out the ingredients and start. Take out your camera and start.

Just. Start. No expectations. No shoulds. No one looking over your shoulder, no one giving you marks on your performance. No one else needs to see it, like or know about it. It's just you creating for the joy of it and for the love of yourself.

Dare to be the one who's in charge. Dare to be the one who holds your dreams valuable. And as you do, others will recognize that value as well. When we dare to pursue our dreams, the Universe steps in big time to support our expansion.

But the first step has to come from us. And that's when we need to love ourselves out of self-criticism and judgment, trading self-criticism and perfection for trust and forgiveness. It's an ongoing process.

As we let go of our own self-judgment and need for perfection, we can be open to be generous about other peoples' growth and mistakes too.

It doesn't shatter us if someone makes a wrong turn, says something inappropriate or messes up. Because we know that everybody will keep learning on one level or another. (Whether we admit it or not is a different matter.)

It's all part of the journey. Accept it! It's not an excuse to not do the best we can or settle for not exerting some willpower in order to secure our growth, but if we accept that even if we do our best we might sometimes fall a bit short of the goal, we might be more easily motivated to try again.

And as we soften the self-criticism, we open up to the possibility of a genuine connection to ourselves and others. We soften the criticism of others as well. We are reachable and we reach out. And we find that we're all the same, deep down. No judgments needed. And love is the only thing that remains.

The Story of Us.

By Hannah Coakley

There are times, when the appealing option, the seemingly natural option, is to view the world and its contents with fear, doubt and jealousy.

It can be so easy to wrap ourselves in the smaller, pettier things. They come quickly to us and cling in a familiar encompassing manner that warms our flesh, and makes us feel less exposed, less at the mercy of the elements.

Perhaps that is why we speak of love thriving in the summertime. Why people from warm climates have reputations for just that: warmth. Loving kindness. With their skin adequately drenched from sun, they do not need the protective layers of cynicism and narcissism. They can remain open – warmed from the outside in. But there are other ways to stoke this inner fire.

I have found it time and time again in the most authentic, honest conversations. It does not have to be with people I have known well or for many years. Oftentimes, it is with individuals I barely know at all.

There is something in the extension of trust, around a dinner table, across a desk, sitting next to each other in a coffee shop that feels illicit. That leaves me feeling on fire, awake and alive.

It lies in the knowledge that we are delving into some deeper, id-like part of ourselves, and showing our animal teeth and claws – not in a threatening way, but as a presentation.

Here is my humanness. Here is yours. And here we are making the space for it, even though we are sitting in confining chairs underneath unnatural light. Here we are telling our stories. Being human together.

So much of our personal narratives, the self-told tales, the monologue we recite in our heads each day, can become stale and meaningless. With a stock of only cold, surface-level interactions to draw from, our continence grows weak and, much like our human gut, our ability to digest new feelings or new ideas or new people grows lethargic and inefficient.

We reject what we cannot understand. We nurture grudges. We highlight small differences. It is essential for us to see that each point of human contact can be an act of love, an opportunity to stoke a fire. A chance to shrug off those temptingly warm blankets of suspicion and frustration that seem to cling so easily to us during the course of our static electric days. We can find the small moments of openness, of vulnerability, of humility in any interaction. We can capitalize on moments of extension, of conversations and connections that feel authentic at a gut level.

We can press into those places, rather than shy away from them. We can set the precedent for what we are willing to share, how much of ourselves we allow to be seen – not necessarily verbalized, but merely shown as being present and available. We get to decide what we permit to warm us. How we map the path of engagement with the world around us.

One of my favorite photos was taken by a good friend during a year spent abroad. It is the picture of the side of a Turkish subway platform, with the words *More love would be better* hastily spray-painted in English.

Something about the sentiment – juxtaposed with both the unnatural Big Bird yellow of the metal and the phenomenon of accessing it virtually via Facebook – seems to me to be such a fantastic encapsulation of the modern dilemma we find within and without ourselves.

With such a big, wide and mechanized world to connect to, instantly and at any time of day or night, how do we keep ourselves open to it all?

How do we prevent an overwhelming influx of information from pushing us to retreat deeper within ourselves? To accumulate all of our blankets and hunker down and shut our eyes to the myriad suffering and heartache that being human in this world can bring? I think the person who wrote that epigram got it right: *More love would be better.*

In a world where the narrative is so often one of fear and anger and doubt: *more love would be better.* In the face of those about whom you care deeply dying or moving on: *more love would be better.* In the uncertainty of yourself, your appearance, your abilities, and your wisdom: *more love would be better.*

We have, within each of us, a tensile strength…

…a long line that finds its name in stories and myths throughout the ages. It is the family tree, the root, the lifeline of the palm. It binds us to our mothers when we are born. It is the magnificent system of arteries and veins through which we are nourished. It is in the pathways and tunnels deep inside the Earth that inevitably claims us. It is both the literal and figurative iron that forges our bodies and builds our cities. And, like iron, this strength within us molds and adapts best when we are warm. When we remain invigorated and passionate.

This requires openness. It requires an honest and forgiving look at ourselves and the myriad people with whom we interact every day. It requires a new kind of awareness and love. *Constant love. Expansive love. Unselfish love.*

In the face of all else, we must find the capacity to remain open. Even when we fail. Especially when we fail. Even when we feel defeated and angry and misunderstood. Even when our hearts are breaking. We must find a moment of exposure and honesty. We must forge new warmth, new understanding, new love.

Because, if the myths and the molecules and the soil under our feet have one thing to tell us, it is that loving – more loving – is what we are meant to be.

Breakthrough.

By Amber Shumake

Yoga is not one more box to check. You don't make a note of it in your phone or day planner and then cross it off. We have enough boxes to check and items to cross off. Yoga is not one more thing for you to do. Yoga is a way of being. Yoga is a lens through which you see yourself and the world, a vessel to help you navigate the earth.

Quality not quantity.
Compassion not competition.
Intrinsic not extrinsic.

Our yoga practices teach us to be ourselves fearlessly. Being doesn't necessarily mean doing. Through yoga we learn to break through our habitual patterns and behaviors.

Perhaps, a breakthrough is kicking up into a handstand for the first time unassisted. Maybe, it's hovering in an arm balance that's eluded you for 2.5 years. Both deserve a fist pump and a high five. Rock on! Look at you! But, yoga should travel with you – from the mat to work, from work to home, and everywhere in between. Because the best breakthroughs happen long after you've rolled your mat up and walked away from the studio.

A breakthrough is a deep breath before speaking.
A breakthrough is a soft jaw you've spent a lifetime clenching.

Through yoga, we find what Panache Desai calls our *unique soul signatures*, our true strengths and mighty gifts the world anxiously awaits. What are you waiting for? Break through. Beyond your perceived limitations, past your ingrained conditioning.

You are not your past. You are not your body. You are a soul, and your soul is rooting for you.

Fractured Beauty and a Fissured Self: Learning to Love Completely.

By Patrick Linder

Part I: Damn you, Walt Whitman.

The great thing about America, they say, is that it is a land of second chances. People come here to make a fresh start. Your ancestors probably did. And it is a land that loves to forgive, to let people try again and start over after their mistakes.

That is a lovely theory. But how do you 'start over'?

There is no Reset button to life. There is no way to erase the past. There are real-life reasons (financial, familial and familiar) why most of us cannot just fold up our tent, hop on a train, and start a new life in a different town. And even if you could, would that really be escaping from the past?

You tote your past with you everywhere you go. It is the invisible baggage that no porter will ever carry for you; only you get to push and pull and tug and lug it from place to place.

Whitman, one of America's first great poets (and a personal favorite), famously claimed that he was large, that he contained multitudes. Beautiful. Lyrical. It is a fundamentally democratic poetic statement, abundant and amenable to differences. I loved it as a college student. I love it as a theory.

The darker side that I overlooked in my first enthusiastic embrace?

What if you cannot stomach some of the past (personal, cultural, national) that you contain? How do you make sense of not just the good that you have done but also the errors and sins that you have committed, the hurts that you have caused? What to do with the part of yourself that you hate, the mistakes that keep beating on the door of your heart?

I contain multitudes. I am a writer, a dad, a marketer, a man, a Kansan (originally), a Washingtonian (now and by choice), a dog owner, a runner, an emotionally intense person, a caring man, a loving man, a man who is prone to excess, a man who has been hurt by others and has hurt others, a man who is more fragile than he wants to admit, a man who has sacrificed to stay in relationships he should have let go, a man who has sabotaged relationships he should have fought to maintain, a man who loves himself, and a man who hates himself.

It is a delicate balance, this effort to contain not only the multitudes that you like, but also those that you want to excoriate and burn and vomit away. For years I could not do it. And the hurt was worse because I could not.

(I can now say that I could not do it 'yet,' but life never feels parenthetical when you are in the midst of it. It is only later, looking back, that the parentheses become clear).

I could forgive, but not myself. I could wash errors of others away and understand that a mistake does not make a lifetime, but not for myself. I'd understand, intellectually, that I was not the only one who had a piece of the pie, then I'd gorge on the entire pie until I made myself sick.

I am embarrassed at both my failings, and my failing to come to terms with them. I have been stuck, pinned to past errors while everyone else moved forward. I have felt marked, branded and tattooed with past failings. I have felt them above my head when I introduce myself. I have worried about them more than an imperfect body when I undress. I have felt the stain of them burn down my cheeks when I cry.

So yes, Mr. Whitman, I contain multitudes. For most of my life, I have wished I did not. I have wished that I were a simple, happy, uncomplicated monad, blissfully unaware of the past and able to leave my mistakes behind.

Part II: Mr. Whitman, meet Mr. Picasso. You two artists, meet Popeye.

I am changing. It has been a forced change. 2012 (to be very charitable) held a 'rough patch' for me. I have since been working to paint a new (or renewed) self.

Among other changes, I want to (re)discover a feeling of fearless love, toward life and toward myself and toward the passion and willingness to be vulnerable and caring that have led to the best things in my life. Somewhere along the line, fear sneaked in, snatched that away, and sabotaged the good. I want it back.

Here is where I am taking direction, as absurd as it sounds, from a paint can. Redecorating requires you to follow a few rules. First, there is prep work. Painting, both walls and the self, is a messy process. If you do not take time to set up your work area, you are likely to do as much harm as good. Set your drop cloth down, tape off the area that you want the new paint to cover, and do not forget to clean the work surface.

No matter how it got there, you are responsible for the gunk and grime on the walls you live in. Simply covering up what is currently showing does not work. For the paint to stick, you have got to clean up the old and repair cracks and scars.

Secondly, you need to give the paint time to dry. Often you will need several coats. Rushing the process does not work and can actually be counterproductive, muddying the finish you want. Patience and a willingness to sit calmly in the midst of a mess are required.

Whitman understood this – that life, art and emotion are inherently messy. This acceptance of messiness has been my turning point. I now embrace that I have a messy soul, mind and heart. They are filled with joy, and filled with defeat. They bounce between success and failure, tears of happiness and tears of sadness, earth-shaking love and underworld-shivering loneliness.

Containing multitudes means not just embracing different facets of the good; it also means accepting the faults and failures. The reason I could not do this before? I could not sit calmly in the mess. I never understood that beauty develops precisely because of, not despite, the fractures we experience.

We make mistakes. Multitudes of them. When you paint your heart and repaint your self, you are not an artist who specializes in the still life genre. Your heart does not belong in a fruit bowl alongside oranges and apples. It is vibrant. It contradicts itself. It causes itself pain. And it also beats with almost inexpressible love and joy.

Painting your self and throwing your colors onto life is less about absolute fidelity to detail and more about capturing and coming to peace with that interplay of contradictory multitudes.

The life you paint is like a Picasso: it is a fissured whole, viewed differently, depending on which angle you choose – disturbing at first, and beautiful the more you accept the failure of unity upon which it is built. It is all about perspective.

Mr. Whitman, thank you. I do indeed contain multitudes. I am living, moving, growing, and evolving. I am constantly repainting my soul. Mr. Picasso, I have come to love my fractured beauty. The hurts and mistakes, joys and loves have made a unique pattern on my heart. I am learning to sit in the pain, luxuriate in the love. We all have stained glass souls, beautiful precisely because of that unique interplay of contradictory emotions, motives, loves and regrets.

Once I understood this, I was able to forgive myself. This does not mean that there is no pain. There is. There will be tears, there will be mistakes. And there will also be smiles and soul-laughter and love. That is how it works. There is no need to deny or tear out from myself the parts I have not liked in the past. You cannot do that anyway.

I have moved from Whitman to Picasso to, finally, Popeye: "I yam what I yam."

I am the base material for living a life of love. That starts with me. I have a new acceptance of my self, warts and wounds included. I am. I grow. I am growing.

My stained glass, cubist soul contains multitudes and competing viewpoints and contradictions and it is messy. Painting your way through life always is. It is not just slapping on some color. Done properly, it is not as much covering up as it is repairing, adding to, and building upon what is underneath.

How to Make Love Stay: 6 Endless Tips.

By Long Distance Love Bombs

"There is only one serious question. And that is: who knows how to make love stay? Answer me that and I will tell you whether or not to kill yourself."

~ Tom Robbins

With that quote, Tom Robbins proposed a big and powerful question, a question about life and everything in it. It's a question that gets right to the point and it got us to thinking, writing and wondering.

We don't know the answer, but we needed to try and find it, if only to start the conversation. So, assuming love is a woman, this is how we'd make her stay.

1. Love her fiercely. Connection is key, vulnerability is bravery, and an open heart breaks down closed souls. We only get one shot at this life, this moment, and this relationship. If you're blessed enough to find yourself waking up next to the same love over and over and over again, please don't think of it as blandness. Choose blessedness.

If you find yourself getting too used to the monotony of your daily existence or if the routine is becoming too obscene, change something. Mix it up. Add some spice. Run off and have an adventure, even if it's just down the road. Go and see something you've never seen, even if it's just across the street. Go and do something you've never done, even if it's just under the sheets.

When you enter a room, let others notice that you notice her first. When you walk next to her, stop and kiss her neck for no good reason other than the fact that she is by your side. When she gets dressed in the morning, smile and appreciate that women are sexier getting dressed than they are getting undressed.

Respect her boundaries, but break down her walls. Crush her fears and free her mind. She's yours, and it's up to you to be hers. Be the hero she's always wanted but never knew she needed.

Be a brazen inspiration. Be a bold revelation. Be a novel innovation. Earn her every day and appreciate her every night. Give her your heart and defend hers at all costs. Be a warrior for love armed with a quiver full of fervor, and love will forever follow you into the hunt.

"Love easily confuses us because it is always in flux between illusion and substance, between memory and wish, between contentment and need."

~ Tom Robbins

2. Make her feel beautiful. This one is pretty simple: girls want to feel beautiful. Unfortunately, as you probably already recognize, women are bombarded each and every day with images from television, magazines, Facebook and everywhere else in our culture trying to show them and sell them beauty.

They should look good. They need to be put together. They must be presented well.

That is total bullshit. Humans were not born to cover their faces in makeup, did not evolve to spend an hour straightening their hair with expensive machines, and did not arise solely to dress up in high heels, or expensive jewels, or an overpriced dress bought to attend that cocktail party that night with those people that we don't really know and don't even care about.

In our society, beauty most often relates to the exterior and although a variety of superficial modifications are now wildly popular, they are all, each of them, a small, dirty, and pathetic lie.

Diamond rings are not beautiful. An open heart is beautiful. New shoes are not beautiful. Kindness is beautiful. Vulnerability is beautiful. Compassion, honesty, courage and confidence are the real beautiful things.

Besides, even with all of the makeup, accessories and clothes in the world, you cannot be beautiful if you do not feel beautiful. Similarly, if you feel beautiful, you are beautiful. It really is that simple.

So, take these powerful ideas and go about setting them free into the world. Make your girl feel beautiful. Compliment her soul. Look her in the eyes when you tell her you love her. Hold her hand. Melt her heart. Be her beacon. When she wakes up in the morning, tell her she looks great, and when she laughs or calls you crazy (and she will), mean it when you tell her that you mean it.

Stare into her eyes until she looks away first. Let her soar, and admire her in flight. Open her eyes, heart, hopes and dreams. Write her a note that says she makes you feel lucky, leave her a voicemail that says she makes you feel blessed and make her a card that says she makes you feel beautiful.

After all, beautiful things create beautiful things. So go ahead and be beautiful together, and love will stick around to watch.

"The highest function of love is that it makes the loved one a unique and irreplaceable being."

~ Tom Robbins

3. Make her feel safe. Girls like being held. They like having arms wrapped around them, simultaneously holding them close and pushing the world away. They enjoy walking with someone that can connect with them, confiding in someone who cares for them and loving someone who adores them. Girls like knowing that they are enough for us and that we are not looking elsewhere for replacements.

Girls want to matter, so let her feel comfortable speaking her heart. When she does, listen. When you listen, understand (not just what is being said, but why). When you understand, relate and remember. Become fluent in the language she speaks. Encourage her to be her best possible, even if that means exposing the hard truths that she tries to avoid, the facts that she can no longer ignore.

It's up to you to make her see that ultimately, no one else will make her happy but her. It's up to you to help her help herself. Earn her trust and then keep making deposits, because helping a woman feel safe empowers her to do the things that her heart tells her they need to be done.

When she is not worried about you or her or us, she is free, an uncaged bird, and freedom is a wondrous feeling. Freedom means safety, safety is liberating, and liberation leads to fearlessness. Without fear, we can focus on the things that matter, the things that set our hearts alight, and the dreams that only arise when we are awake.

Catalyzed by safety, dormant ideas awaken, embolden and enliven our life. Compassion, courage and honesty, love's three younger sisters, will stop by to visit, helping to ensure that our women are as safe and as strong as possible. Why is this important? Because strong women make men strong. And strong men can make love stay.

> *"When two people meet and fall in love, there's a sudden rush of magic. Magic is just naturally present then. We tend to feed on that gratuitous magic without striving to make any more. One day we wake up and find that the magic is gone. We hustle to get it back, but by then it's usually too late, we've used it up. What we have to do is work like hell at making additional magic right from the start. It's hard work, but if we can remember to do it, we greatly improve our chances of making love stay."*
>
> *~ Tom Robbins*

4. Make her feel important. There's a lot going on in the world and we are always on alert. We have to deal with jobs, laundry, stress, temptation, money, family, friends and the future. Distractions pervade. Opportunities proliferate. Obstacles present themselves. We have the Internet in our pockets, a gleam in our eyes and no time on our hands. We're often busy, occasionally stressed, and sometimes overwhelmed. We have much on our minds and to us, normal is nuts.

We have dreams and adventures ahead of us and sorrow and sacrifice behind and yet, through all of the drama and strife, the pains and the panics, the days and nights, love remains. She is there, next to you, urging you on, smiling, and wanting nothing but the best for you because she loves you, she cares about you, and she wants you to be happy.

She is a best friend, mentor and your biggest fan all in one. Your life would be worse without her in it. You would miss her if she were gone. She is the best thing in your world. Don't you ever fucking lose sight of that, and love will have no chance to escape.

Love is addicted to appreciation and awareness. Keep both in abundant supply and love will always be near.

"My love for you has no strings attached. I love you for free."

~ Tom Robbins

5. Fuck her good. Here's the thing: women love sex and they think about it all the time. Although they would probably never admit it, women love getting down and dirty between the sheets, fast and furious on the bathroom floor, and slow and comfortable up against a wall.

If you're a woman, you're probably smiling as you read this. I'm sorry, girls, but the secret is out. We know that you talk about sex with your friends, fantasize about foreplay when you're alone, and dream about the dirty when you are bored at work. And that's okay. It's more than okay, in fact.

Sex is important and good sex is a universal human right. So, do your best to be your best, not only in life but also in bed. However, don't forget that it's far more than just the physical that matters: the most important sex organ is the brain.

Be giving, with words and touch. Be intimate, with emotions and experience. Be thoughtful, with deeds and desires. Seduce her away from her distractions. Excite her.

Good loving is a necessity and if your girl is not getting it from you, she'll start looking elsewhere for greener pastures to fertilize. However, if you can make her shake like a freight train, she'll stick around like a memory. And that's what it is all about – making love stay.

"We waste time looking for the perfect lover, instead of creating the perfect love."

~ Tom Robbins

6. Make her laugh. Cyndi Lauper was right: *girls just want to have fun.* Have you ever seen a bunch of girls going absolutely buck wild on a dance floor? It's a sensation, and fun is the feeling. Have you ever witnessed a group of girls laughing so hard that they're snorting and crying and madly screeching right up close into each other's faces? It's a sanctuary, and fun is the preacher.

Life is hard, and that's a fact. We all know that sadness comes by to play hide and seek, sorrow randomly stops by for a drink, and occasionally, we get overwhelmed, annoyed, or infuriated. It happens. It's unavoidable. It's not her fault.

Being down does not make her a bad person, or a bad partner, or a pain in the ass. Being down does not make her heart any smaller or her beauty any less noticeable. Rather, being down is part of lifting up. Help lift her up. Help make her see. Teach yourself the powerful and noble truth that here is nothing more beautiful than a smiling soul staring at you with love-filled eyes. Make her smile. Warm her heart. Be silly.

Life is far too serious to take seriously and sometimes the bravest thing you can do is laugh.

So do it, and do it often. Goof around. Be playful. Have fun. Locate your inner child and give him a high five. Find some grass and do some somersaults. Enjoy the ride and love will sit next to you, its head on your shoulder, smiling all the while, for where there is laughter, there is love.

> *"But do we know how to make love stay? I can't even think about it. The best I can do is play it day by day."*
>
> ~ *Tom Robbins*

Serve it up hot and let's dig in: *how do you make love stay?*

10 Wicked Morsels for Living a Sexy Life.

By Kristi Stout

In the desire to help a friend conjure tools for the complicated areas of life, I spontaneously compiled these morsels of thought which I now wish to share with you.

Bits of my favorite quotes compiled with my own life experiences, birthed from my love of sharing love, these Morsels were born. Each of them are followed by a question. I feel that questions are the doorways to personal evolution and give us cause to embark on grand and glorious adventures into the boundless realms.

Morsel 1

We must break to become anything different than what we are. Whether it's a broken bone, a broken habit, a broken marriage, or a broken heart, something must be destroyed before something new can be created. It's the hardest most soul-wrenching experience – breaking to the utmost of what you always thought you were – but beautifully blazon and raw, wild as a black stallion and so worth the ride.

When was the last time you broke?

Morsel 2

I could not do this concept better justice than how Henry Miller words it:

> *"Life, as we all know, is conflict, and man, being part of life, is himself an expression of conflict. If he recognizes the fact and accepts it, he is apt, despite the conflict, to know peace and to enjoy it. But to arrive at this end, which is only a beginning (for we haven't begun to live yet!), a man has got to learn the doctrine of acceptance, that is, of unconditional surrender, which is love."*

When was the last time you surrendered to your conflict?

Morsel 3

Don't be limited by feelings of inadequacy. Tell that notion to fuck off. Life is a grand creative project and self-expression is essential to you. Express yourself, always. Divinely. Exceptionally. Grandly. Utterly. Darkly. Lightly. By self-expression we venture further into ourselves. And by venturing further into you, you can't help but become transformed.

When was the last time you ventured down there?

Morsel 4

Instead of placing your identity in other people, friends, lovers, ex-lovers, family life – because this can be precarious and sometimes detrimental – place it into you and the world. Put your identity into your experiences, not the people who you experience with – though love the experiences you have with them. And love *them*. Share – joyously, drunkenly, wildly.

This causes you to fall madly in love with life and yourself in a way that empowers you and everyone around you. Spilling love over like beautiful molten lava! Creating an energy where giving becomes your fuel – what builds you. In this sense life becomes perpetual motion and everything – everyone – around you, including life, as you live it, becomes your teacher.

When was the last time you identified as your experience?

Morsel 5

Brought to you by Hermann Hesse:

> *"Man is not by any means of fixed and enduring form. He is nothing else than the narrow and perilous bridge between nature and spirit. His innermost destiny drives him on to the spirit and to God. His innermost longing draws him back to nature, the mother. Between the two forces his life hangs tremulous and irresolute."*

When was the last time you were okay with not knowing?

Morsel 6

Form a working relationship with your anger. Embrace it. Kiss it in the rain. Caress its sweet contours, then take it home and bang the hell out of it. The beautiful thing about passion is, you create with it. There is no right or wrong way to be passionate. There is merely conscious and unconscious passion.

Making sweet love to your anger is being conscious of the God inside you. Remember, there is no right or wrong – only choice and consequence. Decide the consequences that are unfavorable and don't make choices that lead there. This is one method by which we truly come to know ourselves. Remember, you are always enough.

What was the last time you suffered consequence?

Morsel 7

Whatever you're afraid of, or hesitant to become because you think you can't... Become it. Rawly. Fiercely. Honestly. If you're scared of it, it's probably an indication you're headed in the right direction. (See Morsel 3.)

When was the last time you told fear to fuck off?

Morsel 8

Everything that has happened to you, the stuff you did or did not do or say, was all a necessary happening. It has made you, and you are beautiful in all your perfect nakedness and imperfectness. In your defeats, accomplishments, wisdom and stupidity. Darkness and lightness.

It has all served the you that stands in the now – an organic, malleable expression of Life and Source. If I were to liken this to the forging of a sword, which in and of itself is a violent process, the true revelation and exquisitely sexy nature of this weapon is apparent through not only the forging but in the wielding.

When was the last time you wielded your sword?

Morsel 9

Think of the world you carry within you. Only be attentive to the stuff that rises up and makes you tremble with ferocity. That violent, destructive chaos that makes you want to annihilate the universe and then turn around and re-create it (let there be light!) – set this energy above everything else you experience and observe about you. This passion is worthy of your entire love.

Allow the solitude of this feeling. There is love even in solitude. Being with solitude is necessary, because when life seems mundane and without point, what comes from your innermost world, from the depths of solitude is what lends comfort. It is also here in this place of trembling passion where you find God. In this kind of solitude there is prayer. Such passion is prayer.

When was the last time you allowed passionate solitude?

Morsel 10

It is only with boundaries and limitations that we can create anything. Once created, those boundaries can be pushed. This is the nature of evolution. This applies to everything – art, poetry, life, relationship, love...

When was the last time you established a boundary?

Even in the boundless realms there need be a boundary laid, for how would you understand the beauty of the realm, were it not dualistic and set up in the language of boundaries? Light/Dark. Hot/Cold. Sleep/awake. Conscious/Unconscious. Boy/Girl. You/Me.

Now go live... you wicked, sexy thing, you.

Fight for Your Life.

By Kirk Hensler

Do you ever feel like other people are always letting you down? And that you're surrounded by idiots? Even worse, that nobody will be honest with you?

It's probably because you're overly sensitive and they are afraid to be themselves around you because they are worried that you'll fly off the handle and have a meltdown. Loosen up a bit for god's sake and give people a chance to communicate with you.

Emotions are like friends. We have to accept them or we won't have any. The idea of what we're supposed to feel like dominates what we actually feel like. We are ghosts in our own bodies.

I think about performing a simple squat. I bend my knees 90 degrees and hover my ass above an imaginary chair. And then my legs start to burn and I act like I have just been shot 6 times in each thigh. I build up a big story in my mind, that the burning is so awful and I am a victim of some great crime. I will do anything to not be squatting anymore. I want out and it's all a bunch of mind games really, my little self-doubting thoughts taking over because I'm tired and scared of failure so I'll let anyone talk me into quitting. But really my body could physically squat for minutes, maybe hours longer.

Sometimes I tell my students that I will give them bundles of cash if they can hold a posture for a minute. Or I'll make it a competition. As soon as this happens they all act like they've just taken loads of steroids and can kick the shit out of any physical challenge I put in front of them.

But no challenge or money means they have to do it for themselves, and since people don't generally give a shit about themselves they quit as soon as their brains get the first indication of a fight from the doubting side of things.

I get mad at them for this. I think about walking around the room and screaming in their face and karate chopping them across the shin. But really I just want to give them the little push they need to be self-governing greatness.

Sometimes we quit on ourselves and then go home; and when we get home we don't like who we are.

Animals will fight until death but humans find any excuse possible not to fight at all. And I'm not talking about bare knuckle brawling; I'm talking about fighting for anything. There's nothing wrong with a good struggle, or burning thighs that make you second-guess yourself for a moment. Taking a good look at yourself in these situations will only help you move forward.

Doubt is great. Fear is great. It means we get to prove to ourselves why we matter. We get to stare doubt in the face and give it a dirty-ass look that would scare a terrorist. It's there because part of us wants us to be miserable, so we can have pity parties and blame everyone else for our own problems. And most of our lives we have let that small-minded fearful talk run the show.

The thing is, fear and doubt are the biggest cowards of all. They can't stand up to us; we're way too fucking crazy. Let's stand up and show them how crazy *we* are. We're strong enough to torture ourselves every day by living a half-assed, borderline miserable lives – I think we're strong enough to sit our asses down in a squat for a minute or two and not give in to the first thought that gets us out of a battle.

Challenge is growth. No challenge is stagnation, Prozac, and hours of television every night. It's fucking miserable and it's killing your soul. You should be arrested.

I should be able to come to your house and smash your television on the ground and take you away and unlock you up somewhere near a tree or a body of water and give you a pen and a notepad and tell you to start writing and not stop until you know what inspiration feels like. And you know that it comes from inside and not outside of you. You don't need anyone but your goddamn self to realize who you are.

Is it because we are afraid that when we're tested we won't have what it takes to pull through? Are we scared that we'll fail and nobody will like us anymore?

First of all, nobody cares about us that much, they are too busy worrying about their own damn problems. The world can be ours to experiment with if some other people want to spend their time burying their head up their ass.

Who really cares enough about failure to let it run their life? That's old news. The most successful people in the world fail every day, and they learn to love it. It's learning, it's living. It's so simple I want to reach through your screen and slap you in the face.

Get up and start doing the things you know you should be doing. I don't care about your family or your job or bills. It's all going to pass you by one day, maybe tomorrow.

Animals don't quit because they don't care what they look like; they care about surviving. It's not an option whether or not they give their best effort, irrespective of what other, gossipy animals might be whispering behind their backs. Animals don't give a fuck, they are going for it.

We aren't fighting for our survival the way we should be. We're humans and we're just a little different than other creatures. Food, water, and shelter take care of our cells but not our souls. In order to survive we need to take care of our body but also our imagination. If we don't feel the painful beauty of life every day then we are (slowly) committing suicide. We are letting our souls die and our bodies won't be far behind.

I think we care too much. About the wrong things. We care too much about our feelings, about other people's opinions, about politics, and about Taylor Swift. And I'm certain we care too much about feeling sorry for ourselves. It is some kind of spell that we are afraid to break. A lot of people live under this spell to avoid the work that lies ahead of them in their quest to be happy.

We're all tired of the game. We're just waking up in the morning and mailing it in. Our hope is diminishing. But at the first sign of rebellion we become wide awake. We remember it's not buried too deep. It just needs a little push. Just a nudge.

Don't wait for it. Someone else is waiting for you to do it. Just be the one and do it already. You won't be alone and you'll know exactly what to do once you start.

Let Yourself Be Moved.

By Jeanette LeBlanc

> *"Forget safety.*
> *Live where you fear to live.*
> *Destroy your reputation.*
> *Be notorious."*
>
> *~ Rumi*

Let yourself be moved until you radiate your own *guru-fab* energy. Let yourself be moved until every day begins with a tingle of anticipation that starts in your baby toe and rolls through your body and out into the universe.

Pretend I'm an ancient guru. Yes, it is a stretch, but humor me for a minute. You have got a good imagination, and you probably owe me a favor or two. Come on… put aside your skepticism. I will even help you out.

I am sitting high on a rugged mountaintop and you just climbed the whole damn thing to see me. You are covered in sweat and your legs are all scratched from those damn prickly bushes that lined the trail. Short shorts were a bad idea.

You worked your ass off to get here, and it was one hell of a climb. But I am *guru-fabulous* like nothing you have ever seen before. I am all wrinkled skin and wise eyes and radiating thousand-year-old wisdom. Plus, I am wearing a freaking insane pair of red stilettos and a dress you would kill to get your hands on.

I have got a rockin' body for an old girl. Do not even try to pretend you did not notice. You are in awe. It is a damn good thing – because a healthy dose of awe is the price of admission on my mountaintop, baby.

But still, you doubt. You think, "She'd better damn well make this worthwhile."

I gaze at you – with all my thousand-year-old *guru-fab* wisdom – and you listen. You listen because I am an ancient sage in drag queen stilettos, and you know I've got to be speaking the truth. I say only four words: *"Let yourself be moved."*

You want to live with a wide open heart? Let yourself be moved. You want to break through old patterns and discover yourself anew? Let yourself be moved. You want to fall in love? Heal a broken heart? Make right a deep injustice? Smash through paradigms? Pick yourself up and dust yourself off? Change the freaking world? Let yourself be moved.

We live most of our lives with our guards way up. Well-built walls protect us from threats, both real and imagined. We are splintered and patched and numb to the core, but we keep our game face on, always.

We nurture our skepticism and our cynicism and that tiny kernel of innate distrust until they are larger and harder and more powerful than we ever wanted them to be. We give the bad more power than the good, even when we do not intend to.

This life? It can be hard. On your knees, sobbing for mercy, crazy-fucking-hard. But we all have moments of brilliance – experiences that wake us up to the sheer beauty of the universe and chip away at our cynicism and distrust. Interactions that feed our souls, open our hearts, and convince us that just-possibly-maybe-perhaps life really is inherently good.

And those moments, my sweet friends, only occur under certain circumstances. When we are safe, or brave, or distracted, or bad-ass-crazy-enough to lower the veils, dismantle the walls, and blast the hell through that numbness into a place of deep feeling.

And I mean *deep*, people. Brilliance never settles for superficial. Brilliance only happens when we let ourselves be moved. But there is a catch. One little *guru-fab* caveat that I will let you in on, because I totally think you are ready: Brilliance rarely feels entirely gentle. Yes, it can be transcendent and awe-inspiring and all kinds of fabulous. But it can also be utterly terrifying.

Brilliance exists so far outside of our everyday detachment that it can rock our worlds. Talk about being moved – brilliance of the life-altering variety can feel like a whirlwind around-the-world-in-80-days mind trip.

It can bring up all sorts of baggage we did not know we were lugging around, and test us in ways we never anticipated. Insecurity? Scarcity? Limiting beliefs? Debilitating jealousy?

Yes, yes and yes-yes-yes. How about all of the above, plus a dose of paranoia, all wrapped up in a two-for-one order of heart-pounding fear? Hell yeah. Sign me up. And the only way through that whole mess? Let yourself be moved some more.

Caveat Number Two: Sir Newton was on to something when he formulated that pesky little law of inertia. Dear ole' Newty scored major points on his science quiz with this little gem:

If you ain't been a-movin', you ain't so likely to be moved. It is going to take a little practice at first; a nudge in the right direction or a giant push toward your desire.

You want change? Start seeking out change-makers and soak up their intensity. You want to get over a broken heart? Start by actively falling in love with yourself. You need to stop standing still? Polish up your dancing shoes and start with a slow shimmy.

You want to be moved? Get off your ass and get moving. Refuse to remain stagnant. Stop accepting the status quo. Do not let society dictate how you feel or live or love. Not one more day of allowing your past or your family or your community to choose your life for you.

Reject the idea that you must settle for *breathing just a little, and calling it a life*. No longer feel limited by protective walls or numbness or that tiny voice that tells you to play-it-cool-don't-hope-too-much-feel-too-much-want-too-much-love-too-much.

That nagging little voice? It's gotta go. Just let yourself be moved, dammit.

Read poetry until your body tingles. Go to an art gallery and stare at a painting until you can feel the artist's brush strokes on your body. Gather your girlfriends and laugh until you cry. Then cry until you laugh again. March in a protest and be swept away by the power of the crowd and the madness of inequality. Give 'til it makes you uncomfortable.

Listen to a symphony and let your heart swell to a point of bursting with the power of the music. Lock eyes with someone who makes you feel that *Sing... Tug... Whoosh...* in your gut and just go with it; to hell with taking it slow.

Watch your kiddos play or fight or dream or make art, and feel your own inner child break free. Jump out of a plane and contemplate your own mortality. Read your poetry for a crowd even if your whole body is shaking. Look a homeless woman in the eye and ask her how she is doing; feel her answer deep in your bones.

Take a giant leap outside your comfort zone and experience every last bit of the panic that greets you. Let the abundance of life penetrate you deep, until you lose count of the infinite number of ways the universe can move you.

Sit with your fear and your insecurity and your jealousy and your paranoia and let them push you past that place that holds you back – past the numbness, past the complacency, past truths fed to you by people who hold you with a limited view.

Nurture your genius, your beauty, your inherently trusting nature. Feel your own courage. Fall in love. Create a safe space for someone marvelous to fall in love with you. Dance with fire. Get loud during sex. Shake your fabulous booty while you do the dishes. Make friends with your roaring goddess power. Above all else? Stop. Holding. Back.

Let yourself be moved until you catch a glimpse of your limitless, full-of-potential soul. Hold it within you like the priceless thing that it is, and bring it forth as your gift to the world. Dust off your divine spirit and get down with your groovy self.

Make friends with your heart, and go down on your knees to thank it for serving you well. Fuck inhibitions. If your body wants to make love in the rain, do it. If your spirit wants to sing Beyoncé in the grocery store, let her. If your soul tells you to body-paint a giant canvas in rainbow colors, go and make some supersized art.

If your heart wants to fall in love every single day, give it the freedom to run free and seduce the world. Get juicy, get wild, get wanton and lusty. Get turned on by life. Really turned on. Feel everything. Deeply.

Let yourself be moved.

Let yourself be moved until you are opened wide. Wider. Even wider than you ever thought possible. So wide that you are swimming in brilliance. So wide it does not feel safe. Because safety was never the goal (we were just tricked into believing that it was).

Let yourself be moved until you are ready to love more, feel deeper, change things. Let yourself be moved until you radiate your own *guru-fab* energy.

Let yourself be moved until every day begins with a tingle of anticipation that starts in your baby toe and rolls through your body and out into the universe. Let yourself be moved until you are ready to move mountains with the brilliance of your soul.

But not my mountain. It stays where it is. After all, I am a thousand-year-old-red-stiletto-wearing guru. And what I say, totally goes.

Let yourself be moved.

Writers are from Mars, Readers are from Mars, too.

By Skip Maselli.

You were expecting Venus? So that is where you are; I should have known. The following is a compendium of musings on the balance of reader and writer, teetering on the fulcrum of creativity.

***

A creationist's take on the theory of revolution.

First there was dirt, and God yawned and said nothing, for even He could look within Himself and know that there must be more out there than this.

He paced back and forth across the universe, rolling a piece of lint in his pocket into an immense idea.

Then *God Shuffled His Feet*, and kicked up a spark from the floor of heaven, sending a lightning bolt into a puddle of primordial ooze, squeezed from a giant rock. He looked into the elixir of life, the original heartbeat's ground zero, and saw that it was good… so He rested.

In the pre-dawn of time, stuff began growing and crawling onto land, followed by some monkeys who serendipitously learned to fling their dung against rocks with great deftness and expression (it is always about monkeys). And then some of them stood erect and walked into the evolution of Homo Sapiens Scriptoricus (Human Writer) and Homo Sapiens Lectoricus (Human Reader).

That writers ever crawled out of the ground to begin with, is an event that overcomes astronomical odds. Imagine the frustration of the first human writer, of having no language, knowing no words to convey what he feels, senses, fears, loves, or loathes. This must have sent him to the edge of sanity.

Even today, many Homo Sapiens still relate to that feeling of wanting to share, but having no sense of what sharing means or takes to accomplish.

God really knows His shit. But God didn't make it easy – we are all still evolving as creators… and He keeps jumping up and shouting, "Oh, oh, write about Me, write about Me!"

And we did... and now we get married because of it, and we feel guilty because of it, and we annihilate cultures because of it.

After the above evolution, something happened: Lectoricus began realizing that she needed to break from the descending progression by writing herself in a new direction. Now it seems like just about anyone with opposable thumbs can tap out a creative writing piece. Yep – God does know His shit.

Evolution is a natural inability to accept the conditions of our limitations. But revolution... ah, sweet revolution changes the conditions so there are no limitations. One need only to muse for a moment at the potential of what has yet to be created, and in that moment, creation manifests.

Let us say, and I am just saying, that evolution applies to a writer. Our hearts will one day turn to parchment, and our blood to ink. The letters on the keyboard will fade in synchrony with the march of time, and our thoughts will drip tears into the black well of the soul.

A writer's composition is her footprint through time... traces of heel-to-toe, dancing through the archaeological records like notes on a scale. Her nimble steps and surefooted gait, prancing along the azimuth of passion; leaving behind the artifacts on where she has been within herself, the predators she evaded, and from which watering holes it was safe to sip.

Writers are from Venus, Readers are from Mars.

An irritated friend noticed my pensive distance and snapped, "... were you listening to anything I just said?!"

I thought about this for a moment and replied crisply and with honesty, "No – no, I wasn't. I was listening to what I heard."

To know a writer through his writing is not necessarily the same as understanding what he has written. The dilemma of this writer is whether to sing to your weaknesses or strengths; to play upon your dreams or to lure you into mine.

In seeking to know another, the Venusian writer and the Martian reader should begin with what they seek to observe within themselves.

"What is wonderful about great literature is that it transforms the man who reads it towards the condition of the man who wrote."

~ E.M. Forster

The planet rotates about the spine of a book while the universe expands from the Archimedean point. Getting closer to the source of expression entails opening up to the sensations of its symptoms – the transformation happens at the precise moment the cause becomes the effect.

The identity of the reader emerges through creative conjecture, and destiny is fulfilled when self-discovery within the Marian manifest through the creative clues of the Venusian.

For Earthlings: the writer – lightning; the reader – lightning rod; the planet – energy.

The feeling of writing is akin to that of making love to the mind and heart of the reader – it is this unfettered giving that feeds the ego, the id, and libido.

Mental foreplay will become the distinguishing characteristic of the writer species as palpating fingers on a keyboard play on the flesh of still and silent creatures – until they leap, from repose to rebellion on a steed of words... echoing within our bodies, never fading off the pages.

Archaeology: unearthing the truth.

"Every day we slaughter our finest impulses. That is why we get a heartache when we read those lines written by the hand of a master and recognize them as our own, as the tender shoots which we stifled because we lacked the faith to believe in our own powers, our own criterion of truth and beauty. Every man, when he gets quiet, when he becomes desperately honest with himself, is capable of uttering profound truths. We all derive from the same source. There is no mystery about the origin of things. We are all part of creation, all kings, all poets, all musicians; we have only to open up, only to discover what is already there."

~ Henry Miller

The geological law of original horizontality will be up-righted by the humming glow of phosphor and liquid crystal – millions of computers en echelon pitted and weathered by the ideas of so many unleashed minds.

Impressions and casts, etchings and primitives, potshards of jagged broken ideas buried in situ where overflowing urns were emptied into the bellies of despondent artists and left behind as they maundered off in their besotted dreams.

Reading unfurls the coils of love laid sweetly by a poet. With our shovel, pick, and brush, we clear away the dust and detritus of entombed poems.

With the turning of pages, the lids of the sarcophagi are cracked open to the musty gasps of revelations – page one, see me; page two, feel me; page three, love me; page four, let me go; and so on back to darkness. The turning of one page chases the ink to the next.

> *"Truth is stranger than fiction, but it is because fiction is obliged to stick to possibilities; truth isn't."*
>
> *~ Mark Twain*

The inconceivable truth shifts in the shadows along the artist's path, snapping twigs in the darkness under his feet. There, in the absence of light, a writer learns to tell lies of the stories they have lived, until they begin to live the stories they tell. In the end, the reader finds out that only dead writers write the truth.

I need to feel the predator eyes of the writer upon me, catch the flash of teeth that bite teasingly into her lower lip, recoil from her dripping tongue and the tensioning of her haunches, then the rise of her hips an instant before sharp words spring upon my senses.

Ink is blood. The voracious readers slice their fingers on the paper-thin edge of truth, and fiction is salt pressed into the open wounds of fact.

As for my wounds – when I hand you the rose of honesty, please be aware of the thorns. I have already pricked my hands many times carrying it around on my own.

A writer's pen is the scythe that emblazons the sinuous trails between origins and destinations that are as unique as the traveler – it is the turn in the path, not just the soil beneath the feet.

Fear not that you will read your next great idea somewhere else, before you have had a chance to find it within yourself. There is less treasure behind us that is worth the carrying – left by the others on the ground – than there are our own treasures that we've, ourselves, yet to bury.

My gift at mid-life was received when I dropped a palette of gold that I pulled from the earth so that I might catch a single white feather that fell toward me from the sky. The gold was intended to pave the trail from whence I came; the feather, to be dipped in an inkwell so I might author the direction I should go.

Choose your medium.

When we are through with the pounding pursuit of our myopic objectives, and the chisels of tactics are worn down to nothing but pitted dull stumps, we will find we have created a tall berm of talus and dust between us and the truth, but there stand the *fruits* of our labor nonetheless.

An authentic artist can look at a block of marble and know the true form within it before the chisel is ever set and struck.

Writing is art, and it is especially interested in destructive approaches to building castles of catharsis – it resonates from a dull hum to vibrating harmonics that disintegrate the matrix paralyzing the verve of imagination.

The cement-worker constructs the *forms* with his mind, and then pours the cement. He textures it with stones of syncopation and sounds, cobbles of consonance, and coarse grains of alliteration. He writes an entire sidewalk...for pedestrians to read. The words may be the cobbles in the cement, but the real magic is in the matrix.

In music, it is rhythm and melody, adorning the words, which resonate with listeners on a very deep and subconscious level. Some hear music, some write notes, some read lyrics. Westerners culturally hear the same score of music different than Easterners, despite the scale ranging from monkey poop to honeysuckle. Melody and harmony are a blend of unique notes that are untainted and parochialized by customs and dogma and codicils of culture (which impacts words and meaning). In some way, the magic transcends from musician to listener – it is the blending that is tasted by the ear, not the notes. And of the Martian readers, the magic is the understanding of the story, less the words scribed by the Venusian writer. The Martian reader rewrites the meaning in his mind, and the Venusian lays the tracks of her own inner story.

Writing also is best when it does not rely on language – hard to explain, but so is the musical scale.

Like music, the story is always present in the universal plane consciousness – it is the collaboration of reader and writer in which it becomes manifested as art. It is the fine relationship between the *art of creation* and the *creation of art*. Mars, Venus, what is the difference?

Writing is tricky. It is what the words do not say that gives freedom to the creative machinations of the reader. Left to only to the vocabulary of the reader, even armed with a dictionary or synonym finder, there would be no such thing as great writing.

"Hey, creation happens!"

"The creative adult is the child who survived."

~ Sun Gazing

Of this quote, a loving friend wrote, "Think about it; the most creative moments of your adult life were the moments you allowed the child in you to play."

Sad how growing older often becomes the smothering of the innocent innovator; we are compelled to protect what is within us by never letting it out.

Through the course of becoming adult-ish, our surface becomes as rough and scarred as tree bark around the sapling; the child thrives within, wrapped in thickening wounds. These protective layers are well-intended... but ill begotten in the end as the cork of youth is lost in the depths of time. And then one day, we are so numb that we cannot remember what we dreamt the night before, let alone a sweet and pithy childhood memory. The writer inside the reader hangs on to these moments of youth, for they become the trusted handholds and firm footing for many a slippery slope as we cross into our later years.

Creativity is the uncloaking of passion that is otherwise imprisoned by the broad black lines in our coloring books, with the grown-up instruction, "Shush now, and color within the lines."

I am reminded of a picture from Kent State during the war protest – a college student is placing a delicate green-stemmed flower in the gun metal barrel of a national guardsman's rifle. Images like this are misconstrued as spittle against an institutional wall, a statement of history in conflict, rather than acts of creativity, passion, and love. Make your pen the *prettiest rifle*.

The world can only be saved by the minds of adults with the hearts of children. Of all the animal kingdom, thankfully the only species to not evolve is the child within an adult. It is a misprint in the recipe for man, but it is a delicious irony for mankind. It takes a certain level of maturity to know that you will never outgrow your own youth.

Tomorrow I will imagine the conference table as a sandbox, our coffee cups as pails, and my colleagues as playmates.

You can go fly a kite or go to hell, just be getting somewhere. She who flies the kite should not fear he who snips the string. But both will gasp at frame and sail – careening off on the winds of malcontent, gusts of rapture, cyclones of confusion, and eddies of pain. The impish voyeur and bon vivant – both twisted in the sheets, moaning from within the cave of literary fornication – beautiful revolutionaries in contrapposto.

I have picked up many a stone, etched with words of encouragement…but none so fulfilling to me as those that I have scribed on and chucked into the wild rivers, which skipped and disappeared into the depths of only God's awareness. I am just a reluctant angel with ten unruly typing fingers, who apparently conspire with the warped underworld of my mind to snuff the lanterns at Dante's door.

"…all the love in the world we need can be fit on the tip of a pen. More than the bounty of earth, sea, and sky, it's ink that gets under our skin…"

~ Lovely Dreaming Foxes (who, you ask?)

Your Everyday Guide to Sanity – 21 Ways to Reclaim your True Colors.

By SR Atchley

> *"You know those days when you get the mean reds? The mean reds are horrible. Suddenly you're afraid, and you don't know what you're afraid of... The only thing that does any good is to jump in a cab and go to Tiffany's."*
>
> ~ *Holly Golightly, Breakfast at Tiffany's*

We all have those days. Days when the mean reds rise up inside and spill over into our atmosphere, coloring the entire day with cardinal, carmine and crimson.

Or days when the blues rain down from cobalt clouds, spilling slow sapphire showers. We all experience the ups and downs of the authentic life, but we can't all catch a cab to Tiffany's. So... what do you do on those days?

Having dealt with the mean reds since I learned my colors, I've had ample occasions to try some things out. On some days, I find the best I can do is to add a touch of green as a complementary color, instead of trying to repaint the whole canvas into a rainbow.

In my efforts to repaint my days into something a bit more pleasing to the mind's eye, I have found that a stockpile of varied tools – plenty of paintbrushes, palettes, pastels and pencils – is essential. Having an arsenal of armaments and art supplies can help add a splash of color to those monochromatic days.

In case your arsenal is running low, or if you've not yet accumulated enough effective armaments, I offer you the following magic color change tips to help turn your day around.

When you find the combinations and compositions that work for you, rest assured, my beautiful open-hearted human, you will find those days become fewer, farther between and much easier to forge through.

1. Write it out! The simple act of putting pen to paper can be extremely liberating when it comes to dealing with a hard day. I have had more than a few days colored by fear, anger, sadness, jealousy and regret. In those days, I find I can leave my troubles behind by writing.

Expressing in words those things that are troubling me often lends an air of objectivity to the issue at hand. A letter, a list, a poem, an essay... each is an act of release, an act of putting your colors on the page.

When, and if, you revisit what you've written, you may find a rainbow reaching out from behind the clouds.

2. Dance, sing, play. I've had a song swimming in my head since the moment I opened my ears.

Music allows us to express, enhance, exhort and embrace our emotions. Let the music flow from your limbs, legs, hands, feet and fingertips. From your heart to your lungs, throat, lips. Feel your soundtrack tingling up through the crown of your head as you tap in.

Music has evolved alongside humanity for thousands of years, reflecting our deepest depths, highest heights and everything in between. Use it as your muse, and let your spirit soar.

3. Tell someone your story. Chances are, there is someone out there who is willing to listen. Someone safe, who cares about how you feel. Chances are, they have felt the way you are feeling, or they will at some point. If they cannot help you understand, they may at least lend an ear for a few minutes.

If you are lucky enough, you may find not only a willing ear, but a mouth wise enough to tell you something helpful, such as "...this isn't something you did. This is something that happened." Huh.

There may be something to that.

4. Have a good cry. Crying, though sometimes viewed as a sign of weakness, is actually a healthy body process. Tears carry toxins away from the body and kill harmful bacteria. When based on an emotional response, tears release powerful chemicals such as prolactin, stress hormones, and endorphins.

It's okay to have a cry; it really can make you feel better. Tears also cleanse and lubricate the eyes, resulting in improved visual clarity. And really, what could be better on those days than the strength that results from enhanced clarity and vision?

5. Recall moments of strength. Speaking of strength, take time to reconnect with those days when you demonstrated resolve, determination, steadfastness... and let yourself consciously remember what your body, mind, and spirit felt like in those moments.

Bring those instances to your current awareness and sit with them. Let them build you back up. You are strength and wisdom incarnate, my stardust warrior! Arise!

6. Take a walk. Move yourself, and let yourself be moved. Let the natural world take you back in. Rest in your Mother's arms for awhile, enjoying the sun on your face and the call of birds in your ears.

Become grounded again with the earth beneath your feet. Sometimes spinning out of control just means that you have lost your footing, which is okay. It is one way to gain ground and put your foot down somewhere new. Make a new path.

7. Cleanse yourself. Take a long hot bath. Take a cold shower. Take a swim. Stand in the rain. Water is your friend – you are primarily composed of it, after all. And a good cleanse is... well... cleansing.

While you're at it, drink a couple of large glasses of water... your body needs it, especially if you went with #4 on the list.

8. Find your core. My core is my body. It roots me and holds me to this life. As much as my mind and spirit affect me, I am neither of these without my body.

Yoga connects me to my core…to my body. Yoga is one of the most beneficial activities you can give your body. Yoga leads to enhanced strength, lower stress and an actualized sense of serenity.

Find your core, connect to it, and use it to guide the movements of your body, mind and spirit.

9. Laugh! Allow me to reintroduce you to the phrase *Laughter is the best medicine*. Like crying, laughing is healthy. Endorphins and dopamine levels increase as a result of laughter. Laughing boosts the immune system, reduces stress, relieves muscle tension, and improves circulation.

Take a break from the mean reds or the blues to find something that makes you laugh. Read the comics. Watch a video of your favorite stand-up comedian. Watch children play, or even better, play with children!

One of my favorite laugh-inciters, which is ridiculously simple and completely free, is the following: repeat one word over and over and over and over and over again until it is hilarious. Seriously, have you ever said 'fork' 100 times? It dissolves into a group of sounds that make little to no sense. So do our problems when we let them.

10. Create! Build a birdhouse. Crochet an afghan. Paint a sunset. Mold a man from clay. Create!

Your powers to create are much greater than you know… until you begin to use them, at which point they become boundless. By reaching into yourself and using what you find there, you can reconnect with the basic principles of the universe to recreate your universe.

A broken heart does not consist of holes. A heart breaks open in order to be whole. Opening up to the heart allows for its light and energy to reconnect to its origins. Use your open heart to expand and grow your world. Let your heart become whole by tapping into its creative nature. Pour your heart into your projects – your powers of creation are endless.

Even Picasso had the blues for a while…

11. Stop Ruminating. Replaying your pains, fears, longings, losses, and letting them swirl into hurricanes within your heart and head, does no good. Stop it. There is no changing the past. There is no telling the future.

Stop replaying your story in your head. Stop playing out future scenarios you cannot know. There is no peace in should've, would've, could've. Stop. Pay attention, instead, to Now.

12. Meditate. If you have a hard time with #11, try meditating. I have been meditating for about five years, and though I am far from rigorous with my efforts, I have found that meditation practice is, in itself, the culmination of effort. Developing the ability to sit quietly can bring peace to a difficult day.

One of the greatest benefits I've reaped through my meditation practice is the ability to quiet my mind. Using basic *shamatha* techniques, I can quiet my thoughts and reside in a state of calm abiding.

There are many great books, courses, teachers and instructions for introducing meditation into your life. A favorite reference of mine is the book *Meditation: The Buddhist Way of Tranquility and Insight* by Kamalashila, which outlines *shamatha*, *metta* and other basic meditation techniques. A great secular resource also exists in the Mindfulness Based Stress Reduction program pioneered by Jon Kabat-Zinn, which is appropriate for all faiths and ages.

13. Hug someone. Embrace the nearest living animal to you. Dog, cat, child, spouse, stranger – if you dare! If there is no one near you, hug yourself. Wrap your arms around your own shoulders and give a squeeze.

Hold yourself tightly, cradle yourself. Rest in your own embrace and be reassured by your own warmth. Love makes the world go round – love for yourself included.

14. Be compassionate. Be compassionate to yourself. Be compassionate with your thoughts about those persons, events and circumstances that led you to this day. If someone hurt you, chances are that they are hurting themselves.

There is no better way that I have found to let loose my own troubles than by holding others with compassion and loving-kindness. This can be difficult, to say the least. But it is worth it. It frees the heart from hurt by acknowledging the fragility of each one of us.

Handling others with care, even in your thoughts and wishes, is essential to moving towards a more loving and connected world, and can often turn the mean reds into a mellow mauve.

15. Express gratitude. There is a good deal of truth to the saying *It could be worse*. It could. Find those things in your life that are going well, and be thankful for them. Do you have food and clean water to drink? Start there. That is something to be thankful for.

Are your basic needs met? Are you clean and warm? Express some gratitude for your basic comforts. Then move on... to your lessons, your talents, your support systems. Take a moment to thank the Universe for all it has given you. Gratitude is healing.

Gratefulness can expand your narrow view of red and blue into the visions of bright white light that fill us all.

16. Clear away the clutter. I have found that my inner world often mirrors my outer environment. When my home is cluttered, my mind is often cluttered as well. On really red days, I clean out my closets and cupboards, removing those items that are no longer needed or wanted.

Take some time to get rid of the things that are in your way. Grab your mop bucket or your feather duster, turn up the music, and wipe away the cobwebs that are hanging around. Wash the windows and mirrors so that you may see yourself and your world more clearly.

Wipe away all obscuration, paying attention to the cracks, crevices and corners – those are where the deepest delusions lie.

17. Donate. Give something away. This is a good follow up to #16, as you may find yourself with a garage full of clutter when you are done with your clearing. It is also a natural consequence of #15, as gratitude often leads to thoughts of the less fortunate.

We live in a confusing world that is characterized by excesses and deficiencies living side by side. What greater way to find balance, both within and without, than to give of oneself for the benefit of others. Whether you give away your treasures or your time, the result will be beneficial to all involved.

18. Avoid intoxicants. Simply put, bourbon rarely makes a bad day better. Trust me on this one.

19. Rest. Take a break. Have a cup of tea. Take a nap. It's okay to check out for a bit. And when you wake up, pull back the curtains, open the blinds and let the sun shine in.

> *"Every now and then go away, have a little relaxation, for when you come back to your work, your judgment will be surer; since to remain constantly at work will cause you to lose power of judgment."*
>
> *~ Leonardo da Vinci*

20. Distract yourself. If you simply must, then by all means, hop in the cab and head for Tiffany's! While avoidance can be detrimental over the long haul, a healthy distraction can be good medicine, especially when facing a significant hardship.

Shortly after the death of my beloved husband, I feared for my eldest, as my child seemed less affected by the loss we were experiencing than I would have imagined. I assumed I was witnessing my child's avoidance of the issue of death, as demonstrated by the inclination to continually fill time with friends, games, parties, books, and social activities.

On one occasion, while languishing in my own pain and simultaneously trying to determine if my child was on a path of effective coping, I asked a simple question. "How do you maintain your carefree attitude amidst the loss of your dad?" My wise child simply told me, "I distract myself." My child was not ignoring the issue, had not forgotten or blocked out the obvious loss of his father from our home, family and lives. My child was not denying his death, but simply choosing not to focus on it every moment of every day.

My eldest chose, instead, to find activities, people and places that allowed for a break from the difficulty of the loss. A wise child, indeed; had he penned this piece, it may have included only this tidbit, for many of the other armaments in my arsenal boil down to just this.

Distract yourself. It's okay not to give those days more attention than they deserve.

21. Let it be. Step back, set down your paintbrushes and just have a look at your canvas. So... maybe this day's color scheme is not a bright sunny yellow. This day's composition is not a walk in the park or a sailboat on calm seas. Regardless of the subject matter or color scheme...

You are a work of art! Some days the colors get muddled and the paint goes every which way... but these, too, can be happy accidents. From different perspectives, different colors stand out. The truth is... All of your colors are beautiful, and together, they combine themselves into the most fantastic masterpiece of all: You.

The Art of Loving Yourself.

By Patricia Biesen

Writing a Valentine's Day blog provided me with the opportunity for a little road trip down relationship memory lane. I reminisced about the good, the bad, and the crazy (which was often me).

Everyone says that to love anyone you have to love yourself first. Many of us have high self-esteem but not a deep self-love. This means that besides admiring your gifts and talents and the good hair days, can you love yourself when you are being tested? Can you love yourself when you try out something completely new? Can you love yourself in the face of rejection? Can you love yourself when you are in an argument? Can you love yourself as you get older?

"I don't like myself, I'm crazy about myself."

~ Mae West

Many of us with high self-esteem may also be lacking in self-care. Good self-care practices would include getting enough sleep, eating the right foods, proper exercise, and drinking enough water. While most of the time I eat a healthy diet, there have been times I've had too much wine to keep up with other partygoers. If I really loved myself, I would have kept it to a two-drink maximum. I would have respected my body and not woken up with a skull-crushing hangover. I valued being cool with the cool kids more than I did my own well-being.

"Self-love is the unconditional love and respect you have for yourself that is so deep, so solid, so unwavering that you choose only situations and relationships – including the one you have with yourself – that reflect that same unconditional love and respect."

~ Christine Arylo (The Queen of Self Love)

How different would my life be if I were madly in love with myself?

How would it be if I couldn't wait to share myself with the people who are right for me? I've often given my love, support, money, attention and energy to people, organizations, and things that were not right for me. I tried to push my way in. Self-love is also about being patient and letting things happen in their own natural time, or not happen at all.

There will be those friends who just want to love a little bit of us, and we are okay with that when we truly love ourselves. Loving yourself gives you the freedom to let those around be who they truly are without manipulation, assumptions or expectations. I confess I am not good at this!

> *"To compare yourself to another is an act of violence against yourself."*
>
> *~ Iyanla Vanzant*

It also takes faith to love yourself. It takes patience and strength to wait for something you want to show up. It takes a knowing that if you hold true, then it will feel good when it finally shows up.

And there's another clue: *feeling good*. When you love yourself, you can sense when something is right and feels good. It takes courage to bless the audition that didn't work out or the invite to a fabulous party that all of your friends got but you didn't. It takes courage to know that life is happening exactly as it should.

> *"It's not rejection as much as it is selection."*
>
> *~ Coach Robert Notter*

A healer I know once said to me, "I love myself as much as I do a lover." I've never jumped on a couch in praise of how awesome I am. I've never phoned a girlfriend and said, "Guess what, I'm so in love with me. The other day I was so cute while I spilled coffee down my shirt. Blah blah blah."

I know myself more than anyone else knows me. I have collected tons and tons of data. Not all of it is very good. I'm with me all the time. I cannot get away. I think loving myself as much as possible is also practical and more fun than not. It's just new. My generation didn't grow up with these concepts. Hopefully future ones will.

Perhaps it happens much in the same way as you fall in love with someone. At first you get to know them and collect little bits of *like*: "Wow! I like his taste in music." "I like that he always has the right thing to say." "I like that he wears vintage bowling shoes even when he's clearly not anywhere near a bowling alley."

Then one day you realize you have captured all these *likes* and turned them into *love*. This can happen with ourselves if we take the time to appreciate how amazing we are.

Embrace the Mystery.

By Thomas Qualls

"To be lost is to be fully present."

~ Rebecca Solnit

We're afraid of the unknown. It is a fact of recorded history, of psychology, of spirituality. As a result, all manner of myths have been created – and institutionalized – to make us forget that the world is uncertain. When this doesn't work, we develop obsessive-compulsive disorders in order to perpetuate the illusion of control.

Our best minds and our brightest souls continue to tell us otherwise, still the vast majority of us cling to an imaginary belief that certainty is possible.

More profound than this, we humans continue en masse to operate under the illusion that certainty is desirable. To believe that flexibility, surprise, curiosity, spontaneity are not far superior qualities.

"As far as the laws of mathematics refer to reality, they are not certain; and as far as they are certain, they do not refer to reality."

~ Albert Einstein

Most of us live in a world that is not real. The government is not what we think it is, and neither are our friends or foes. Those we blame for our woes are almost entirely without fault, those we believe are aligned with our best interests are in truth aligned only with their own, and a shocking number of the things we would call important are really just meaningless distractions we've pasted to the walls of the imaginary dioramas in which we live.

This phenomenon of not having any true grasp of reality necessarily means that most of us are – in spite of all our beliefs, and quite often because of them – the secret harbor of our most debilitating delusions. And these delusions are snakes that feed on their own tails.

"There are no solids in the universe. There's not even a suggestion of a solid... There are no surfaces. There are no straight lines."

~ Buckminster Fuller

We say, over and over again, in countless different ways, that we want certainty, that we need it in order to get up and tie our shoes in the morning. That we must define all the things and places and people around us, so we understand exactly what we are dealing with. All the while, we become depressed when our lives become dull, routine, and predictable. We are torn between wanting to be surprised and not wanting any surprises.

The mind wants certainty. The soul wants mystery.

"To really ask is to open the door to the whirlwind. The answer may annihilate the question and the questioner."

~ Anne Rice

In order to make peace with the dualistic ideas of certainty and mystery, imagine for just a moment a life without uncertainty. What would be the point? No adventure, no new discoveries, no anticipation, no inspiration, no desire, no growth. This would be enough to kill even the most risk-averse of us out there.

What if there were no mysteries to investigate, no stones to turn over, no wonder to wander through...

Think of the excitement and possibility of a first kiss, the longing, the uncertainty, the hope, the thrill, the waiting that almost drives us mad. What if we knew exactly what would happen while we stood on the threshold of that sacred space? What if we knew how a painting would turn out the moment we picked up the brushes? What if we knew exactly how our characters would tell their stories, our children would live their lives, our gardens would yield, and our loves would unfold?

"Knowledge is an unending adventure at the edge of uncertainty."

~ Jacob Bronowski

The truth, of course, is that the mysterious holds sway over our hearts, our bodies, our souls, in ways that certainty can never even aspire towards.

It is the unspoken – even if minuscule – danger of the unknown; it is the possibilities of flowers, of color, of kisses, that makes life worth getting out of bed for, that moves us towards today and tomorrow. It is the search of that indescribable and almost invisible feeling of aliveness in all the little, daily unknowns that gives life purpose, meaning, depth, and feeling.

So the next time you find yourself walking the razor's edge between knowing and unknowing, don't panic. What you're feeling is simply the exhilaration of what might come next.

It's called life. Drink it up. That's what it's there for.

My Declaration of Creativity and Love.

By Saran Kaur

Hunger has always shown me the way. My emotional hunger and my years of a troubled relationship with food have always shown me where I'm disallowing the Divine Flow, where I'm hiding my longing or where I'm squashing my creativity... where I'm not telling my truth but instead swallowing it along with a bar of chocolate to ease the bitter taste of self-betrayal.

It's only now, as I sense that I'm really stepping into my life purpose and that I've graduated from the process of becoming myself, that I see what the food-addictions, eating disorders and problems were about.

They were driving me towards just that: myself – toward the expression of my being, my unbridled creativity, my greatness and my light. As I've been opening the floodgates to my creative expression, I'm awestruck by this force, the sheer force of the creative impulse pushing to get through the ego-ridden filters and layers of conditioning.

Why is this important to talk about, you may ask? It is important because creativity is freedom. It is absolute self-sufficiency. No wonder we're not taught to be truly creative at school, a system that puts numbers on each individual and has a hard time understanding the limitlessness of absolute creativity.

Don't get me wrong; discipline is needed for creativity to blossom. But it can never act as a substitute.

So, back to hunger... hunger for many of us has become a way of life. Sometimes we're so hungry that we don't even feel it anymore. We're hungry for meaning, for life, for love. For me, hunger represents emptiness. For me it's associated with death and loss of the physical body. But unlike death which is a kind of limitlessness and infinite spaciousness, hunger is a kind of talking void, a vacuum that actively asks to be filled and also gets associated with lack, scarcity and all other kinds of suffering.

The feeling of physical hunger has been one of the scariest things for me personally: What will I do with that emptiness inside? How do I fill this, make it go away? This feeling has been followed by shakiness and jitters as cellular memories of scarcity and death are triggered.

Physical hunger has been the painful reminder of another emptiness deep inside that doesn't bear to be spoken. (That huge space where my creativity is now living and thriving.)

My experience is that we carry memories deep within us, but also learn to be hungry in many more ways than just physical food-related hunger.

There are millions of commercials telling us what to want and what to be hungry for. Mainstream society and media are constantly telling us what we should first want and then how to still our wanting by pointing at what we should consume.

We are being bombarded with an ideal of all round perfection that can never be attained; it's like eating candy instead of food; it gives an initial buzz and then makes the blood sugar levels drop, triggering a deeper feeling of hunger.

We live in a society that demands that we stay hungry. It feeds us with images and rules of being that have no substance; that ultimately leave us feeling empty inside and keep us coming back for more. We're taught to be hungry for a new pair of shoes, a bigger car, a slimmer body, a certain amount of money, fill-in-the-blank, and it's never enough. And it will never be enough.

What truly satisfies us is connection and self-expression. Connection. To another human being, to a group, to an animal, to your own Soul, to a spiritual path. Connection to something living that makes you feel alive and seen and accepted. Self-expression in any form that paints your sense of being, sings your feelings or exposes your truth.

So now I'm asking you the same questions I asked myself: What are you hungry for? Why do you want? Do you need to be feeling hungry in your life? Where are you putting your fulfillment and contentment on hold? Where did you learn that you should be collecting scraps on the sidelines? What rules are you holding yourself hostage by (can't/couldn't/shouldn't/not allowed/not good enough/etc.)?

There's a cure for the hunger. And that cure is called creativity. It doesn't matter what you create as long as it expresses itself as you. As you create from your original originality, you free yourself. You become unrestricted by rules, regulations, conventions and cultural mores. You are that being that is creating and as that is being created. You flow on both sides of the matrix. And no one can hold you down, because you are that force.

You are that God that seeks expression through your form and your unique composition. Can you see how beautiful it all is? Can you see how beautiful you are? And at this moment of creation and creativity you are sufficient, contented and enough. There are no needs because there is only abundance. There is your richness of being. There is no place for hunger inside you anymore. There is only room for joyful expansion and a deepened contentment.

Here's the million-dollar question: Do you dare to become satisfied? Do we dare to let our hungers dry up and be contented with who we are, with what we have? Do we dare to start feeling good, Divine, exactly where we are right now? Or do we make up conditions on how it's supposed to look or feel or what enough-ness and creativity is for us?

Let's do it together, right now. We are that love, that creativity, that Divine Force in action.

Happily Ever After? In Defense of Marriage.

By Tracy Wisneski

"Until one is committed, there is hesitancy, the chance to draw back, always ineffectiveness. Concerning all acts of initiative (and creation), there is one elementary truth the ignorance of which kills countless ideas and splendid plans: that the moment one definitely commits oneself, the providence moves too. A whole stream of events issues from the decision, raising in one's favor all manner of unforeseen incidents, meetings and material assistance, which no man could have dreamt would have come his way. I learned a deep respect for one of Goethe's couplets: 'whatever you can do or dream you can, begin it. Boldness has genius, power and magic in it!'

~ W.H. Murray

There is a multi-billion dollar worldwide industry built around the quest of *Happily Ever After*. They study it, analyze it, and formulate it. There are courses, books, steps, retreats, and yet, there is a growing number of people who claim it can't be done.

As we advance in so many ways, we tend to complicate matters that are so much simpler than we make them out to be and marriage is perhaps the most tragically distorted of all.

Is it hard? Sometimes. Is it for everyone? Maybe not. Is it complicated? No. So what's the secret to commitment? Commit. Fish or cut bait. Shit or get off the pot.

That's it. Hand to God! Please don't confuse this with fixing broken people or finding perfection. Most certainly do not take this to mean that you should make a life with anyone who doesn't respect you or treat you well. But all of this hemming and hawing and looking for perfection? Nonsense!

Remaining in a loving, functional adult relationship for years and years and years, just in case this person isn't "The One"? Probably the worst thing you could do. You won't commit, until you truly commit.

This dance of *maybe* is the kiss of death. You're an adult. Presumably, you have at least a semi-healthy sense of self. Once you've been on more than ten dates, you know if you're interested enough to go further. Once you move in and get your growing pains over with, you know if you're compatible.

If you've got all of the above, you've lived together without abuse or attempted homicide for at least a year and you still love each other, I recommend you put on your big-kid underwear and talk about marriage.

It's not a relationship until you've worked for it.

And you're not likely to truly work for it until you have to. Why would you have to if you haven't committed? The dance of maybe means that you'll be together while it's still convenient, still fun, and still new. But life isn't always convenient, fun or new.

If you haven't tried it yet, let me tell you that commitment is so much sexier than you might think. Only a ride-or-die gets to be by my side. Marriage is not all flowers and kisses, sweetness and support. Ask long-term married people if they've ever had to suppress the urge to choke their spouse. Ask them if they've ever considered cheating, leaving or maybe setting the house on fire. Ask if they've ever feared that they'd made a colossal mistake.

But here's the catch: if they loved their partner in the first place and they've truly, deeply made that commitment, they stay. They work it out. And while it sometimes takes longer than others, they fall in love again. That scarred, rebuilt love is so much stronger, so much more satisfying than fleeting butterflies.

Think of marriage like the vast ocean. There will be high tide, low tide, even violent storms, but it always comes back around. It is enduring and powerful. But what if you change and grow?

Of course you will change and grow, but if you've committed, then your relationship will adjust with you. You can have friends, pursue new endeavors and re-invent yourself while still keeping that one enduring anchor (your anchor doesn't keep you down, it keeps you grounded). And grounded is a good thing, a wonderful thing. What about imperfections, baggage, and all that annoying stuff?

Once you've put over a decade into each other, that annoying stuff becomes almost endearing. There are things you will iron out and others you'll just learn to accept. My favorite of all is that the longer you've been committed, the stronger your love, the deeper your commitment, the more enchanting your treasure-trove of memories. And freedom?

Nothing has ever made me feel so free and confident and secure as the passage of many tides and the weathering of many storms with my best friend by my side, giving me the confidence to take chances and live life to its fullest.

If you are healthy, respectful, loving people, if you are best friends, then please don't allow all the hype and the fear to keep you away from something as beautiful and venerable as promising before family, friends and the God of your choice to love and honor someone, for better or for worse, in sickness and in health, until death do you part.

Like any great adventure, even if it should go awry, it would have been worth it.

I Want to Burn it All Up.

By Shasta Townsend

I want to burn it all up.
The plans,
The pain
The past
Ideas about who I should be
As a woman,
A wife,
A sexual being.

I want to burn it all up
With love
True love
Fierce love
Not a pretend to be nice and well-behaved so you feel good love.
I am Kali on crack with a cracked open heart.
Dancing, dancing the beautiful into being on the pyres you despise.

I want to burn it all up
All this domesticated bullshit
All this fear
All this insecurity, mistrust, jealousy,
All this you not showing up in your majesty,
All this mailing it in and stuffing it down,
All this keeping it small, good and polite because it's what nice girls do.

I want to live like an inferno.
Raging the wildfires of love across the plains
burning that which is not love,
the fire releasing the seeds of what can be,
like those California pines which need the heat to burst forth their seeds.

I want to live like an inferno.

Burning, burning
As Ferlinghetti says, "and everyone says, Ahhh"
But also "Aha"
This is how it can be.

8 Wondrous Ways to Restore your Wild Spirit.

By Victoria Erickson

This week was terribly mundane. It was one of those weeks filled with laundry and schedules and coffee pots and ticking clocks. I was never a schedule-loving person, for my drive for freedom and adventure overthrew sameness like waves, swallowing any idea of such a dreadful notion in their foam.

Yet, I still do it. We all do. Structure. Rules. Routine. It gets draining, and naturally, I crave more. Don't we all instinctively crave more?

I work in an oncology program for women and my patients often talk about feeling and being more often than women who are not sick. In fact, in my time directly working with the energy and emotion of oncology patients of all ages, I have noticed that nearly all of them talk about their primal needs, even long after they've recovered.

They have been rocked right to the core by an unforgiving disease that causes great pain, even beyond recovery, yet also incredible humbleness. And while they maneuver that unpredictable jungle of medical treatments, charts, and needles, it is their spirit that they face head on, and most are astounded by who they find: a warrior.

They also learn early on that it wasn't the cancer cells that made them warriors; they were born that way. We all were born that way, but sometimes it takes extreme diversity to unleash it again. It doesn't have to be this way.

That is why tonight I write from a fierce place, a place made of fire, and a slow-burning truth. She inhabits my ribs and breathes her flames, sometimes quiet, and sometimes a roar I cannot purge. It is on nights like these when she presses until I can no longer stand her howls, rising like the moon and forcing me awake. She is a force to be reckoned with, and a familiar memory – the primal me, the warrior, and the human. The human in us all.

To be fully human is to be wild. Wild is the strange pull and whispering wisdom. It's the gentle nudge and the forceful ache. It is your truth, passed down from the ancients, and the very stream of life in your blood. Wild is the soul where passion and creativity reside, and the quickening of your heart. Wild is what is real, and wild is your home.

Tonight, I throw my advice to the wind to reach those who feel painfully restless and forgetful of spirit. Our souls are naturally filled with great vitality and ageless knowing, that flow through us freely until they get blocked by modern living.

Right now, I urge you to unravel the listless, rigid parts, and feed your wild, because it is the wild you, not the barely alive, embedded-into-routine, zombie-like you that is now struggling for air. For a turn-on. For sweet prana. Restore the wild and the warrior.

You shouldn't have to get sick or halt domesticity to find it; you just need to remember that you are human, still very much alive, and wickedly, wildly extraordinary.

"We are all as much extraordinary phenomena of nature as trees, clouds, the patterns in running water, the flickering of fire, the arrangement of the stars, and the form of a galaxy."

~ Alan Watts

"How," you beg, "do I restore it? How can I truly be human in this modern society that keeps us so terribly tame? How can I manage the me that longs for fresh air free of concrete and traffic lights and ugly parking lots? How does one breathe life into the wild parts that crave connection to themselves, to others, and to the earth?"

"The way to maintain one's connection to the wild is to ask yourself what it is that you want. This is the sorting of the seed from the dirt. One of the most important discriminations we can make in this matter is the difference between things that beckon to us and things that call from our souls."

~ Clarissa Pinkola Estes

Let's go there. To the primal place you can reach in everyday life. Here are eight incredibly simple and direct ways to feed your wild spirit – for these are some of the very things that can call to your truth quickly, even if you don't know it yet:

1. Garden. Gardeners are cultivators and regenerators – harvesting new life and replacing the old, stagnant energy with new seeds. Dig into the dirt with bare hands and breathe the essence of herbs and flowers into your wise body, for it will recognize them as home. Get earthy and gorgeously dirty.

2. Feed on raw food. Energize, alkalize, and heal your body on a deep, cellular level. Nourish yourself with vibrant greens and fresh juices with nutrients you know the story behind; nutrients that heal illnesses instead of creating them with chemicals born in a lab.

> *"The food you eat can be either the safest and most powerful form of medicine or the slowest form of poison."*
>
> *~ Ann Wigmore*

Start buzzing with aliveness from food that is also alive, and feel your body's wisdom beat with every breath.

3. Find live music. Find the kind of music that makes your soul soar from the sound. From drum circles under ancient trees, to jazz on city streets, to underground clubs that keep people dancing through the night, music's rhythmic beats exist to tell universal truths that awaken us from everyday hibernation.

Have you ever seen crowds of 60,000 people at music festivals? They sing with the bands under enormous summer skies, erupting into applause, dance, and smiles so large they ache. If that isn't the wild, primal roar of the human spirit, than I don't know what is. Find it, because music, my friends, is life.

4. Play. Find the most hilarious person you know, whether it's over social media, lunch, or the work water cooler and laugh. Even if you only have 20 minutes, take a random car ride to somewhere even more random. Dance to

80s music while you clean the house, paint the inside of your garage neon, or watch a Pixar movie with your favorite kiddo.

Personally, I love swing sets. I don't care what your age is or how busy you are, play is essential to promote a youthful mind which is dynamic, curious, and enthusiastic; that will open you up to new possibilities, which will feed your wild spirit even more. A playful mind is fluid, creative, and of course, wild.

5. Make love. Make love like it's your last night on earth, gasping for air and sanity, frantic under clouds and stars and sheets. The kind of animalistic lovemaking that's written in books – one that hypnotizes and captivates. The kind that's made of heartbeats, intertwined flesh, and fiery, blazing, all-consuming passion.

> *"Despite what you've been conditioned to believe, sexual desire is sacred and virtuous. When you and your beloved merge physically and emotionally, you go beyond the boundaries of the ego and experience timelessness, naturalness, playfulness and defenselessness."*
>
> ~ *Deepak Chopra*

6. Get wet. These are cures that open you in places you forgot could even open, for salt and water are a miraculous mix. Release disappointment through tears, sweat from awesome, bodily pumping movement, and swim in the soft caress of water.

These wild activities often launch you into the feeling of vulnerability and renewed power at the same time, while carrying you to a clearer place inside your mind. Yes, there you are again, wild one.

7. Tell your stories. Tell stories of your childhood, of deep-rooted pain, of intense loss, of blood, and of your greatest loves. Tell them by firelight under violet, star-filled skies, or by sending words into cyberspace. Tell them over cups of strong espresso or glasses of sweet red wine. Tell them with tears and laughter and faith in the human race. Tell them to friends, to lovers, and to strangers.

Everyone has stories that need to be told, and there is always someone to listen. Make sure you tell your stories while you still have the chance.

8. Shine. Show who you are, authentically, and completely unapologetically. Be fearless in your ambitions, goals and decisions. That energy will then spread itself into the universe and boost the human race, for one drop can indeed, raise the entire ocean.

> *"As we let our own light shine, we unconsciously give other people the right to do the same. As we are liberated from our fear, our presence automatically liberates others."*
>
> ~ *Marianne Williamson*

And as you work on these wondrous things to restore your wild spirit, do remember that even when you're still not quite there, you are a miraculous human warrior and that...

You are beautiful. Wildly beautiful.

Love Is in the Air: Don't Settle.

By Valerie Gangas

"I could not tell you if I loved you the first moment I saw you, or if it was the second or third or fourth. But I remember the first moment I looked at you walking toward me and realized that somehow the rest of the world seemed to vanish when I was with you."

~ Cassandra Clare (Clockwork Prince)

Once upon a time, I jumped from one long-term relationship to another, without a second thought.

It seemed so natural to me. I liked guys, and they liked me back. It was always like that. I was kind of a tomboy, and having a boyfriend felt like having the ultimate play pal. I was not exactly mature, so it just seemed like one giant party. We all had fun, and nine times out of ten, no one got hurt. The men I have dated have all been exceptional people. I always felt very fortunate and loved. I thought I had it all together...

Then it happened. My mom passed away. Everything stopped. I was frozen, and the last thing on my mind was dating. I felt no desire to be in a relationship. I longed for solitude, time to reflect on my pain. I needed to make sense of my world that had been turned on its head. Spending time with people who subsisted like ornaments on the surface of life, and talking about nonsense over bottle after bottle of Cabernet, no longer appealed to me.

I repeatedly told my friends and family, "It is going to take a miracle to get me to date someone." My mother's death forced me, for the first time, to focus on me – and only me. How to live without her – the longtime love of my life – took center stage, and everything else seemed mundane and pointless. In the cracks of my broken heart, new questions emerged: How did I want to live? Who was I here to be? What values were important to me? How was I going to help others?

I turned to the spiritual side of myself, which had always been important to me, and jumped off the high dive right into the body of my soul. I felt a

117

deep connection with the world, and realized that God was in everything around me, including myself. It is pretty hard to compete with the source of creation and ultimate intelligence.

Match.com – are you serious? What planet are all these people living on? I did not have time for that; I had to think about the nature of my existence. I have learned more from not dating than I ever did from continuously being attached. Not dating was the best decision I ever made.

Were there days when I felt concerned by my lack of interest in dating? Of course! But at the same time, after years of being in relationships, it also felt pretty awesome. It was different, but not in a bad way. It gave me the chance to take a breather and redirect my life. I think we all need that from time to time. No big deal, just a little break.

I had to adjust to all of this. It was new to me. For once, I did not have to check in with anyone. Gone were the days when I worried about what I was going to make for dinner or if I could hang out with my girlfriends on a Saturday night. No need for a second opinion. I could roam the earth at will without someone else's seal of approval.

It was all up to me. I, alone, was free to write the next chapter in the story of my life. How liberating! Freedom – freedom like I had never experienced before – it almost overwhelmed me.

Over the past couple years, I have come to understand exactly who I am: a child of God; a woman with a deep longing to make her mark on the world, to connect with people, and above all, to be kind.

I started a company I love, picked up a meditation practice that is the backbone of my existence, road-tripped all over the country, began writing a book, realized my love of flying airplanes, and met a group of people that I consider to be my soul family. I finally became the person that I always wanted to be. I was whole.

Prior to my inner pilgrimage, it felt like I was just spinning my wheels. I was always happy, but a bit confused. I knew there was more, but I just could not get there. It was out of my reach. Now I felt distinct, fulfilled and happy – a wonderful combo platter.

Ultimately, as a result of my introspective time spent not dating, I figured out the best way to enter into a meaningful relationship: Be the love you want; be the person you want to meet; be solid.

There is no point getting involved with another human being when we need them to complete us. That is a recipe for emptiness, confusion and disaster. We are already complete; we just have to open our mind and soul to see it. It is inside all of us. The key is that you have to experience it for yourself, and not just read about it. You have to walk the walk, and there will be days that it is going to hurt like hell.

Sometimes it takes losing your mind in order to find your soul, but there is a major upside to all of this. We attract exactly who we are to ourselves. With that equation, how can we lose? When you come together with another self-actualized person, the energy fueling that type of relationship is indescribable. It is pure magic and much different from anything you may have experienced prior to your metamorphosis.

"Where there is great love, there are always miracles."

~ Willa Cather

Time gave me the gift of realizing that I was not my parents, my friends, or anyone else but myself. This is my feature film. My love song. The fear of having the same experience as another person's horrible relationship, or re-living a bad break-up, went right out the window.

Take the time to explore, meditate, pray and enjoy your life, alone. Figure your shit out, however painful it is. On the other side of that pain is a rainbow with unicorns that live in the land of possibilities. When you think about it, what are six or twelve months in the course of a lifetime? It is a blink of an eye. We are setting the stage for the rest of our lives.

Settling, in our relationships – be it with a partner, the person we chose to be the mother or father of our children, or even with our friends – is not a viable option. Our time is too precious to waste it on the wrong relationship just because we are lonely. Blast through that lonely feeling; it is not real. We are never alone.

I am reminded of the solid advice my wise Irish grandpa once gave me, "Marriage is the biggest gamble you will ever take, but give it a shot, at least once." This coming from a man that married a woman he never stopped loving, even after she passed away 30 years before him.

I know it will not always be easy, but anything that is truly amazing never is. I can say to Gramps with confidence now, "You were right."

This is a no-limit game. My chips are on the table and I am holding a made hand. I am all in.

Tattoos Do Not Belong in Spirituality (and Other Complete Bullshit).

By Chris Grosso

It's obvious that anyone who desecrates their bodies in such an appalling way as those who get tattooed couldn't know the first thing about spirituality, compassion, loving-kindness or well-being, right?

As ridiculous as I'd like to think that question sounds to most of you reading this, the unfortunate thing is that for many people, it's not – they actually believe this bullshit.

Being heavily tattooed myself, I've heard sentiments like that shared by judgmental people more times than I care to remember, however, it's also worth noting that it usually doesn't stop there. The stereotypes often carry over to anyone whose lifestyle deviates from what's traditionally considered *acceptable* as a cultural norm.

It pretty much goes without saying that if you live in such a way that can be deemed as *risqué*, or outside of the norms, you're subject to find yourself at the butt end of the occasional mockery by people who fear what's not familiar to them in everyday society. This is just a fact.

What I find even more disheartening, however, is that many of us who do live outside the confines of the traditional norms also find ourselves automatically equated with a complete lack of authentic spiritual living, or understanding, by many of those who consider themselves to be conventional spiritual practitioners.

And I'm not singling anyone out here because I've personally caught it from Christians, Buddhists, Yogis, non-denominational spiritualists and more, and all literally for nothing more than my outer appearance.

The thing is, no matter how closed off certain people are toward lifestyles they don't understand; it's not going to stop us. There's an emergence of people just like me – the ones who are immersed in independent culture yet also have a sincere, dedicated spiritual practice, and we're just as worthy of others' respect as anyone else.

The number of young, independently-minded spiritualists is growing, and for many of us, our conscious awareness is shifting from that of ethnocentric (some of us) to world-centric (all of us). What this means is that many of us are no longer only interested in the wellbeing of our selves, our friends, families, communities and nations, but are just as interested in the wellbeing of the entire global community as a whole.

Isn't this something to be rejoiced by everyone rather than being scoffed at? I'm grateful for no longer feeling the need to judge others whose outsides don't coincide exactly with mine, though it certainly wasn't always like that for me.

Relinquishing material-based judgments is something I've made a diligent effort in working on, and through years of practice, today I can honestly say that I couldn't care less about your style of dress, or haircut, or whatever other material things seemingly make us different. I'm much more interested in what's happening on your insides, and not in what's outside.

And so it's in the spirit of acceptance, which I've come to understand as a pretty universal spiritual theme, that I offer you – the ones who find it necessary to judge and vocalize your disapproval of those of us who are externally different – this to ponder: the next time you feel the need to pass judgments and write us off simply because our lifestyles are different from yours, how about instead of acting on it, you use that as an opportunity to turn inwards and explore why you have those opinions and judgments in the first place?

I mean, if you truly consider yourself *spiritual*, please take a moment to sincerely contemplate whether those who live differently than you, or practice differently than you, are affecting your life's wellbeing, spiritual or otherwise – and if we're not, then really, why do you care?

I'm asking you this from a very sincere place, a place that is attempting to try and find some reconciliation rather than to create more separation. I recognize that by using words such as *us* and *you* in this article, as I have, may contradict the point I'm trying to make, but please know it's truly nothing more than my own limitations with prose.

Accepting one another for exactly who we are, as we set foot onto the spiritual path, is of paramount importance, because regardless of our differences in personal tastes, styles or beliefs, bettering ourselves through conscious and intentional living is always for the greater collective good, which includes both you and me.

Each moment that any of us (and I mean *any* of us) sit in meditation, say a prayer, practice yoga, count a *mala* or rosary bead, or even, simply take a mindful breath while skateboarding, hiking, making love or rocking out at a concert, truly benefits all beings.

So for fuck's sake, seriously, how is it 2013 and we're still not in this thing together yet?

Outrageously Alive: The Art of Letting Life Chew You Up and Spit You Back into the Cosmos.

By Anna Mattinger

If art reflects life, then there seems little point in a life spent blocked off, tucked away from experience. So many of the artists I know sacrifice those unified experiences life has to offer in the name of making time for their art.

They skive off personal connections, they avoid adventures, they stifle too much movement or activity, and they become perpetual homebodies, because they need to live within an incubator so they will have time to fiddle around ceaselessly, honing their skills or scrounging for materials...

And the result is kitsch – aesthetics-driven art that appears to carry some weight at first glance. Preachy-pulp-fiction-pop-culture-palatable writing. Technical writing, when people write about something they have no personal interaction with, because they read, and they think, and for many that is enough to replace firsthand experience.

Hypothetical treatises of self-discovery. A robot's account of feeling alive, of primal love.

Reading Tolstoy or Camus or whatever other long-dead thinkers gleaned centuries ago can enhance your appreciation of humanity. Following a path to *enlightenment* via Christ or Kundalini Yogis, reciting benevolent words...

But their wisdom, no matter how it resonates with you, is not yours, because they walked, and bled, and felt things like abandonment and regret, in order to get there. Their truth may coincide with yours, but it is not identical to your truth.

Relating to the suffering, lust, and relief of others is not a substitute for experiencing them for yourself out in the world, for working through your own real demons of jealousy, humiliation or guilt.

At worst, all that reading about life from a detached, *objective* perspective can cultivate that academic or spiritual narcissism of those well-educated enough to trick themselves into thinking they know how everything works, into thinking they are experts.

I was there as well. And then I realized I did not know shit. I still do not, but I know a little more now than I did back when I thought I knew everything, pontificating from the safety of an emotional condom.

Take it off. Dare to look stupid. Dare to misspell. Dare to ask an elementary question, rather than pretending you understand. Dare to be proud of something you made that was born of your own truth rather than extrapolated from the truths of those before you, even if it is not *marketable*, even if someone calls it *low-brow* or *sophomoric*.

Dare to sing, dare to scream, dare to forgive yourself of your mistakes and dare to never apologize for your glories. Dare to deplete yourself and push yourself to the outer limits of your existence – and then dare to exercise true patience and forgiveness, to nurse yourself back to homeostasis, taking notes of what happens along the way.

And I will admit, most of the artists I know who live this way have technical skills that surpass mine. It is true that if I invested more time into practicing my craft, on the surface I'd probably look like a better artist.

But I'd just be churning out pretty stuff, not really knowing why. Stuff to put on a T-shirt that would sell at Urban Outfitters, stuff to decorate your house with and stick on your trendy coffee table. Stuff to stock a festival vendor's booth. Not just useless – arguably a defining characteristic, maybe even a virtue, of art – but also meaningless.

That work may be able to shock you, but it will not haunt you. It may present social commentary, in disorganized rants or cutesy platitudes, but its source is media and late-night conversations, not sweat and trauma and flirtations with death and the bitter tears born of experiencing injustice. It will titillate or fluster, but it will not give you indigestion.

That kind of work is crying wolf – it is self-righteousness, silicone passion. If you ask me, it is those who have at some point been broken down who have beautiful things to say. And I do not want to make social commentary – I want to make existential commentary.

I want to suffer Hell and Nirvana and Purgatory before deigning to let them peek through my work. I want to mess with my own head until I feel like I have lost control, and then come back to tell you about it, and maybe you will come with me next time, and maybe we will fall in love and maybe we will tear each other apart and lose ourselves, and years later we will learn how to rise above those ugly thoughts and feelings and harness true compassion, and forgive ourselves and each other – and then, maybe that is when, I will write something true.

I want my path to wisdom to involve a lot of stumbling, landslides, and pits, because the significance of your path is measured in how high you have risen from the depths into which you have fallen – I do not want to reach the mountaintop via some wide, meandering trail and then claim enlightenment.

If I am going to create anything I could call *art*, then I do not want it to shock. I want it to stir up, even disturb. I want to drug you – by proffering myself as an example that shows you a glimpse of your shadow, a dark truth that you cannot quite deny relating to.

More than that, I want to compel you to do it back to me – to do your very worst. I want my writing to be, not a soapbox, but a dialogue across time and space – a divine argument between us, strangers. I want you to boomerang back so I can learn from you too.

I hole up too, sure, as a reprieve from my otherwise torrential life – for just long enough so that I can write it all down, paint it, sing about it, recover from it, recalibrate to Center and practice Being over Doing. Lick my wounds and embrace what I might have previously called *boring*. Then I run back out into the storm again. Because it keeps me organic, keeps me human.

Our work is more stirring when you let life chew you up and spit you, tumbling, back into the cosmos. How else do we figure out what we are made of and who we are?

Pinching At Poetry: A Lifetime Affair.

By Catherine Ghosh

"Everywhere I go I find that a poet has been there before me."

~ Sigmund Freud

The year I turned 13, poems began trickling out of me like drips out of a leaky dam. My poems were born of loneliness and were the orphans of the country I'd left behind. Their cries would send me to the eucalyptus grove across the street from our house – writing tablet and pen in hand – to catch the desperate sound of sea breezes rustling through leaves before sunset.

It seemed as if I was becoming Kierkegaard's definition of a poet: an anguished heart whose cries sounded like music.

My songs of solitude started with an enumerated series of short poems that were nearly haiku-like, called, simply, *The Tree*. They all began with light, ended with darkness, and with the brush strokes of a naturalist, painted simple psychological portraits of the parts of me that needed the most attention.

So I disguised my feelings as bark, roots, trunks that swayed in powerful gales threatening to break them, and leaves that were always falling.

In the years after we abruptly left my childhood home, each time I felt alone and unheard, I poured myself into a poem. This filled me with such addictive satisfaction that by the time I was 16, my trickle of poems had turned into the fierce waters rushing from a broken dam after a record-breaking rainfall.

I scribbled poems in school when I should have been listening to the teacher. I spent many school lunches in the library, looking for quiet corners that would feed my compositions. I wrote on the bus ride home from school, and in my room after school, and in the middle of the night when I could not sleep.

I wrote with such intensity that my finger grew a little bunion where the pen rested. Today, that little bump on my finger stands as an endearing testament to how poetry created a firm passage for me to walk upon when it felt like all other ground under me was crumbling.

The poems I wrote as a teenager were, for the most part, not pretty poems. They were laden with achiness, prickly perspectives, and itchy feelings that their readers needed to shake off as soon as possible.

My poems were raw, jagged-edged, emotional outpourings that hit the pages at 100 miles per hour, independent of any rules or mentors, splashing in all kinds of uncomfortable directions. They morphed into studies of my pain and inevitably became screeches to my mother – as any mother would cringe upon discovering that her baby is hurting – and music to my shrink!

To me, my poems were my emancipators, galloping down hills of adolescent turbulence with shiny swords raised and wild manes blowing in the wind. My poems even made my depression look beautiful! I think Shelley was most fond of that function of poetry: its ability to infuse even the ugliest of subjects with beauty. Framed in poetry, the unapproachable suddenly becomes approachable.

Poetry seems to get away with successfully presenting what others might find objectionable in prose. Its playful use of words makes it language's endearing child, delightfully beyond reproach. I took full advantage of this and never limited the topics I explored in my poems. Reservations dissolve when intoxicated with the exhilarating process of pouring oneself into a poem.

I would not say that my adolescent poetry was good by any literary standards, as no one ever taught me about meter, rhyming, diction or alliteration. I was never formally educated in poetry composition. But form proved secondary to me when substance reigned supreme, for my relationship to my poems was utilitarian: they were my brave liberators. They were fearless explorers of uncharted terrain.

My poems were the wild and uneducated swings of an intuitive machete as it blazed trails through the existential jungle of my adolescence. So, as a teenager, I wrote poems to flirt with boundaries of where I began and where I ended.

I used them to deconstruct myself and carefully stitch myself back together again. Like patchwork on a quilt, I wove many sides of myself into a singular poem. Each poem was like a code which, if deciphered, opened windows into places I wanted to explore: landscapes of my being. The process of composition doubled as an adventure in self-discovery. Sometimes the journey was terrifying, as I scratched at words and pinched at sonnets, looking for myself to the tune of individuation.

Like an underground river, my writing of poems disappeared as I exited that period of my life. And yet, though poems no longer rushed from me, they continued to swirl in me, as poetry had permanently inundated my being.

Robert Frost once described being a poet as an unshakable *condition*. Thus, being a poet is not only what happens when one splashes words on paper: it is a continual state of being. Poets view the unfolding of life as a poem in itself. As I experience it, being a poet is a heightened sensitivity. It is a continual dialogue with nature, both inner and outer. Poetry is what spontaneously injects perspective with metaphor even as one washes the dishes, weeds the garden, stuffs kale into a juicer or scrubs the bathroom tiles.

Consequently, I noticed that some of my best poetry gets written when I am showering or doing dishes, and not when I am sitting at my laptop. I am tempted to say that, at a certain point, poetry simply merges with one's very essence. Voltaire called poetry "the music of the soul, and, above all, of great and feeling souls." I believe that if we excavate deeply inside ourselves, we all eventually hit poetry's treasure chest. There are poetic gems to be mined, if only we let ourselves be used as the tools that will do so.

For poetry to flow, assuming a yielding stance is required. To the Greeks, poetic skill was synonymous with becoming open and receptive to the celestial muse Polyhymnia. Many ancient cultures believed that poets yielded to the divinities, and were thus able to speak in their language. All Sanskrit verse, for example, is regarded as a passage to the sacred, for poetry weds words to sound, and – according to quantum physics, sound threads connect us all at a subatomic level.

This sonic oneness was poetically expressed across cultures and throughout history, as the sharing of poetry has an oral origin. As a child who simply adored the Museum of Anthropology in Mexico City, I loved imagining tribes gathering around fires to ingest poetry, drumming out exciting rhythms that matched the beats in nature and syncopated with the thumps in a listener's chest.

As I experience it, the process of gestating a poem in me certainly plays with my heartbeat. I can definitely feel a poem in my body first before it emerges. Poems grow in my core, and kick right before they are ready to come out. Sometimes, birthing them hurts.

Robert Frost once wrote that a poem begins with a lump in the throat. And once it is born, a poem takes on its own life! Poetry makes its way into the lives of readers through books salvaged at yard sales, readings in cozy coffeehouses, blogs that others accidentally stumble upon, and posts on Facebook. The mischief they get into after that is a subjective affair.

Leonardo da Vinci paralleled the enjoyment of poetry with experiencing a painting that is felt rather than seen.

Writing poetry was like that for me in my teen years: a form of expression that teetered between painting and prose. I used to oscillate between the two, and when neither medium was equipped enough to hold me (and all my complexity), poetry worked each time. Consequently, I filled whole journals with my poems. It was an emotional purging of sorts. When I was done, I had created a beautiful new life for myself, and my poetry went into hibernation.

It was not until that life began to crumble, over a decade later, that I started writing poetry again. Picasso once said: "Every act of creation is first an act of destruction."

As life around me began to fall apart, my poems, predictably, began to rise again: like little suns lighting the way, in sync with my own intuition. My poetry blazed through outdated images of myself in a frenzy of reinvention. It was the good kind of destruction that erupts in colorful flames and dances wildly like Lord Shiva, burning soil to provide nourishment for the next seeds.

Audre Lorde spoke of poetry as that which "lays the foundations for a future of change, a bridge across our fears of what has never been before."

When my first marriage began to evaporate, I built such bridges in secret, wriggling in a cocoon of transformation from which I finally emerged 10 years later. My poems were not reproducing like rabbits as they did before, but the process of writing them was powerful, and it became a kind of a companion to me: the kind that holds a mirror up to you. It was a visceral journey that reached toward spirit.

So, making poetry took me and shook me, and unexpectedly reminded me of beauty I had misplaced. It also discarded a few stagnating parts of me which I later tossed into coffins and happily erected gravestones to – for sometimes, poems resemble epitaphs, and sometimes, they twitch like fresh butterfly wings drying in the sun.

As for me, after much twitching, I think my wings are finally beginning to dry now.

Sex, Yoga, Ethics and the Guru.

By Cameron Shayne

This discussion will serve as an important exercise for yoga instructors and students alike. Prepare yourself to suspend your beliefs, perceptions, and values in order to receive new information. Be willing to learn something outside of your own experience in order to develop compassion and understanding.

We must stop identifying with stories, and beliefs that paralyze possibility and promote judgment. Every person's truth is absolutely true for them, until it's not. What you believe now will continue to evolve as you gather more experience to contrast with what you now know.

As you read further, try on both sides of truth so that you can see beyond black and white, good and bad, evil and sanctification. Learn to be a student by listening, rather than hearing what supports your pre-existing limited beliefs.

First, suggesting that a consenting adult teacher/student relationship is social, ethical or even criminal misconduct, is the projection of sexual shame, pain and blame.

Second, this is a conversation about consenting adults' personal liberties, not rape or sexual exploitation. Any person who seeks to collapse this conversation into "the right to f*ck vulnerable students," cannot be taken seriously. It is the weakest form of debate to demonize the counter culture perspective, rather than addressing the issue.

Below I will present a number of points in support of the pro-choice position.

Pro-choice does not equal pro-exploitation.

Pro-choice does not imply the abuse or mistreatment of another person. It implies the right to exercise personal liberties on the part of consenting adults.

I do not support or promote exploitation of women or men, as students or teachers. I do not support the use of a yoga classroom as a space to seek out sexual partners. It is not, and should not be. Engaging a person sexually, in a deceiving way, is contradictory to all ethics I uphold. Using authority or power for personal gain is in stark contrast to transparency, honesty and consideration of others.

I also believe it is absolutely safe and ethical for consenting adults in modern yoga environments to date. Why? Because these same consenting adults can die in war, procreate, and vote. The suggestion that they are competent only until they enter a classroom, stretch their bodies, and consider that they may be more than a physical manifestation, is contradictory to high standards of reason.

I do not condone any person, teacher or student, to use my experience as justification for their actions. I emphatically support the freedom to exercise personal judgment and ethics, as long as they include the careful consideration of others. I also strongly support any teacher who has a policy that restricts them from dating an adult student.

Adult students can and do assign meanings to experiences they are having with adult teachers in any field of study, i.e., linking their improved state of mind to the teacher. This projection or transference of feeling onto a person due to circumstances, means that caution and care must be taken by both parties, to be clear. And least we not overlook the indisputable point that projection of feelings onto people who inspire us, occurs under numerous uncontrollable conditions.

That was then, this is now.

Yoga has evolved. The Yoga classroom environment has evolved to include different styles, props, and especially women, as they were once forbidden to participate. The relationship between teacher and student has evolved from "guru," to "certified instructor."

Traditional Indian cultural values, which promote cast systems, restrictive gender roles, religious ideologies, and guru worship, do not work in the west. Making policy for modern western yoga using transitional Indian yoga values, simply does not translate.

I strongly believe that orthodox yoga practitioners, who strictly adhere to ancient rituals, should be respected, as they should respect those who choose an unorthodox approach to yoga. There is space for everyone's views and practices without judgment.

There is a time and a place for everything.

The yoga sutras, considered the Bible of Yoga, contain important and relevant guidelines that transcend time and culture. One specific guideline is restraint from sense driven living. It clearly serves the common good when people are not urge driven consumers, yet we are all driven by the urge to be safe, loved and accepted.

The problem stems from one yoga practitioner judging another's urges as right or wrong. This only underscores the hypocrisy of a community that strives to instill non-judgment as a core value. Drinking a glass of wine, eating good food, being socially accepted, and making love all stem from urges. There is clearly a time and place for all urges.

I personally see the classroom as the wrong place to act on sexual urges. I do however believe that consenting adults, in western yoga classrooms, have the right to conduct their private lives, including intimate relationships, outside of the classroom without interference and judgment.

Adults need to learn to be competent students by discontinuing blind devotion of teachers, projection of accountability, and seeking outside of themselves for ethical and moral guidance.

Why we are all attracted to teachers.

People are attracted to skill, talent, and charisma inside or outside of a yoga class. If the teacher or student possesses these qualities, they are naturally going to be attractive. A musician, dancer, lecturer, or an artist performing can inspire the same feelings that a dynamic teacher can. All are provoking emotion and feeling. I am personally attracted to anyone who is skilled at their craft.

However, attraction doesn't cause me to lose sight and application of my personal ethics and values. These are however, my ethics and values, and should not be adopted by anyone. As independent agents operating without force or pressure due to career or financial consequences, an adult teacher and adult student are fully capable and accountable individuals.

I believe that if a female yoga teacher were attracted to a male student, there would be a much less biased proposal, as there would be an assumption that the male would have enough sexual agency to resist his teacher's advances. Also, suggesting that a female student cannot engage a male teacher with as much competency as a man, discredits the intellectual and emotional power of all women.

You can't date your guru.
When you deconstruct the differences between the "yoga guru," and the "certified yoga instructor," you find stark contrasts that many people are simply collapsing into one archetype.

The guru model clearly demonstrates several problematic power differentials. In order to have a yoga guru, a student must seek a religious teacher, surrender to his or her authority, and be initiated into a specific discipline. Sex or an intimate relationship between these two suggests a complex dynamic to say the least. I believe it would be extremely difficult for the student to see the guru as an equal in or out of the yoga classroom.

The western yoga teacher, in contrast, is holding a casual space for people to come and go, with no commitment, or agreed religious or spiritual discipleship. Yoga certainly implies general spirituality, but this does not suggest people are in danger because they can date in this environment.

Gurus or teachers dating students carries a high risk of conflict of interests. However, whether you or I agree to its merits, there is no controlling consenting adults intimately engaging one another. In fact, partners meeting in yoga class is quite common.

I also recognize that some men see women as sexual objects and not as people. Some men behave in a manner that travels the scale from disrespectful to criminal. That however, cannot be controlled by policing a yoga class, but rather by teaching yoga practitioners to establish their personal ethics and values.

When students stop seeking a spiritual leader to follow blindly, and teachers stop encouraging discipleship, things will inevitably change.

Stop the guru complex.

Teachers need to stop encouraging co-dependent followers by providing them with answers, and start cultivating independent thinkers and competent yoga practitioners.

Western yoga teachers must stop trying to play the role of guru, enlightened being, or one who possess a commodity on truth. We don't. We are as limited, challenged and deep in it as our "students." In most cases we are the ones with the greatest pain, seeking hardest for the answers.

Students need to stop believing that teachers possess something they do not. A true teacher is always guiding you back to your own universal wisdom and truth, which we are all endowed with. We have nothing special to offer, other than being able to ask questions that further and ultimately direct you back to yourself.

How to Be Afraid and Do it Anyway.

By Andréa Balt

"I must say a word about fear. It is life's only true opponent. Only fear can defeat life. It is a clever, treacherous adversary, how well I know. It has no decency, respects no law or conventions, shows no mercy. It goes for your weakest spot, which it finds with unerring ease.

It begins with your mind, always. One moment you are feeling calm, self-possessed, happy. Then fear, disguised in the garb of mild-mannered doubt, slips into your mind like a spy. Doubt meets disbelief and disbelief tries to push it out. But disbelief is a poorly armed foot soldier. Doubt does away with it with little trouble.

You become anxious. Reason comes to do battle for you. You are reassured. Reason is fully equipped with the latest weapons technology. But, to your amazement, despite superior tactics and a number of undeniable victories, reason is laid low. You feel yourself weakening, wavering. Your anxiety becomes dread.

Fear next turns fully to your body, which is already aware that something terribly wrong is going on. Already your lungs have flown away like a bird and your guts have slithered away like a snake. Now your tongue drops dead like an opossum, while your jaw begins to gallop on the spot.

Your ears go deaf. Your muscles begin to shiver as if they had malaria and your knees to shake as though they were dancing. Your heart strains too hard, while your sphincter relaxes too much. And so with the rest of your body. Every part of you, in the manner most suited to it, falls apart. Only your eyes work well. They always pay proper attention to fear.

Quickly you make rash decisions. You dismiss your last allies: hope and trust. There, you've defeated yourself. Fear, which is but an impression, has triumphed over you."

~ *Yann Martel (Life of Pi)*

Fear, for me, started when I was five. Up until then, I'd never heard of it. I thought we were immortal, let alone my own superpowers – what else could account for all the miracles I was making with my invisible magic wand? – and there was nothing else but life: unlimited, unedited, eternal, juicy, tactile life, with giggly breath and bubbly toes. And I touched it.

One day, after an unusual "but why? but why? but why?" my mother broke the news... "What do you mean we're going to die?" I asked, nearly stabbed to death by this awareness. "Even us?!..."

"I'm afraid so," she replied.

"But...I thought only bad people get Death..." I had been suspicious for a while though – like when some kids I knew lost both of their parents in a car accident...It didn't make any sense. Parents are generally good people...it must have been a glitch in the system?...

"So we're not special?... Like, does this mean we could die in our sleep?" I tried hard to understand, as a thick, dark cloud was getting ready to rain and thunder over my head for years to come. It didn't seem fair to me that our life could be stolen without any previous warning.

"Well, not necessarily in our sleep but... at some point, we will..."

That was my first Introduction to Terror. Looking back, I wish I had been spared this course 'til college. Perhaps it wouldn't have been as tragic had I grown up in a society that viewed death as a natural, side effect of life.

But most people don't experience the first death – the death of the ego, of their social construct, of their possessions (dead plastic things, much deader than death); the destruction that brings new life, the painful letting go, the hall of shame out of Eden, the walking through fire, the ache, the faceless void, the abyss, the fall, the insurmountable darkness, the dark-blue choking loneliness, the demons in the mirror, the irreversible loss. And when they do, they cover it up with lifeless distraction.

They don't, as C.S. Lewis put it, "die before they die," so when they finally leave the world altogether the pain has doubled (if not tripled or quadrupled) – they have to say goodbye to both, their neglected, inner treasure and all their other imaginary, plastic selves. This is the real tragedy of death, the excess of goodbyes. So we should travel light.

But I was accidentally born there and then – and nurtured by this type of scared and scary people.

***

There are three types of fear that have shaken my life up to date – from the most basic to the most complex, overlapping each other and intertwining with my sense of self, ever since that early Age of Innocence collapsed.

I'm sure you can see yourself in at least one. After all, you're 99% Me…or I, You – or Us, Life.

Fear of Death.

My worst enemy during the first decade of my life. After finding out that we weren't in fact, immortal, I'd stay up and pray every single night, pray that we didn't die that night, pray that I could see the world again, tomorrow. And woke up tired every day, with gratitude instead of eyes.

Maybe this is what made each hour intense and infinite, filling it with indescribable childish wonder. While I was alive, I could do anything! Only death was impossible. So when the night came, I shivered. I couldn't control life while asleep. I tried to stay awake as long as possible. And I kept praying.

Fear of Love or the Lack Of.

My second decade on earth was plagued by this fear. The awkwardness of going from child to adult in just a few years, the ew, the awww, the oh, the ouch, the om…

Why did love hurt? It's like discovering America when you're headed to India. What the hell is this new planet, and how did I end up here, and why are people hanging upside down?

Why the sweet pain? Why not just SWEET or just PAIN? Who had this idea of mixing both? Are pain and love inevitably linked? Does every Utopia rise from the ashes of its entropy? Do you also have to die to the hands of so-called-love in order to eventually experience it in its depth and wholeness? I was sick to my stomach.

Fear of Failure.

Third decade: welcome to Adulthood. And I failed (often miserably), failed at nearly everything I tried, about 100 times out of 101, only to confirm all my fearful, misguided assumptions. My initial question, being asked and answered by Life, in the same tone, again and again... And the frustrated protest in the back of my still-5-year-old throat, growing fainter and older and wearier with each blow: "But I had thought, I had hoped, I had wished..."

In my forever optimistic childish mind, I would have never imagined that my mother's answer to my tragic question regarding our mortality would be, *Yes*. And never, not in a million years, could I have anticipated all the blows that followed, in nearly the same fashion... Or did I secretly do?

Just like our trust in ourselves and our basic goodness is a map to life's hidden treasures, isn't our fear also just another map to the self-authored tragedies that do their best, time after time, to keep us from these treasures?

It's the same script being written over and over. The same movie playing. The only elements rotating in and out of our carefully built, domesticated universes are the supporting actors and the settings. But the protagonists – the storytellers, we – remain unchanged.

D.E.A.T.H (Dirt Enters At The Heart)

~ Saul Bellow

So how do we stop running from our worst enemy? How do we turn around, and – shaking like a leaf – face our giant shadows? May cause excessive urination.

I'm afraid of relationships ending, of people leaving, of creatures dying, of nature degenerating, of mutant food, of pesticides, of falling in love (again), of not falling in love (again), of having children, of not having them, of Monsanto, of illness, of idiocy and illiteracy, of being hit by a truck or a train, of being in a plane crash, of sharks, of bats, of spiders, of jellyfish, of cockroaches, of breaking my neck and being paralyzed from the head down, of getting struck by lightning, of losing my mind, of ghosts, of zombies, of pandemics, of Ebola, of the end of the world, of being unloved, of being too loved, of being different, of being ugly, sick, stuck, old and alone, of failing, of suffering, of being lied to, of being hurt...

As Montaigne so wisely put it, "My life has been full of terrible misfortunes, most of which never happened."

But when you turn around and face the monsters in your closet, strange things *do* happen. I call it The Alchemy of Enough, the Power of I, the Here is Where this Chapter Ends Because I Am the Author of this Book and I Say So – the strength that comes when you realize that no one else can save you, because you truly are "the captain of your soul, the master of your fate" in the deepest sense of the word.

Could it be that our fear is more afraid of us than we are of her? Even crazier, all it takes to disarm her is to say it is so. You leave the Matrix the moment you decide to leave the Matrix. We are symbolical animals. We live through signs. Nothing means anything until we agree to it. We have that authority.

The shadow is real – it's not imaginary. You can see it on the wall. It's huge, grotesque and terrifying. But it's just that, a shadow of your smallness. And your smallness, well, quite small... it couldn't interfere with your greatness if it tried – unless *you* let it. You're both, the author and the main character in your story.

A demon's shadow grows five times its size on the walls of our imagination. (I know this because I used demon measuring tape.) I can sense their discomfort when I go past the Shadow to the Thing, past the Symptom to the Cause. They don't want to be found out – because truth disarms, aids and abets love and love sustains life and life conspires with you, not against you, you are her child!

So say your fears out loud. Shout them over the rooftops. Come clean. It's embarrassing. It hurts a little to even try. But when you dare to look them in the eye, your demons lose their power.

It's like falling in love with an empty (pretty) head. After you face it long enough, a face is just a face. What more is there to it? It's human nature. Once you assimilate anything (a new face, a new world, a fear, a condition) it becomes a part of you and, as such, it ceases to constantly affect, surprise or disarm you. The only thing that amazes is Life – abundant flowing life. The rest gets boring.

And so it is with Fear. What more is there to fear other than the fact that, yes, I'm afraid, I'm terribly afraid, pee-my-pants-scared-shitless…Now, what needs to be done? Get it together!

Georgia O'Keefe, one of the most relevant artists of the twentieth century, recognized as Mother of American Modernism, shared her scary little secret: "I've been afraid every single day of my life, but I've gone ahead and done it anyway."

This life often plays like an indie film where the main character is allowed to inexplicably disappear 20 minutes before the end. I used to accept this. I used to think: *It's okay, I can take it, I'm so Indie… It was too good to be true, anyway, I should have known this was coming.* And then sit through the rest of the film, watch it end because hey, I paid for my ticket, so read the credits upwards and backwards, say them out loud, in French, maybe there's meaning hiding in between, endless question marks popping out of my eyes days, months, even years later.

I wrestled and argued with reality, tried to understand the intellectual behind the "lectual" – thinking, just wait, just give it another turn, just compromise your heart a little longer, the *aha* will come…at some point. Maybe not now, maybe not later, maybe twenty years from now or on my death bed (or in the afterlife, whatever that means)… Someday I'll understand the Bigger Plan, the Destiny, the Purpose, the Amen, the Hallelujah. All the mute Angels will finally sing to me then.

They say this is "trust" in things not yet seen – I say this is fear, of things already seen, the ones we hide from, the ones that could shake our foundation to the core and truly transform our life from the inside out.

Marianne Williamson, said it best:

"Our deepest fear is not that we are inadequate. Our deepest fear is that we are powerful beyond measure. It is our light, not our darkness that most frightens us."

So now I disagree with my previous self. Lately, I think that whatever is great it has to be true, right here and right now. And if it's not yet true, then let me help it materialize. And if I'm not allowed to make a dream come true, I better stay awake or dream another. I now punch screens that show me lies and I use the books I don't like as toilet paper. I don't rewind anymore, I delete. I get rid of all the stories I'm not allowed to co-author with life.

I don't have time for the stars to align (and neither do you). It's later than we think. And those rocks are a million years late for everything. So spare us your galactic flashlights, Universe, here on earth we're used to seeing in the dark. Our life is ours and nobody else's. And here's one irrevocable truth about this Life: It's passing through our fingers.

Every step is a second chance to make it or break it. Whatever has been written about and for you by others is not valid. It doesn't – it shouldn't – exist. You can safely delete any story that doesn't belong to you and ask your so-called-Destiny to get her fake hands off your soul. She sure as hell ain't got your copyrights.

Only life can generate more life. I have no idea what Death is but I hope they let me write you a letter once I get there. So this leaves us Fear as the Number One Enemy of Life.

"The matter is difficult to put into words. For fear, real fear, such as shakes you to your foundation, such as you feel when you are brought face to face with your mortal end, nestles in your memory lie a gangrene: it seeks to rot everything, even the words with which you speak of it.

So you must fight hard to express it. You must fight hard to shine the light of words upon it. Because if you don't, if your fear becomes a wordless darkness that you avoid, perhaps even manage to forget, you open yourself to future attacks of fear because you never truly fought the opponent who defeated you."

~ *Yann Martel (Life of Pi)*

I wish I wrote this from the future, and I could happily confirm to you, dear twenty-first century prehistoric creature, that we, *homo sapiens creatives* of 2149 AD (or however long it takes us to figure this out) have still not gotten rid of our fear, but we've finally understood that we're not supposed to, that our parasites are good sometimes. They get the dirty job done and help regulate our body functions.

Be glad you're afraid of jumping out of a third-floor window.

At this point in the future – post-earth, sad to say – we've finally learned how to co-exist with our fear, how to use it to fuel our imagination, how to create more fearlessness out of it, how to blend it with our wildest dreams; how not to sweep it under the rug, how not to disappear on it… But to show up, every day, to look her in the eyes; and if need be, even hold her slippery reptilian goblin hand and then, and just because we can, do the unthinkable, the I can't believe I fucking did it, the wonderful, the crazy, the impossible, the impractical, the uncomfortable but necessary, the real you and the truthful me. With, not without, our fear.

But why do we have to wait another 200 years? Why can't we dance right now?

Facing the Darkest Side of a Beautiful Person.

By Tanya Lee Markul

> *"Beauty comes in many forms – and there is no form more beautiful than you. Just exactly as you are, this minute, right now, without changing a thing... you are beautiful. Beautiful enough to take God's breath away. You do believe this, don't you? Oh, you must. You must. How can I believe in my beauty if you don't believe in yours?"*
>
> *~ Neale Donald Walsch*

May every single one of us find the space to really appreciate life. Your life, my life, just a small speck, a tiny offering, in the grand scheme of everything.

At the end of the nineteenth century, Otto Lilenthal, the Glider King, a pioneer of aviation, was the first person to make well-documented, repeated and successful gliding flights. He died of injuries in 1896 when his glider stalled. He was unable to regain control and fell from an estimated 50 ft, fracturing his neck. On his deathbed he said: "Small sacrifices must be made." His death, his courage, a small sacrifice in the grand scheme of everything.

> *"Hello darkness, my old friend, I've come to talk with you again, because a vision softly creeping, left its seeds while I was sleeping, and the vision that was planted in my brain still remains within the sound of silence."*
>
> *~ Simon & Garfunkel*

The darkness what is repressed, suppressed, enraged and encaged.
Your life, my life, just a small speck, a tiny offering, in the grand scheme of everything.

I am not bad, you say. It is debatable if we are born a certain way, bad versus good, but throughout our lifetime due to controlling, repressive influences, it is safe to say that we all manifest, conjure and create the dark creatures that fester within.

We acknowledge and reflect them in and through the eyes of others often feeling provoked, angry, deeply hurt or sad, misunderstood, hopeless or confused, judged. Lost.

The birth of shadow: Be a good girl, don't be bad, they say. Our wounded ego from quite a young age turns defensively fierce and creatively delusional and a master at distracting us from what is real.

It is more acceptable for me to hide my emotions. To silent my voice… To hide my creativity… To believe that no matter what I do, even if I follow their path, that ultimately I will always be unacceptable. So I must hide. Not be seen. Not truly live.

Over time we become angry and cynical. We start to live in denial and confusion with all the masks we wear that truly are not who we are. We dehumanize ourselves. We become creatures of superficial habit. Careless. We become addicts, abusers and course because so many aspects of the profound infinite beauty and mystery of being human are deemed unacceptable. Our passion, our inner calling becomes nearly irretrievable. So as we age we stray even further from the essence of who we really are we lose sight, sensitivity, we disconnect from our vessel and we lose all trust. We become prisoners of our own pain.

Who's telling the truth? Nearly everyone becomes a liar. Nearly everything becomes a betrayal. The journey of life becomes so insignificant that we seek only the dark we dim our lights until we can no longer see. We can no longer feel (yet we so desperately want to we yearn for it somewhere in the depths of our own personal well).

Silently and shamefully, we retreat from this experience. We barely recognize ourselves and although we pray for its end, death becomes our most frightening nightmare because we acknowledge, only to ourselves, that we aren't living as we are meant to be.

But why, you ask. Haven't you had enough? From yourself and every dark suppressed shadow?

"As one soul sinks lower, so do those around it."

~ Unknown author

Lead us all from the unreal to the real, from darkness to light.

Your life, my life, just a small speck, a tiny offering, in the grand scheme of everything.

Trust that despite your ignorance, despite all of your conditioning and hardships, despite the dark collective shadow that covers significant masses of our existence on this planet, you are meant to be here as you.

This experience is not in vain. You do have the ability to release pain, to transform the darkest parts of you into the deepest offering of healing, nourishment and transformation... for you, for those around you and for all life forms. The healing elixir exists within the poison. Your issues, your trauma, your pain can set you free. Make forgiving yourself the greatest act of courage. Make forgiving those around you, the world, the smallest sacrifice. Tap deeply into life. Invite the possibility of transforming the darkest aspects of you into something that is malleable and something that is *allowed to be released.*

Trust beyond your current understanding that you don't have to be swallowed by the shadows. Change your interpretation. Own your darkness like your life depends on it because it does. If you never embrace it, it will never, ever let you be. It will never, ever let any of us be. You deserve better. You are more than you've ever imagined possible. There's nobody quite like you. Step into the magic of who and what you are.

You beautiful human being, confront your darkness and connect with the life you were meant to be living and the person you were meant to be. Live so that at the end of your life, your death will be the most encouraging offering, a small sacrifice for all of mankind.

A Beginner's Guide to Change: Love the Questions, Don't be Afraid.

By Shavawn M. Berry

> *"I would like to beg you, dear sir, as well as I can, to have patience with everything unresolved in your heart and to try to love the questions themselves as if they were locked rooms or books written in a very foreign language. Don't search for the answers, which could not be given to you now, because you would not be able to live them. And the point is to live everything. Live the questions now. Perhaps then, someday far in the future, you will gradually, without even noticing it, live your way into the answer."*
>
> *~ Rainer Maria Rilke*

Have patience with everything unresolved. What's most perplexing about life these days is this overwhelming sense of limbo that most of the people I talk with feel. Everything is raw, ragged, confusing. There's no sense to be made or found anywhere. It seems there aren't answers to any of our burning questions.

It is as though we are forever in flux, walking a dead landscape of uprooted trees, smashed cars, swollen rivers spilling their banks. We wander in neighborhoods of broken houses full of random (and often useless) belongings. An eggbeater. A wheel. One lonely shoe.

Love the questions like locked rooms or books written in a foreign tongue. We want to feel some sort of solace, but there is none. There's just a sense that everything in this wide world is shifting, but nothing has shifted, yet. Live the questions. And, perhaps, as Rilke wrote a hundred and ten years ago, we cannot live the answers. Yet. So we must live the questions.

This is what this particular time is all about. Living with this sense of foreboding. Living with the acid burn of negative potentials – catastrophic climate change, the rapacious over-use of our natural world, the senseless killing of our own wildness, simply for the sake of killing. We must live inside these terrible questions. These questions that make us ache, so we will become larger, more pliable, and more open.

Finding our way into the answers. We cannot solve the problems we face with the same sort of thinking that created them. We cannot be so certain of which path to take. We must all become beginners. We are slowly cracking and breaking the outer shell (ego) in order to reveal the true. We have never been here before. We are brand new.

As I sit shaking in my boots and shitting my pants at the mere thought of all this change — of these paradigm shifts that are unseen in any lifetime before ours — I keep reminding myself, always be a beginner, always realize there is something to learn, always remember that you know far less than you think.

Be a novice. Be a blank page. Be embryonic in your sense of yourself. You are just learning the steps. You are just starting out. It is okay to be stupid or blind or to not have the answers. It is okay to be wrong, to make mistakes, to muck it all up. This is all part of the process of becoming, of enlightenment, of living.

Love it all. The confusion. The mess. The raw, red rims of your eyes. Love the experience of being born. Love the experience of watching the old way of life die. Watch everything burn. Watch everything go. Don't be afraid.

This. This is how you find your way. You don't notice the changes as they come. You just wake up, one bright morning – sky the color of robin's eggs – and you realize that you are there. And you open the door and smell the restless air and say a prayer of profound thanks.

Falling in Love? Only on Days Ending in Y.

By Macaile Hutt

A friend texted me out of the blue last week and asked if I ever feel like I want to be in love with someone other than myself. I had to chuckle at the last part because I'm sure he assumed he would get some soapbox "I love myself and that's all that matters" answer if he didn't add it to the end.

Without missing a beat, I immediately responded, "only on days that end in Y."

And it's true. I want to be in love so badly. I want to wake up next to my best friend, sip coffee on the patio while listening to the birds chirp on Saturday mornings, and chase each other with squirt guns in the fresh cut grass on hot summer days.

I want to cry on his shoulder while watching classic black and white movies, and I want to be the first person he calls when he's had a bad day.

I want to speak in secret codes, reference inappropriate jokes using memories that only we would understand, and call each other the most absurd nicknames when we are in the privacy of our own home.

I want to travel the world with him; to another country, another city, or maybe even just another room.

I want to take mini vacations to the grocery store and hold hands the whole way home.

I want to fall asleep to the sound of his heartbeat and wake up to the tickle of his eyelashes fluttering on my back – stuck in the moment between being sound asleep and wide awake, one of my favorite places to be.

I want to finally love someone I'm scared to lose, instead of losing someone I'm scared to love.

I want to memorize his freckles, add depth to his laugh lines, and always give him a reason to want to come home. I want to slow dance in the kitchen while sipping red wine and shoot whiskey on the weekends when we just need a good time. I want to be the best buzz he's ever felt, his favorite hello and hardest goodbye. I want to find something worth fighting for.

I want to find someone who knows what he has before I'm gone, sees the beating heart hiding behind concrete walls, and views all of my flaws and scars and broken pieces as stained glass windows for my light to pour out of. I want to find someone who isn't afraid to make friends with the monsters in my mind or take me on a journey to even the dustiest corners of his soul.

I want someone who wants all of me – every tiny piece – all of my hopes and dreams and flaws and insecurities, all of my demons and mistakes and haunted memories, all of my love that I've kept locked away, saved for the day that I finally found what I was looking for.

I want to save that love until the moment I find him. And once I find him, I want nothing more than to give it all away.

I could go on forever about all of the things I hope to find within the puzzle piece person that fits so perfectly alongside all of my jagged edges. The yin to my yang, the happy ending to my story, the answer to all of the questions I was too scared to ask.

I could tell you about how I've written him letters and prayed for him to find me when times got really rough, and then secretly thanked him for not showing up yet simply for the fact that I proved to myself that I could get through it alone.

I could tell you that I get scared sometimes that I'll never find what I'm looking for. That maybe I live in a magical land within my mind, dreaming up someone who doesn't even exist. That maybe my standards are too high and my inner romantic is too hopeless and all of the days I've spent with my head in the clouds, stuck in a daydream are just that – a dream.

And if that's the case, then so be it. I'll live there happily, peacefully, comfortably.

I'll pack my realistic bags filled with realistic goals, stuff my suitcase self with thoughts and ideas and dreams and plans, and I'll carry on, the way I always do.

All the while wondering,

If there's a starry eyed boy that also lives in this fairytale world,

Sitting in his kitchen,

Fingers tapping lightly on his keyboard,

Sipping tea,

Texting his mom,

And thinking about me.

The Art of Chasing Rainbows: A Pocket Guide to Daydreaming.

By Simone Datzberger

"You'll never find a rainbow if you're looking down."

~ Charlie Chaplin

Chasing rainbows is a delicate business – practically, emotionally, and mentally. To begin with, it is hard to catch the momentum of a rainbow. Once we spy it, it can disappear in a moment's notice.

At times, rainbows shine just ahead of us, but for some reason, we focus only on the grey and do not even catch a glimpse of all the magnificent colors. Rainbow hunting is a craft to be acquired with patience and great care.

A beginner's introduction to the art of chasing rainbows:

Facing the dark sides of life. You can only witness a rainbow if the sun is behind you and the rain is in front.

Changing perceptions. From airplanes, you can see full-circle rainbows.

When dreams become delusions. There is no gold at the end of a rainbow, only an optical illusion resembling it.

Reawaken a sense of wonder. Not only double, but triple and quadruple rainbows also exist.

Nothing lasts forever. The longest lasting rainbow is reported to have appeared in North Wales, and shined for over 3 full hours.

The power of interconnectedness. The largest human rainbow consisted of 30,365 participants – organized by the Polytechnic University of the Philippines at the Quirino Grandstand of Rizal Park in Manila, Philippines, on September 18, 2004.

Finding pleasure in the sheer superficialities of life. *Vogue* magazine studied every outfit the Queen of England wore for a full year. The result is a chart called *Rainbow Queen* that breaks down all the colors she wore, ranking blue (with 29%) as her favorite.

Not everything is supposed to be colorful, and yet it is wonderful. The print of the movie *Chasing Rainbows*, released in 1930, survived a major fire that erupted in the MGM studios in 1967, in which hundreds of movies were destroyed. *Chasing Rainbows* lost its only two Technicolor scenes, and remains, to this day, a fully black-and-white movie.

Bright creativity is a ripening process. Radiohead's album *In Rainbows*, released in 2007, was probably the strongest collection of songs the band had assembled for a decade.

Despite being unpredictable and temporary phenomena, rainbows serve a particular purpose at a particular time. They can entertain us, mesmerize us, and every so often, even rescue us.

> *"Sometimes it's important to work for that pot of gold. But other times it's essential to take time off and to make sure that your most important decision in the day simply consists of choosing which color to slide down on the rainbow.*
>
> *~ Douglas Pagels*

It is scientifically proven that daydreaming helps sustain a healthy mind. Hand on your heart: Would you ever publicly admit that you have been lost in a daydream? Letting our minds wander in dreamland is often associated with laziness, irresponsibility, and being unfocused. Especially in Western societies.

Yet the cerebral benefits of daydreaming are often dismissed. According to Eric Klinger, Professor of Psychology at University of Minnesota:

> *"Daydreams help us to get the most out of our brain power, and are an essential personal resource for coping with life. Sounds like something we should all be doing more of."*

Prof. Klinger further argues that daydreams help us realize our goals and reveal our innermost hopes, desires, and fears. Likewise, an article in *The New Yorker*, entitled *The Virtues of Daydreaming* highlights the fact that leading psychologists and neurologists found a correlation between daydreaming and creativity. Thus, in Steve Jobs' words, "Dream big." Or, put differently:

"Forget your politics for a while, let the color schemes arrive!"

~ Mates of States

There is nothing wrong with chasing a rainbow until we realize that it is not the gold we are after, rather the manifold and miraculous elements that are perfecting its appearance. As long as we do not twist all colors in our minds to fit our own image, we will not blunt our own senses of wonder.

Rainbows are omnipresent and often appear in our life when we at least expect them.

"Two bubbles found they had rainbows on their curves. They flickered out saying: 'It was worth being a bubble, just to have held that rainbow thirty seconds.'"

~ Carl Sandburg

Plastic Tiaras and Living the Dream: Give me Truth.

By Braja Sorensen

There's so much out there telling us what we could or should do, emulate, produce, look like, wear, buy, promote, eat, read, think, say.

How to be beautiful, slim, popular, rich, successful. How to live the dream, be the queen or king of your own carefully constructed palace. What a life-challenge it is just to wake up these days (are the sheets the right thread count, which side of the bed should I get out of, how raw is my breakfast and organic my coffee?).

I tell you, it's hard keeping up with the Joneses these days: for starters, they changed their name to Kardashian…

Trashy pop culture has produced a violent thug called Illusion with strongarm-tactic issues who seems to drape himself languorously around half the free world, forcing them into a drugged-like state of uber-consciousness about how they look to everyone else, always very careful to be seen living the dream, uploading endless streams of photos of themselves into the social network strata with Photoshop filters ratcheted up to the stratosphere, images that don't carve inroads into what is reality but which they perceive as a barren desert, photos eternally lost in space.

These obedient lambs of slaughter worship at the altar of designer religion in the Church of the Acquirement of the Ultimately Worthless, whose Mecca, Wailing Wall, and holy river is the Internet, where words and images are the currency and the "whores" have all the money.

In epic tales of yore, entire worlds were created by the spoken word; in spiritual cultures, words are the carrier of the grace and power and will of God; in the times of the Mahabharata, words carried weapons of mass destruction. Yet never in history has the world experienced the effect of the written word in the same way as we do in this 21st century…

Social network sites have created a culture of people armed with words in their lifelong efforts to desperately sell their living-the-dream scenarios: 120-character ether-bites to prove their happiness, success, achievements, humor, wit, beauty, their own selves…all impossible in such a medium, where the very idea of "self" is built on a platform of arbitrary artificiality.

> *"All our words are but crumbs that fall down from the feast of the mind."*
>
> ~ Khalil Gibran

So what are we feeding our minds? Not "they"– the other half, the lower forms of human life. What are *we* feeding our minds?

We're all on this shame carriage – admit it. I confess I watched an episode of the Kardashians on the plane but I swear I simply couldn't get past 10 minutes, and that included the horrifying fascination and irresistibility factor already having happened and been dispensed with. But the effect it had on me was… mind-rape.

How is it we can "wonder" at what happens in the world when this is the fodder being poured from the never-ending numbers of massive silos of uselessness into the millions of minds parked in neutral – doors to the consciousness wide open, senses on overdrive, and brains locked on uncontrolled?

This is how "words" are produced in this pop culture, whose hallowed halls our minds are stalking daily on the internet. How much can we say we're not influenced by it, even if we find it off-putting? It makes me wanna' pull my own plug…

Words are my craft, my life, my only resource for intellect and heart and mind, my go-to, my shelter, my love… Their misuse disgusts and repels me, destroys my social resolve, makes the fire of renunciation and simplicity start to burn within me… The contemplation of a life lived on the banks of the sacred Ganges (about 150 m down the road – ohhh so close, can I do it?!) seems an increasingly attractive option.

I am intrigued, romanced by the dynamics of thought, speech, action, and the written word. The random use of any of these elements of communication can create disturbance to those around us, to relationships, to knowledge, education, morals, ethics, spirituality, and ultimately to ourselves.

Like the master of the poetic word Wallace Stevens said,

"Perhaps the truth depends on a walk around the lake."

Or, yes, a wander down the riverbank. Both are certainly far more potent soil in which to plant our thoughts, carefully sow our creepers of phrase and speech, and from which pluck the fruits of gently-blooming words…

Imagine if we were all conscious of every word we spoke or wrote, of our thoughts before they formed into words, of our words before they tore into the ether, of our actions before they inflicted harm… if we only heard or read words constructed with infinite care that produced genuine acts of kindness, words rich with thought and meaning, edited with a soft yet controlled mind, and shared with love.

If only we were conscious, always, of the ability we have to produce such art with words… whose ultimate fruit would be truth.

"Of all types of security I am consciousness of
the eternal soul within.
Of secrets I am pleasant speech and silence,
and among seasons I am spring.
Among jewels I am the ruby,
and among beautiful things I am the lotus cup.
I am the steadiness of mountains
and the fragrant aroma of the earth…"

~ The Bhagavad-gita

Love is Everything and Sometimes not Enough.

By Melissa Smith.

> *"I love you without knowing how, or when, or from where.*
> *I love you straightforwardly, without complexities or pride;*
> *so I love you because I know no other way than this:*
> *where I does not exist, nor you,*
> *so close that your hand on my chest is my hand,*
> *so close that your eyes close as I fall asleep."*
>
> *~ Pablo Neruda*

To behold the kind of love that touches the space between my breasts, where my soul resides, is the humblest form of love.

And if that love can be tenderly layered with an abundance of compassion, it is nearly perfection. And yet I strive to become more, better than I am, because of love.

> *"We loved with a love that was more than love."*
>
> *~ Edgar Allan Poe*

Love is kindness, quality time, service, and the spilling of words that edify across real paper, across a million miles of sea. It is respect – friendship and commitment.

And just when I start to feel the inadequacy of giving this kind of love, the impossibility of it, I find it. It resides in me, waiting to pour onto the One who is willing to receive my love just as I am.

Love is moment-to-moment mindfulness, where communication becomes a spiritual transaction.

And when love fails to be mindful, falling again and again, it stops and takes a breath – opening up rather than closing down. It listens and forgives, and grows deeper through all the trials and errors. Love is forgiving grace in action, instead of bolting the other way.

"...forgiveness is a lovely idea until they have something to forgive."

~ C.S. Lewis

Could the notion of a soul mate be a fairy tale? If you believe in serendipity, which I do, then you might just meet someone who is exactly right for you, fitting you like a coat.

Neither of you is perfect. Instead, you are imperfect with your combined flaws arranged in a way that permits two separate humans to hinge together as one.

The flaws are like wet paint on paper – folded, then mashed together, and opened to reveal two of the same design, only slightly off, and with colors blending and bleeding into the next.

Love. Let go. Then love some more when you'd rather hold on tight. Love accepts when you choose to follow the longing in your heart, until you have exhausted all the roads and alleys in order to uncover your path.

And when that path turns out to be something completely different from the dream in your heart, love morphs into an outpouring of support and understanding. It floods the veins to resuscitate you when the blows of life are more than what you can bear.

Love is touch, holding you as if you were a delicate flower. It allows for moodiness, gossip, and unfolds deeply into understanding when sheer exhaustion causes the body to collapse.

Real and physical love is like going to church, but it is unlike any other church you have ever attended. Its sacred passion moves electricity between your legs and into the tips of your fingers, hugging your skin like a silk sari elaborately draped over your body.

Love is vulnerable, accepting, giving – and when you give, you risk losing it all. Rumi says, "…gamble everything for Love if you're a true human being." Heartbreak is inevitable, but then the heart breaks open, not closed.

"We are not the same persons this year as last; nor are those we love. It is a happy chance if we, changing, continue to love a changed person."

~ William Somerset Maugham

To be embraced by love is to know that I am home. Love takes the breath from my lungs so that I can scarcely move, and suddenly, I am more alive than ever before.

Love is everything and sometimes not enough, all at once.

How to Heal a Broken Heart: A Rebelle's Guide to Grief.

By Amber Shumake

(Kubler-Ross meets Drama Queen.)

1. Unmask your Pain. Diva up. Channel your inner opera singer. Create cleavage. Sing soprano. How many times can a person die inside!

Exclaim this as Emily Dickinson would. Stand in the stairwell. Stomp your feet. Wave a white scarf of surrender. Get into character. Evita meets Titanic. Don't cry for me, I'm the king of the world. Whatever comes to mind. Conjure every cult classic. Watch your own demise on the big screen. Oh pain – what hast thou to teach me?

Replay this question on repeat. Let the CD skip. Scream on a page. Record the softer side of you. Speak your truth in tongues. Give a foreign accent a whirl: Italian meets Hungarian, crossed with Jamaican. What elicits a response? What stops the bleeding? Something's gotta shift. The only constant is change.

2. Simmer in your Darkness. Dive down. Close the curtain. Change the scene. Hot bath. Cold shower. Get really clean and clear on what it is your heart needs from you – which is perhaps the opposite of what your logical mind would have you do. I have a yoga student who when he really loves a pose says, "Oh, I hate this! This is terrible." He is joking. He thinks if he says, "Oh, this feels so good," that I'll never teach that asana again. Healing is like reverse psychology. Drown in your sorrow. Never underestimate the power of a single Earth shattering tear. Sift through the rubble.

Steep. Inhale the steam. Let the salt in the water remove the shrapnel from your weeping bones. Hug your knees to your chest. Cry inside your mouth. Rock yourself silly. Savor the moment when you begin to shiver – a signal that you're alive, on the verge of chemical reaction. Entropy. Homeostasis.

One can only hope. Dry off with the ragged hope that this too shall pass. Rub the towel across your shoulders as you would a small child. Just beyond the horizon is a feeling far superior to this pain. This pain shines a flood light on the joy you've yet to have

3. Romance your Soul. Bring Sexy Back. Rub oil all over your body until everything you thought you knew slips from your hands. Unlearn all that you think you remember. Calm your unnerved. Rewire your brave. Slather yourself in all things sensual. Mantra: I still got it. Get it. On.

Put on the panties you save for those special nights. Pull off the bra that's holding your hollow heart hostage inside, the sweat pants you should've thrown out years ago, and the T-shirt leftover from a few different relationships ago. Close your eyes and bring the so-soft-it's-almost-organic cotton fabric up to flush your red nose.

Six degrees of separation. Inhale the scent of who you've been – past and present – even if you can't remember yet. Swaddle your sordid self in the memories of vibrant vestiges from past lives. The holes in the fabric only add to its appeal. And soon – tomorrow or next week or in the next breath – you'll realize it's true for you, too.

You break wide open and hemorrhage, only to bandage yourself back up again. In the cracks – Rumi and Leonard Cohen were right – that's how the light gets in. Don't rush it. Feel the tear stream down your right cheek into your inner ear, through the left side of your brain, flushing away the logic. Love knows nothing of logic

4. Indulge. Sin. Do something decadent. If you're fanatical about cleanliness, clutter your space. Let it look like your life. If you're cluttered, clean something especially dirty and ridiculous like the inside of a trash bin. Miss the mark. Feed your addict. Give in to a vice. Just one. Maybe two. Stop at three. Call your sponsor if you need.

Choose the least restrictive addiction for your heart. Avoid the vodka that would drink her underneath the table. Now's not the time to take up smoking as a sport. Instead, eat the chocolate, milk, not dark. Preservatives do a broken heart good. Forget that you're lactose intolerant. Drink milk out of the carton. Pretend it's raw. Lap it up. Kitten, meet your saucer. Curl up in a ball. Pet yourself. Lick your wounds clean. Ah, you see, this is the way the other half-lives. Realize they're on to something. This shit tastes damn good. Bartender, hit me again. Wonder why you don't indulge more frequently. Let yourself go. Let high fructose corn syrup move you. Briefly remember that you're lactose intolerant. Remind yourself that in this moment it's okay to forget.

5. Sleep. Wake. Reincarnate. If you can't sleep, rest. If you can't rest, pace. If you can't pace, sit. Sleep and rest and pace and sit all at the same time. Breathe in the stagnant stillness; bask in the seismic shift. Put cucumbers on your aching eyes, Mentholatum on your grieving chest. Humidify your aching heart.

Treat yourself as a child with a chest cold. Be your own mother minus the guilt trip. Stages 1-4: your homeopathic expectorant. Turn your head and cough. Dry heave if you need. Match your movement with powerful intention. Get. It. Out. Even if you don't know what it is. That's okay. The placebo effect is stronger than you know.

We forget to remember what's true. The truth is, you're remembering how to return to you, your core, your essence, all facades aside. And tonight that means you must die a little more inside. Applaud yourself for your resilience. Bow to your wickedly stubborn resolve. You don't merely exist; you're not here just to survive. Beyond your sorrow – you know – in joy, you'll thrive. Hang on. The only way out is to breakthrough.

Now I lay me down to sleep.
If I should die before I wake,
I pray my soul reincarnate.
And so it is.
Amen.

Whispers of Wisdom for Children.

By Sarah Voldeng

There are no mistakes, only lessons.

Life is short, but also long, and at any point you can change direction. Listen to your gut feeling. Anxiety means you need time to settle before making a decision. Falling in love is like falling through space, you will know it when you feel it.

Tell the truth because it feels better, lies create holes in the heart. Feel the earth with bareness; it is the greatest grounding gift—let the sand slip through your fingers and the icy waters splash over your feet. Let the pebbles feel your pain and wash it away.

Smiling makes you feel better, laughing until you cry is amazing. Fear is there for a reason, it lets you approach with caution.

Place your memories in your heart and be selective about who holds the key. Discover your passion: music, dance, poetry, art, or athletics; and do it every day. Ride the bull. Take it by the horns and never let go.

Fill your life with people who support and inspire you. Guilt, shame and remorse do not belong in your vocabulary.

Do the right thing for no other reason than because it is the right thing. What matters today may not matter as much tomorrow. Do not overly focus on it.

It is totally healthy to cry. Crying sheds sadness and opens up the heart for more love. Holding in tears does nothing but create blocks of sadness.

I know it seems obvious, but do what makes you happy. You will spend much of your time doing it, so find something you enjoy. Take the time to figure out what that is. There is no hurry in life. The only hurry is in all there is to do, see and accomplish.

Travel because it allows you to see how the rest of the world lives. Do not isolate yourself into the small world of your own reality. Expose yourself. Allow yourself to be touch by the world. Allow the world to be touched by you.

Love is the answer to everything. Forgive easily. Do not hold a grudge as it lodges arrows deep into your heart. They are hard to remove.

Look after your physical body. You only have one. Do not abuse it but nourish, hydrate and exercise it.

Learn to master your mind and control your thoughts. When it seems impossible, work it out physically. Learn to release being trapped in the labyrinth of the mind.

Be yourself, even in darkness and sadness. The light will shine, just dimmer some days more than others.

Try to have a good sense of humor and light disposition. Do not let the poison of others penetrate. Let it drip and roll away like a bead of sweet oil.

Breathe in deeply and soak it up. All of it. Appreciate.

Most of all, enjoy life. We have only one.

The Heart Breaking Open: Release Me.

By SR Atchley

And just when I start to break open again, I find it hurts.

Love. Requires. Openness.

If you have ever been hurt in love (who hasn't?), you know that allowing yourself to begin again, to release the gates, open the door once more… is… difficult to say the least.

Sick. Twisted. Essential Masochism.

Return to the starting gates and re-run the race? But what if I lose yet again? Would the universe be so cruel?

Yes, without a doubt it would. So, instead of simply letting the universe take its winding course, I turn to the buddhaverse this time. Having reaped karma, having experienced the results of my actions time and again, I begin to look at the whole situation from a perspective of insight, introspective analysis. Attention. Awareness. Mindfulness.

I choose, in this time, to allow myself to feel more. And to be mindful of what I feel, allowing it to pervade me.

The hurt, the fear, the energy, the rush of blood as I flush, as it happens. And if I feel something I've felt before, I turn a spec of attention toward it. And if I feel something new (is that even possible?), I examine its spec as well. That spec can save me, I'm certain. Save me from running blindly. Save me from missing the mark.

Because we are only given one chance in this dreamlike trance of life – one chance to recognize the importance of the spec. It is the spec that connects us to everything. The spec is everything. One chance, over and over again without end, without beginning.

As a woman who has experienced the heights of passion, pleasure, partnership and purpose, as well as the unfathomable depths of dark, thick, black pain, the possibility of allowing myself to be alive is frightful. With life, authentic life, comes feeling. And with feeling comes… a multi-limbed bitch of a beast that tries to tangle and twist all that is.

Maya comes when we expect her and when we don't. She tempts us all to give up, give in. And the only way to overcome her is to do just that. Give up and give in. to feeling, to pain, to pleasure. Resisting either can become a fatal flaw.

The only way to overcome the eons long programming to protect the self is to give up the self. I don't exist, anyhow, outside of this lovely dream, so what is the harm in giving myself up? No harm. But, it requires a great deal of inner strength, derived from a spot that most of us have been conditioned to characterize as weak, our soft spot.

The place where we are vulnerable, the ego clinging, me-victorious, pain aversive nature that lies within us all. This is the attachment to self, to be more specific. Letting go of attachments is the name of the game.

I have found that the most effective way for me to loose my self-clinging is to be mindfully aware of what I am feeling. Then I can go two different ways with it. Search for the underlying causes of the feelings, which lead to insight, or hold those feelings with compassion for as long as they persist. In doing so, I find a changed perspective – perspective that allows me to hold and then release the feelings without judging.

When we stop judging the self, the self becomes more free. As the self becomes more free, it becomes less *me, mine, I, ego* and connects to the larger space and time wherein all beings are interwoven. Joining the race of all time, all space. In these moments of mindfulness, I become less attached to myself, and I find my Self attaches to something vaster.

In the universe, we have a place, an area that can be pinpointed, mapped, documented. In the buddhaverse, we are place. We are time. We are no longer limited by me or my. In the buddhaverse, the race can only be won if you don't run it. There is no race. No I. No me. No you.

Exposing the heart and soul to the openness required for growth requires letting go of the constructs of our individual identities, in order to become a part of the larger, unquantifiable, indescribable, indestructible loop. It requires extreme vulnerability and attention to uncertainty.

The vulnerability is unbearable, yet is the only redemption there is. It is the truest source of strength I have found. For we are all fragile, delicate, feebly pretending we are not. We get lost along the way because we are not willing to follow the signs. Some never even notice them. The rushes of adrenaline, the fuzzy headed tingle of shared thought, the energy that moves between bodies heavenly or not, the ache in the gut-pit.

The moments of recognition precognition superstition that create volition. The signs are there. They are the same arrows leading to the finish line which does not really exist. The dreamlike path through the buddhaverse traverses and twists and turns. It teaches. So we may evolve. Vanquish fear. Fear is nothing other than uncertainty.

So, I am certain. Certain that breaking open is not that bad. It hurts. It happens. Shit happens. Better to have loved and lost than never loved at all. Everything happens for a reason. Yes, magic eight ball, the signs point to Yes and it is decidedly so.

Pick a cliché, any cliché, and you will find a spec of truth, of humor, of happiness. Find the spec and pay attention to it. Be certain it is there. And then remember it is only a dream.

> *"Do not take life's experiences too seriously. Above all, do not let them hurt you, for in reality they are nothing but dream experiences… If circumstances are bad and you have to bear them, do not make them a part of yourself. Play your part in life, but never forget that it is only a role."*
>
> *~ Paramahansa Yogananda*

Imperfect Advice to Perfectionists.

By Elise Museles

> *"At its root, perfectionism isn't really about a deep love of being meticulous. It's about fear. Fear of making a mistake. Fear of disappointing others. Fear of failure. Fear of success."*
>
> ~ *Michael Law*

Dear Control Freak, Type A, Classic Overachiever, better known as Perfectionist. Welcome to your imperfect home, your life.

Other than the fact that neither of us is perfect, there are other symptoms we share. For years, I've searched for the perfect diet, relying on books to dictate what and how to eat. I am a classic overachiever, in that I dot every *i* and cross every *t* (and then some).

Even when it came time to put together this article, I procrastinated. Could I sit down to write on such an important topic? How could I talk about it like an expert? Do I really know enough (besides living it every single day)?

Perfectionism isn't usually a tamed beast. People who have perfectionist tendencies tend to be that way in other areas of their lives as well. Diet. Exercise. Appearance. Parenting. Work. Plans. The list goes on...

On the one hand, it can drive us toward excellence with lofty goals that are certainly impressive. On the other, it can prevent us from achieving, feeling, trusting our instincts and being realistic.

But most importantly, it can be a chronic level of stress that can wreak havoc on our overall health and wellbeing.

Here are some of the negative consequences that result from perfectionism:

- We procrastinate because we are waiting for all the stars to align before we begin something new and exciting.

- We are less efficient with our time as we analyze and agonize over all the details.
- We have unrealistic standards that are impossible to achieve.
- We can make things unpleasant for those around us with our overly rigid behavior.
- We are too worried about doing things the right way, so we miss out on the enjoyment or pleasure in our experiences.
- We are releasing cortisol due to the continual, self-imposed stress.

And here are some imperfect (but healthier) alternatives:

What if...

You subscribe to the philosophy that good enough is good enough during times where those ten extra steps of effort really don't add any additional value?

What if...

You abandon your overly dogmatic approach and try not to get so caught up with rules or labels? Vegan? Raw? Paleo? High carb? Low Carb?

Imagine being liberated from thinking about following the perfect diet, which is most likely some other expert's plan anyway. Of course, setting up a foundation with healthy habits that includes eating whole, real foods is essential.

But, instead of obsessing or beating yourself up about breaking the rules and restrictions, you learn to listen to the signals your body sends you... all day, every day.

What if...

You relinquish control (just once in a while) and become a passenger instead of always being a driver?

The upside is that you may learn to complete a task, make a recipe, plan a vacation (someone else's – and not just your – way). And you could end up with extra time to use productively in some other manner. Liberating!

What if...

You stop the inner dialogue of *should* and *must*, and just feel your way through?

I know, the rational side would not approve, but try tuning into your messages and not dictating them because you have a preconceived notion of how you should feel or must think.

What if...

You ban the all-or-nothing mentality? You know... that destructive thought process that leads you not to try something unless you are certain that you can give it 110% (or do it perfectly)?

Don't wait for the perfect moment to start a business, write a book, tackle a big project, or run a 10k race – it will never come. Begin it now, imperfectly.

What if...

You accept your body right now?

You stop waiting for it to look like it did when you were 18. No hate. No judgment. Just pure gratitude and thankfulness for the life it gives you with each breath, creative thought and enduring emotion.

What if...

You embrace the deviations?

You enjoy the slow Yoga class you take on the day when your body says No to the 10-mile run you had planned for your upcoming half-marathon training. You learn to become flexible instead of insisting on following the prescribed *plan.*

Just thinking about the unrealistic expectations is enough to elevate your pulse and raise your blood pressure.

While we – perfectionists – have spent years, or our entire lives, trying to be perfect (and exhausting ourselves in the process), we're living with that chronic level of stress which releases the hormone cortisol that can impact everything from weight to sleep patterns to disease prevention.

Letting go of perfectionism… or at least considering it, is as close as it gets to a perfect plan.

How does your perfectionism show up in your life? Get it off your chest and start breaking free.

10 Travel Truisms – for a Swollen Heart, an Open Mind and an Inspired Soul away from Home.

By Long Distance Love Bombs

A girl we know was about to take her first trip overseas and she wanted some advice. Here is what we came up with…

Truism #1: There is only one first.

So you're off to see the world are you? Off to lose yourself in the unknown? You're off to explore distant lands to see what the light feels like on the other end of the horizon?

I could not be happier for you or more envious of you. And that's a great feeling for me to have because it means that you are doing things right.

The first big trip out of the bubble is one that you will never forget and one that I long to experience again. Alas, like so many things in life, there can be only one first. Keep that in mind, and do not forget: You only get one. Hold this thought in the palm of your hand and squeeze it with all of your might — you only get one first trip overseas just as you only get one bright and shining moment at a time.

Live in it. If you don't go out into the great blue yonder of this world to discover what you're capable of, you'll never know the boundaries of your potential, the possibilities you can create or the joy this pursuit may bring you.

The only thing sadder than undiscovered potential is unused potential. Do not bring this sadness into your life.

Seek intimidation. Hunt fear. Overwhelm yourself. Search for the opportunities that scare you and try to make each day an insatiable quest to question, not only your ability, but your confidence and faith in who you are and what you can do.

Why? Because you must learn on this journey that deep down you already have all of the answers. And the only way to do that is to live the questions.

That's my best guess at least. I don't know for sure, but I'm okay with that. I'm okay with not knowing. I'm alright with chasing mysteries.

For instance, I'll walk around a rundown village in Africa and I'll see little kids with big hearts walking around with no shoes, dirty clothes and a runny nose, begging me for money in the only English they know.

And I'll talk to great men about their dreams, men with kind hearts and soft eyes who live amidst filth and squalor and poverty, and we'll discuss their lives and their hopes, and I'll hear about how the government wastes money, about how public officials are corrupt, about how selfishness and greed destroys entire cultures, about how society is starving, not because of a lack of food, but a lack of will, a need for courage, and a desire for kindness to prevail.

I'll see these homes, these people, these lives, which seemingly have nothing to fill them, and yet I'll witness such pure, unadulterated joy oozing from the very essence of their souls in such a completely overpowering and forceful display that I am taken aback, dumbstruck and amazed as to how it all works.

Why those with the least to show have the most to give, why the richest hearts seem to lead the poorest lives, and I'll read Albert Camus' observation that "There is solitude in poverty, but a solitude that gives everything back its value" and I am humbled, and curious, and intrigued about life and everything in it. And for a long time to come, each and every day, I can honestly say that I'm working on it, that I'm trying to understand, that I'm challenging myself to do more, to do good, to do better.

Are you?

Truism #2: The darkest night is no match for the dimmest light.
The ugliest facts of life will find you no matter where you hide. No matter how bright you shine, some will always find you dull. No matter your beauty, some will see ugliness. No matter your grace, some will only notice your shortcomings.

However, this is not your fault or is it your doing. Do not concern yourself with the perceptions from others and do not take anything personally.

Take nothing from strangers except directions, kindness and knowledge. Because why take anything else?

You have everything you need right in front of you. Everywhere you look, literally, there is light. Everywhere you look, literally, there is life. Even with your eyes closed, there are many beautiful things to see. Focus on these things – the light and the life – and you will be okay.

You will be okay because deep down, you know that you find only what you search for. Deep down, you recognize that what you decide to search for is all that matters.

This search has a name. It is called Life. Go and find that fucker every chance you can. However, sometimes things will go awry. People may force you to confront a situation you never wished to see and sometimes you will have no choice but to engage the darkness in a staring contest.

Do not be afraid to ask for help. Asking for help shows strength not weakness, just as being reliant upon others is a necessity, not a choice.

Once, on the streets of Vietnam, an angry man began screaming at me. "Fuck you," he yelled. "Fuck you and your family. I will kill your mother."

What would you have done? Would you have yelled back? Would you have run? Cry?

I chose to smile. I chose amusement. I chose not to believe my eyes and ears, but rather, to trust my heart. And do you know what? He smiled back at me. Just like that, it was done.

So, when you come across the angry street vendor harassing you to buy his goods, what will you do? Shake his hand and wish him well.

The paranoid backpackers with pockets full of complaints and dark scowls threatening to scare off your sunrise? Offer them a hug, buy them a beer, and tell them a joke.

The cafe owner who overcharged you for lunch, the shady local policeman pestering you for money, and the disrespectful tourist littering on the street and loitering in the heat? The advice for dealing with them is the same for dealing with life itself: smile, and keep moving.

The best revenge is a happy life and this is true regardless of country, creed or color. I encourage you to prove me right.

Truism #3: Just because people aren't advising you what to do or showing you how to live does not mean that people aren't advising you what to do or showing you how to live.

My upbringing was about as normal as it gets. I graduated high school, got good grades and then studied at a community college. I had no idea what I wanted to do with my life at that time, and, spectacularly, that seemed like a great thing to do with my life – to just dwell in that terrifying, yet strangely comforting, unknown.

So, I followed my heart and I worked hard and I moved to other countries. I fell in love and I got depressed and I had adventures. I met dazzling people, did fun, once-in-a-lifetime things. From these experiences, I learned about myself and I learned about the world and I grew to love people.

Eventually, at long last, what happened was that I began to tolerate myself. Slowly, I started to like myself and eventually, I began to adore humanity, to believe in who I was becoming, and to love the life I was creating. Trust me when I tell you that it is a wonderful feeling when you start to think like this. It took a while though. All good things do.

The other day, I was thinking about my family. I thought about what advice they'd offered me along my journey, what pearls of wisdom they had given me to get my ball rolling.

I thought about what they had told me about my life, and about life in general, and I thought about it and I thought about it, but I couldn't think of anything specific. There was, for example, no revolutionary insight passed through the generations down into my heart.

I can recall no occasion in which they sat me down and told me, for instance, to "Stand with like-minded men, when possible," or "If in a fight, hit first and hit hard." There was, it turns out, not much of that at all. Why? I'm not sure.

However, my family gave me advice by showing me how to live and by supporting me, always and unconditionally, in how I chose to live my life. Though my choices were undeniably different from theirs in nearly every degree, they loved me fiercely, they supported me wholeheartedly, and they set a truly admirable example for me along the way.

"Work hard, love your family, be humble…" They taught me these things not by telling me, but by showing me.

"Don't forget where you came from, be polite, be proud…" They led by example.

"Enjoy yourself, don't be afraid to cry, never forget where you came from…" They were good teachers.

These lessons, these undeniable pearls of good, vibrant living, were their advice. They weren't always quick to come right out and tell me, but I learned a tremendous amount from them.

Their advice was their experiences and their lives were my lessons. And, just as there will be lives and experiences all around you on this new adventure, so too will there be lessons. Take note of them, but also remember that you, too, are a teacher and as such it's also very important for you, too, to live your lessons.

Truism #4: The journey is the destination.

Relax. Relax. Relax, my dear.

You're off on an adventure and you have a lot planned: yoga retreats, temples, beaches, parties, hiking.

You're going to see it all, do it all and remember it all. Well, here's a funny story: No, you're not, no, you shouldn't, and no, you won't.

But that's okay. The open road doesn't necessarily lead to anywhere, and about all of those curious sights, smells and tastes that will blow your mind each and every day? To other people, those are normal, commonplace, or boring. Those people you will meet with those new accents, different clothing and entirely unique ways of living, doing, and being? They are not strangers. You are the stranger.

They are not different. You are different. They are not odd. You are odd. These people are not weird or funny, crazy or complicated. Rather, you are those things, you are those thoughts, and you are those opinions. Never forget the power of perception.

Truism #5: Optimism is a worthy investment.

I was in Indonesia last year and a local man told me this story:

"I born in Bali, but I go to Java when I young, maybe ten. Twelve? I go to live with my uncle and I work for him. All day, I work. Every day. So long days. So hard. I work in the house.

My uncle he very mean man. He hit me. He scream at me. Every day, he scream at me! My aunt, she worse. No good, no good… Never happy for me.

I so sad. I not go to school. I have no money. I have no friend. I stay in the house working, working, working. All the time working.

I don't know when I ever go back to Bali. I miss my family, my mother, my sisters. Everybody. I stay there maybe three years and I so sad. Every day so much sad.

One day, I sit on my bed and I crying. I crying so much. I never happy in long time. My uncle, he hitting me and my aunt she always screaming me. Never good. Never happy.

So, I sitting on my bed and I take rope. I take rope from the yard up to bedroom and I make a loop. I make like a loop, yes, and I put the loop around my neck. I crying, so much crying. I put rope around my neck on the bed and I crying, so sad. I want to die. I think I make suicide now.

I sit with rope around my neck, yes, and I make tight. Very tight. And I sit for maybe one hour and I crying so much and I think about my family and my sisters and I think – I cannot die. No. My sisters would be so sad for me. So I take the rope off my head and I put it down and I sit on the bed and I cry.

I work for my uncle maybe two more years and then his brother come and find me. He see what happen to me and he feel so bad and he take me away. I come back to Bali and I go to school and I working. I working so hard and now I so happy. I always laughing! Life is so very much happy now! I have good wife and daughter and my house is good house and we have Western toilet and TV and everybody happy.

When I grow up in my uncle's house, I was like frog in a well. I cannot do anything. I cannot go anywhere. I so much sad. But, I keep going and I keep trying and now I am so very happy all the time!

People they say to me 'How can you be so happy all the time?' and I say 'Because I am so happy!' When I child, I so much sad, but I very, very lucky for the sad. Very good for me to be so sad, because now I so, so happy! All the time I am happy because I am a so lucky man!"

Pain is a prelude to pleasure. It's as simple as that.

Truism #6: Be inspired or be expired. The choice is yours.

Here's the thing about travelling: it's all up to you. If you want to sit around and complain all day about the trip, the food, the culture, the people, the toilets, the roads, the language, the internet and the lack of the regular comforts of home, feel free. By all means, go right ahead and do it. That's entirely your choice.

But, it's also your choice to embrace disappointment, to cuddle up with craziness, and to slow dance with all of the severely messed up things that make their way into your life. And don't kid yourself – there will be a lot of unexpected slow dances on this trip.

But, like on the dance floor, just because you don't know the words, doesn't mean that you can't sing along and just because you don't know the steps, doesn't mean that you can't dance like a motherfucker until the sun comes up.

Setbacks are speed bumps and fears are fuel. Get moving, get shaking and don't ever stop.

Truism #7: Life is funny. Don't forget to laugh.

Once, I sat on a pier in Puerto Rico and watched a man walk his dog at sunset. It was a quiet night, with a light ocean breeze dancing through the air. The man stopped to admire the view before calmly bending down, picking up his dog and then throwing the little guy right off of the end of the pier. There was no apparent reason for this. He simply threw his dog straight out into the ocean. My mind blown, I wandered the beach trying to make sense of what I had just seen. Words escaped me. Ideas were elusive.

Months later, I thought back to that man and that dog, I pictured the pooch flying through the air wondering to himself about how maiden voyages are always the most delicious (remember Truism One?), and I imagined the man, arms crossed in satisfaction, observing the magnificent splendor of his small dog in flight, and it hit me: you've got to take risks, you've got to live unexpectedly, and, sometimes, you have to pick up something you love and throw it out into the depths of the unknown just to see how it'll fare without you, just to see if it will somehow find its way back into your arms.

For you, I hope it does.

Truism #8: Say yes, and say it often, but do not forget the powerful importance of saying no.

I've had enlightened conversations with third world prostitutes, taken motorcycle rides with strange French surf bums, and cuddled a Vietnamese chicken on an overnight bus ride. I've crossed borders on boats, taken taxis to nowhere, and been mugged in the daytime streets and robbed on a moonlit beach.

I've made mistakes and I've made amends, but I've also made a life and I encourage you to do the same.

Go and do that thing that scares you. Climb a mountain, take that chance, and be that person that leads that group to do that thing that time that you've always wanted to do because that will be a good day. Express your heart, loudly and clearly, every chance you can. Sleep under the stars, cry under the moon and stumble face first into all of those glittering gutters that so many never escape from.

Make mistakes (but never the same one twice). Get sick. Fall down. Have adventures. Inspire yourself. Love everything. Create opportunities. Pinch potential on the ass as it walks past searching for a place to rest its head. Be raw. Tear yourself open and have a look around inside. Smile at a sunset and break dance with a break down. Push your memories aside and let the present have a turn at the wheel. Get up and get going. Live. It. Up. But not too much.

Don't forget that you're in a faraway foreign land where everything feels different for a reason. Be careful. Be mindful. Take heed. Mind your own business, and pay attention. Seriously. Pay attention.

Trust your gut. Nurture your awareness and give some thought to uncertainty when it seemingly appears from nowhere, pokes you in the arm and begs you for attention. When you're scared, take note. When you're not scared, take note. Grow. Learn. Evolve. Be better than you thought you could be.

Above all else, through the pouring rainstorms of your soul and down across all of the frozen wastelands of apathy and evil that you may witness, never stop celebrating. In time, you will learn that every emotion is a gift, that hardship is a younger, dirtier version of wisdom, and that we are all, each of us, miracles in a constant state of grace.

You may not believe me now, but I'm right on this. Trust me.

Truism #9: Remember to forget, but don't forget to remember.

Don't forget yourself; remember who you are. Remember why you are there, doing those things, seeing those scenes and living those dreams. Remember what you want to gain from this experience. Recall that you've been looking forward to this trip for a long time. You will be in a different place every day with different people talking different languages.

You are your only constant. Find comfort inside yourself. Lose yourself in every moment, but never forget where you've been, who you are, and what you wish to become.

Truism #10: The open road can close your heart. Don't let it.

Crowds can make you feel alone, just as full rooms can make you feel empty inside. Fortunately, you are blessed with family and friends that love you. They will be thinking about you each and every day. They will miss you and even though you cannot feel it, you will carry your loved ones with you in every decision you make. Make them proud. Leave a noble legacy.

I am sad to see you go, I will miss you every day, and I will appreciate you even more the next time our eyes meet. But that's a tale for another day. For now, it's time for you to go and have the trip you've been dreaming about. Go make memories. Go create stories. Go collect experiences.

If I can sum it all up in one little sentence, let it be this: Live a life that would make you jealous.

Fearing Unicorn Horns or How Awesomeness is Made.

By Rasmus Hammarberg

When I was 12, I was afraid of fat and ran mile after mile on an empty stomach. When I was 16 I was afraid of failing to become my father. And this is what I want to speak about, this fear shoved down our throats since we first fell over the kindergarten doorstep.

It is everywhere, this fear. It greets us from ads and reality shows; says hello whenever a cop walks by and it cries for our attention from newspaper headlines. It asks for a dollar from our favorite coffee shops. It claps its hands from holy print, and screams our names whenever two clenched hands emerge from behind the corner. It eats us alive, and never yields unless we force it down from its pedestal. And the pedestal is high.

After all, society runs on fear, and would cry burned bills if something would change. And it would be right to do so. Because if we had not any fear, we would no longer work, or obey laws we do not agree with. We would stop caring for tomorrow, and we'd keep putting our hands on the stove no matter how many times we felt its heat. We would crumble, and take what we know as society with us.

But it is not all fear that is this crucial for our survival. There is the fear of not being accepted, of doing something extraordinary, of kicking a hole in our comfortable world and kiting up to that special place where everything is more awesome than cotton candy, as healthy as kale, and more beautiful than defined calves holding a lover against another.

There is also the fear of standing out. There is the fear of being your very best. What we have here is a fear that does not help us to survive but functions as a muffler for our creativity. What we have here is a fear that makes us less alive than we could be, and less productive than we should. And if we should be something, just a sole thing in this huge world of ours, it is productive.

We should live to produce our very best, create our very best, and make our lives a sheer outcry of what this very best does to our hearts. We should let it be spelled out across our ribs and tattooed across our fingertips, so that everything we touch bears the mark of what we are meant to do and be and leave for our children to look upon with supernovas dripping from their retinas.

If only we could get rid of this fear, that is. And to do this we need to go past our comfort zone and enter that which lies beyond; shrug off our trembling lips and tell the shadow to go suck a pear somewhere. We need to trust ourselves to survive in this unknown territory, tell ourselves that we are indeed strong enough to live in a state of constant awesomeness, and awesomeness cannot be reached without the movement of our feet.

There is more to the issue though. After all, I had no problem going outside my comfort zone when I was 16, and still I raged through every night and told my father to call his secretary if he needed to talk. Still I did this shit, felt worse and then I did some more. I was afraid of failure back then, and thought it would be better to never try because if I never tried I would never fail. Being a loser demands less of you than being the most successful piece of unicorn horn in the world. And this has to change. For all of us. We have to see that there is nothing to fear in failure, we can laugh in its face and say tough luck and I will nail it the next time.

Society has, of course, provided assistance for this fear to grow, and this is why it is so hard to let go of it. Because as with all these other kinds of fear we have been fed pictures of what it looks like; horrible images that only serves to make us not try and then we are back in that comfort zone, and the television is there as well.

We have to do something about it; shove the fear full of dynamite and let it explode someplace where tons of curtains hide every square inch of its remains. Then we can say I will be my very best and mean it. Then we can start running and never look back, and then we can stand on our toes until our calves are strong enough to hold us tightly against whatever we love most. Then we can grip our full potential, and be the most awesome piece of shit we can.

"Be Not Afraid of Greatness." – A tribute to William Shakespeare.

By Richard LaRosa

> *"Be not afraid of greatness. Some are born great, some achieve greatness and some have greatness thrust upon them."*
>
> *~ William Shakespeare*
>
> *"He was not of an age, but for all time!"*
>
> *~ Ben Jonson*

William Shakespeare is in the Poetry Lounge and his ghost haunts the pages of every book of poems by every poet that has written poetry in the past three hundred and eighty-nine years.

In the literary sense, Shakespeare's words are written into the genetic code of every speaker of the English language and that language is woven into the neurons of our brains when we think, and drifts along the currents of our breath when we speak. We cannot escape his influence on language and culture any more than we can escape the gravitational pull of the earth, for to do either would send us spinning off into the void.

In sooth, I can say with complete certitude that everyone with the desire to have a deep understanding of the myriad elements of poetic language will find no greater teacher than the Immortal Bard.

> *"The remarkable thing about Shakespeare is that he is really very good – in spite of all the people who say he is very good."*
>
> *~ Robert Graves*

Reckless hyperbole, you say? Ah, but remember that you are in the Poetry Lounge, where there can never be an overabundance of descriptive language. Herein you will find the velocity of verbosity is akin to Einstein's theory of relativity – it is the energy of words equaling the mass of poetic language times the speed of thought squared.

All the world's a stage,
And all the men and women merely players:
They have their exits and their entrances;
And one man in his time plays many parts,

William was a country lad from Stratford-upon-Avon, a market town in the county of Warwickshire, located in the West Midlands region of England.

He was born sometime between the 23rd and 26th of April in that plague year of 1564 that struck dead 237 residents in six months. Elizabeth had been Queen for five years when the infant poet arrived on the scene mewling and puking in his nurse's arms and the first public theatre in London would not be built for twelve years.

As the son of a Stratford alderman, Will would have been entitled to a free education at the King's New School in Church Street, where he would learn Latin grammar and rhetoric and hone his reading, writing and memorization skills in preparation for his future vocation.

However, the dialect of Warwickshire also found its way into his writing, most notably in Ophelia's mad flowery prose in Hamlet and in various scenes in *A Midsummer Night's Dream*.

I imagine he had ample time to observe his surroundings as a boy with his satchel and shining morning face, creeping like snail unwillingly to school, and later to contemplate the poetry of obsession as a lover, sighing like furnace, with a woeful ballad.

His plays are full of regional words, such as the couplet that completes the following example from Cymbeline:

Fear no more the heat o' the sun,
Nor the furious winter's rages;
Thou thy worldly task hast done,
Home art gone, and ta'en thy wages:
Golden lads and girls all must,
As chimney-sweepers, come to dust.

Shakespeare was a wonder with the rhyming couplet and the ending couplet above provokes imagery with a double meaning. In the Warwickshire dialect, the "golden lads" in the closing couplet are also dandelion flower heads and the "chimney-sweepers" are the dandelion seed heads that we scatter to the winds with our wishful breath when we are children.

Shakespeare also used heroic couplets, when two lines of a rhyming couplet are in iambic pentameter. Here is an example of three glorious heroic rhyming couplets, spoken by Helena in *A Midsummer Night's Dream*, that make up six perfect lines of iambic pentameter:

> *Love looks not with the eyes, but with the mind;*
> *And therefore is winged Cupid painted blind.*
> *Nor hath Love's mind of any judgment taste;*
> *Wings, and no eyes, figure unheedy haste:*
> *And therefore is Love said to be a child,*
> *Because in choice he is so oft beguiled.*

The study of Shakespeare's use of the arts of language gives us access to every possible scheme of grammar and topic of invention we can possibly imagine and many so anachronistic, we never knew they existed.

As a native English speaker, partially schooled by the American system but mostly self-taught, I approach Shakespeare in the manner of a student approaching the study of a foreign language. The difference, however, between the study of a foreign language and my love affair with the works of William Shakespeare is that I must also continually delve into the historical, mythological and literary sources of Shakespeare's day to actually understand all the nuances of what he's saying.

Shakespeare cannot be fully understood without a background check of his life and times – and there's the rub. Most people don't want to work that hard to read an author or a poet. Furthermore, most people think of Shakespeare as a writer of plays and not as a proper poet. But, back in the day, he was called a poet, as well as being known as a player and a playmaker.

Indeed, his most popular and best-selling works when he lived were two epic poems he wrote before he was thirty, in the early nineties, called *Venus and Adonis* and *The Rape of Lucrece*. These poems were so popular with the youth of London (the average age of the citizenry in those days was twenty-five) that they were kept underneath bed pillows and literally read to pieces.

Even as the sun with purple-colour'd face
Had ta'en his last leave of the weeping morn,
Rose-cheek'd Adonis hied him to the chase;
Hunting he loved, but love he laugh'd to scorn;
Sick-thoughted Venus makes amain unto him,
And like a bold-faced suitor 'gins to woo him.

Shakespeare was a true rebel, bold and original. It's estimated that he invented some 1,500 words and phrases, which seem to have made their debut appearance in his poetry and plays.

We are thinking and speaking Shakespeare whenever we await with *bated breath* the *crack of doom* or *fight to the last gasp*. When we finally recognize that *jealousy is the green-eyed monster* and we give in to the *cold comfort OF one that loved not wisely but too well*.

In the *salad days* of our *flaming youth*, Shakespeare followed us whenever we went on a *wild-goose chase*. And, just as he was a rebel of invention, in many of his sonnets he bucked the conventional habit of comparing the qualities of women to such things as the sun and the moon and the stars.

To wit:

My mistress' eyes are nothing like the sun;
Coral is far more red than her lips' red;
If snow be white, why then her breasts are dun;
If hairs be wires, black wires grow on her head.
I have seen roses damask'd, red and white,
But no such roses see I in her cheeks,
And in some perfumes is there more delight
Than in the breath that from my mistress reeks.
I love to hear her speak, yet well I know
That music hath a far more pleasing sound;
I grant I never saw a goddess go,
My mistress when she walks treads on the ground.
And yet, by heaven, I think my love as rare
As any she belied with false compare.

Shall I compare thee to a summer's day? I think not.

Shakespeare's wiry-haired mistress, with her reeky breath and unmusical voice, has been pushed off the Plutarchian pedestal and put in her proper place in the dirt where we all live. But, the closing couplet rescues her from the mud, even though the goddess Venus in the heavens above doesn't get an honorable mention.

Compare the first four lines of this excellent sonnet by Bartholomew Griffin, from his Fidessa sequence published in 1596, which illustrates the typical tradition of comparison:

My Lady's hair is threads of beaten gold;
Her front the purest crystal eye hath seen;
Her eyes the brightest stars the heavens hold;
Her cheeks, red roses, such as seld have been;

Griffin's example is lovely and well written and follows the syllabic scheme perfectly, but I much prefer the mischievous Shakespeare's sly satire of the form.

And, sonnets were still in vogue when Shakespeare was just beginning to make a name for himself as a playmaker and player on the London stage in 1592, though his own unauthorized sonnet sequence would not appear in print until several years later.

He wrote 154 sonnets, comprising 2,156 lines of pure poetry. This is one of my favourites:

When in disgrace with Fortune and men's eyes
I all alone beweep my outcast state,
And trouble deaf heaven with my bootless cries,
And look upon myself and curse my fate,
Wishing me like to one more rich in hope,
Featur'd like him, like him with friends possess'd,
Desiring this man's art, and that man's scope,
With what I most enjoy contented least;
Yet in these thoughts myself almost despising,
Haply I think on thee, and then my state
(Like to the lark at break of day arising
From sullen earth) sings hymns at heaven's gate,

For thy sweet love rememb'red such wealth brings,
That then I scorn to change my state with kings.

As an actor, I prefer getting my Shakespearean poetry fix from his plays, which are filled with the finest expressions of poetic language ever writ down on paper in the English hand. Speaking the language of Shakespeare gives shape to the imagery his words evoke and my approach to his verse began as an actor searching for a key to playing a character showing vulnerability.

I found that key in a scene from *Romeo and Juliet*, when the young lover from the house of Montague gets the news from Friar Laurence that, instead of being put to death for killing the cousin of his girlfriend from the house of Capulet, the Prince has been merciful and is merely banishing Romeo from Verona.

This proclamation sends the star-crossed lover into such a fine frenzy of hair tearing that he cries out:

'Tis torture, and not mercy: heaven is here,
Where Juliet lives; and every cat and dog
And little mouse, every unworthy thing,
Live here in heaven and may look on her;
But Romeo may not. More validity,
More honourable state, more courtship lives
In carrion-flies than Romeo: they may seize
On the white wonder of dear Juliet's hand
And steal immortal blessing from her lips,
Who even in pure and vestal modesty,
Still blush, as thinking their own kisses sin;
But Romeo may not; he is banished:
Flies may do this, but I from this must fly:
They are free men, but I am banished.
And say'st thou yet that exile is not death?
Hadst thou no poison mix'd, no sharp-ground knife,
No sudden mean of death, though ne'er so mean,
But "banished" to kill me? "Banished"?
O friar, the damned use that word in hell;
Howlings attend it: how hast thou the heart,
Being a divine, a ghostly confessor,

A sin-absolver, and my friend profess'd,
To mangle me with that word "banished"?

And, at the end of the scene when Friar Laurence tells Romeo to arise and hide himself, when there is a knock at the door, Romeo says...

Not I; unless the breath of heartsick groans,
Mist-like, infold me from the search of eyes.

...the silence that greeted me at the end of the scene, followed by a collective exhalation of breath and a rousing display of applause, let me know that I had done justice to the emotional intensity of the character. I had completely lost myself in the act of portraying Romeo and it was a magical act of expression that transported me into an entirely new state of being.

The play's the thing. This is how I got to know and love Shakespeare – through the poetic language of the plays. Shakespeare's use of iambic pentameter in the banishment scene directed me on how to speak the speech trippingly on the tongue, not to mouth it as if the town crier spoke the lines. I did not saw the air too much with my hand in the very torrent, tempest, and whirlwind of my passion, but rather suited the action to the word and the word to the action.

My study of Shakespeare's use of language taught me when to pause and how to color words with meaning because he has embedded the emotional and psychological state of his characters in the language and rhythms of their speech.

That is the reason 'tis crucial that actors fully understand the rules of iambic pentameter. Understanding allows us to discover who our character is and the underlying meaning of their speech.

"In Shakespeare the birds sing, the bushes are clothed with green, hearts love, souls suffer, the cloud wanders, it is hot, it is cold, night falls, time passes, forests and multitudes speak, the vast eternal dream hovers over all. Sap and blood, all forms of the multiple reality, actions and ideas, man and humanity, the living and the life, solitudes, cities, religions, diamonds and pearls, dung-

hills and charnelhouses, the ebb and flow of beings, the steps of comers and goers, all, all are on Shakespeare and in Shakespeare."

~ Victor Hugo

And all of this imagery is presented in the most excellent of poetic language. Moreover, Shakespeare is not merely a conjurer of imagery and writer of flowery verse. With the plays we get all the witty wordplay, poetic punnery, and astonishing alliteration that makes Shakespeare so much fun to read and hear and speak.

Love's Labour Lost, "perhaps the most relentlessly Elizabethan of all Shakespeare's plays" (according to the editors of *The Riverside Shakespeare*) is a playground of the new language "filled with word games, elaborate conceits, parodies of spoken and written styles and obscure topical allusions."

The title alone promises excessive alliteration to come and it makes good on that promise in the following passage, spoken to Nathaniel by the pedantic Holofernes, as an epitaph to a deer:

The preyful Princess pierc'd and prick'd a pretty pleasing pricket;
Some say a sore; but not a sore till now made sore with shooting.
The dogs did yell; put el to sore, then sorel jumps from thicket,
Or pricket sore, or else sorel. The people fall a-hooting.
If sore be sore, then L to sore makes fifty sores o' sorel:
Of one sore I an hundred make by adding but one more L.

This passage is a perfect caricature of proparalepsis – a rhetorical scheme that occurs when a few letters add an extra syllable to a word, such as Hamlet's creation of the word climature from climate and temperature. In the example above, the added syllable is -el.

I can go on and on about William Shakespeare for another three thousand words and still only scratch the surface of his genius.

Somewhat like Hamlet's advice to the players, when he tells them to speak the speech trippingly on the tongue, my advice to the reader is to read the history of the Elizabethan and Jacobean eras and learn about the social, political and mythological influences that informed Shakespeare's writing.

Read the plays and poems aloud with friends. Hear his words spoken and performed by skilled stage actors and watch televised and cinematic productions. Dive into the bottomless well of Shakespeare's language and explore the depths of his imagination and invention.

One last warning about getting to know Shakespeare:

He may become an obsession if he isn't already the Sweet Swan of Avon in your coffee. I know this from experience, for a day hasn't gone by in nine years that I haven't felt the presence of William Shakespeare in my blood. Beware and have some perspective – and a sense of humour.

It delights me to read such a fervently orgasmic expression of bardolatry from this fellow named William A. Quayle, who wrote a book in 1900 that was called *Some Words on Loving Shakespeare. From A hero and some other folk.*

> *"We shall never overestimate Shakespeare, because we can not. Some men and things lie beyond the danger of hyperbole. No exaggeration is possible concerning them, seeing they transcend all dreams. Space can not be conceived by the most luxuriant imagination, holding, as it does, all worlds, and capable of holding another universe besides, and with room to spare. Clearly, we can not overestimate space.*
>
> *Thought and vocabulary become bankrupt when they attempt this bewildering deed. Genius is as immeasurable as space. Shakespeare can not be measured. We can not go about him, since life fails, leaving the journey not quite well begun. Yet may we attempt what can not be performed, because each attempt makes us worthy, and we are measured, not by what we achieve, but by what we attempt."*

However, I absolutely adore this passage by 19th-century fanboy, Thomas Carlyle, which I beseech you to read aloud in a grand and bombastic style:

> *"And there are Ben [Jonson] and William Shakespeare in wit-combat, sure enough; Ben bearing down like a mighty Spanish war-*

ship, fraught with all learning and artillery; Shakespeare whisking away from him – whisking right through him, athwart the big bulk and timbers of him; like a miraculous Celestial Light-ship, woven all of sheet-lightning and sunbeams!"

The lights are dimming now in the Poetry Lounge but William Shakespeare's words whisper forever from the stages of his pages; the best poet-actor in the world, either for tragedy, comedy, history, pastoral, pastoral-comical, historical-pastoral, tragical-historical, tragical-comical-historical-pastoral, scene individable, or poem unlimited.

Efficient Procrastination while on the Creative Journey.

By Zofia Cartlidge

"Writing is 90% procrastination: reading magazines, eating cereal out of the box, watching infomercials. It's a matter of doing everything you can to avoid writing, until it is about four in the morning and you reach the point where you have to write."

~ Paul Rudnick

There are mornings when I wake up with a fire in my mind and I feel excited about what I will achieve that day. I spring out of bed, feed the cat, feed myself and then, as if a switch has been flicked, I fall into procrastination – the perfect art of doing nothing, whilst doing everything.

Breakfast is accompanied by my opening Internet surf of the day. I sink into the couch and scroll through status updates. I choose the mindless over the productive, and I wonder why I am letting myself slow down so soon after leaving the starting blocks.

The minutes that pass, as I overload with unnecessary information, are minutes that I will never get back, but I do it anyway. Somehow I find a way to justify it to myself by likening it to starting my day with a warm-up instead of a sprint.

I clean my apartment and wonder if I will ever be one of those people who tidy up as they go along. I call my mother. I call my brother. I call my father. A worthy use of my time but still, time moves forwards and I have not written a word. A moment of guilt registers inside me and I push it aside. I practice yoga. I shower. Finally, I sit down and begin.

I want to write a post for my blog. I want to write a contributing post for another blog. There is the work I do for the non-profit I volunteer with, that is on my list too. I'd like to work on my book, but that always takes last priority, even though in the long run it may have the biggest rewards. The scale of the project, and the mental energy it takes, often feels too big.

It feels too big because whenever I walk into a bookstore, the number of books on the shelves is overwhelming and I wonder how I can ever stand out in this ocean of writers – it's the fear of not being good enough.

Then I remind myself that there is still space in the world for further successes. We are a society of hungry consumers always on the lookout for the next wonderful thing. We love great art, great literature, great gadgets, and there is always room for more.

It is true that I often see the end of the story before I have even read past the first page. I won't apply for that job because I won't get it. I won't enroll for a French class because I will never be fluent in another language. I make things up. Instead of taking a few steps to see what is around the corner, I procrastinate, or even worse, don't do it at all.

Yes, there are times where I can make an educated guess at what the outcome of my efforts might be, but I frequently sell myself short. The truth is that I have no idea how anything will end. Life is not a train line with fixed stops, it is a map and compass and the freedom to walk in any direction I choose. I can drive the train anywhere I want, as long as I turn on the engine.

And the longer it takes to turn the key, the less time there is to enjoy the journey. It is like spending all morning thinking about going to the beach, when the forecast says that the afternoon will bring rain.

> *"The secret of getting ahead is getting started. The secret of getting started is breaking your complex overwhelming tasks into small manageable tasks, and starting on the first one."*
>
> *~ Mark Twain*

A little while back, a new friend said to me, "You know who you are, you just need to fucking do it." She'd only known me for a week, and she was right.

My life right now is rich with possibility in a way that it never has been before. I do know who I am, I do know what I want and I do know what I must do. I think about her words while I am ironing my knickers or arranging my books alphabetically, and they provide me with fuel.

The belief that everything I begin needs to be finished, and everything that I finish needs to be perfect, can be a hindrance. Not everything I write needs to be published; in fact, I need never show most of my work to anyone. The only thing that matters is that I start and consider my work as an exploration that might lead me to the pot of gold at the end of the rainbow, or one that might take me somewhere that I never want to go again.

And then what I have is a lesson, and an experience. Maybe it will give me something else to write about.

I might know who I am, but without beginning, I will never realize it. Instead of becoming accomplishments, my dreams may become regrets, smoky memories of the things I didn't do, or memories to which I only have my own made-up ending, and not one that I lived.

Part of my struggle is my misconception that if I will be successful at something, then it will just come to me with ease. There are times when I sit restless at my computer, feeling like there are no more words left in me. I reassure myself that although we may not see it, success is usually the result of numerous hours of work, and many attempts. The result of many hours spent procrastinating, hand in hand with many hours spent not procrastinating.

I wonder if my list of things to do is too long; perhaps this is causing my delay. I tell myself that if I never start, I will never finish. I question if I am too hard on myself, and need to stop measuring what I believe to be success, with time.

Even though I don't start until 3 p.m., I work on and off until midnight. I drift in and out of a state of deep flow as I write absorbed in how a word sounds, how it feels and how it connects with the words around it, coupled with a healthy obsession with punctuation.

When this feeling hits, I contemplate why I continually put off beginning. Why do I forget how good this feels?

Perhaps the problem is not procrastination, maybe it is efficiency. Maybe this is just the way a creative journey goes, maybe I should stop being so hard on myself. Despite the hours it took me to get there, when I look back, I can see progress, a series of achievements that is growing. In between my Netflix addiction that was seven seasons of *How I Met Your Mother*, I must have done something.

"I have always tried to hide my efforts and wished my works to have the light joyousness of springtime which never lets anyone suspect the labors it has cost me."

~ Henri Matisse

You're Stronger than You Think: Understanding the Body of Fear.

By Jessica Durivage

Author and spiritual teacher Tara Brach asks: How do we gradually embrace, not all at once, but the life that's here?

How do we show up to live fully and presently complete with our entourage of emotions, fears, thoughts, worries, joys, dreams, expectations, attachments, etc.?

Of course, part of the journey is learning to let go of some of the baggage, but there are days and weeks and months when I feel like a travelling three ring circus, no matter where I go. You might never know it from the outside, but in my mind my ego takes up residency as the Master of Ceremonies directing my attention to stomach dropping and heart-clenching tightrope walks and trapeze swings with no space for error or mistake. Must. Be. Perfect. Or you're dead.

Fears lie beneath the surface. It is not something to show up to taking it lightly.

Fear puts our nervous system in a grip. Fear is our anticipation of loss. We can spend our whole life consciously and unconsciously organizing our lives around avoiding fear and never really understanding that being afraid is actually a part of being human and more importantly, we can tame this so-called beast by cultivating a committed intention, quiet understanding and acceptance.

"Committed intention, quiet understanding and acceptance." I feel like someone is mocking these words back at me. "Oh yeah, Jessica? It is that easy, right? Let's just all channel our inner unicorn and deal with our fear by using words like *cultivate, mindful, understanding, intention* and blah, blah, bah."

Hey, I get it. It's not easy. And until I got it (and some days I don't) I didn't get it. But once you do, it is impossible to turn away without realizing that the answer is right there within you and you are free to use whatever words you like to have it make sense. Just don't deny it and don't make excuses.

> *"Give over being idle; be a night traveler like the stars. What do you fear of earthly beings, since you are a celestial rider?"*
>
> *~ Rumi*

However you want to look at it, say it or phrase it, *you* have to make the choice to deal with it. You have to exert some willingness or energy towards even uttering those three dreaded words, "I am afraid."

That is just the first step, folks. Not to burst your bubble, but if you are waiting for a plane cross the sky with a grand message about your life or how to get through whatever it is you are dealing with, I have five more words for you: Shit just ain't gonna happen.

I think a lot of us on the spiritual path go through a period where we hope our burdens will just *lifted* from our shoulders for no good reason or no participation on our end. I'll admit, miracles do happen, but for the most part, you are the synergistic center to a miracles happening in your own life. Not a book, a person, a white turban, a prayer, a mantra, a yoga class or a diet or detox.

You are the catalyst of change in your own life. It is almost as if we become inner couch potatoes trying to do all of the right things on the outside, but on the inside we are still replaying the same episodes over and over again, glued to the comforts of our own strategies to avoid discomfort and real transformation in our lives.

Understanding the *body of fear*.

Fear takes approximately 1.5 minutes to run its course through your body.

Fear is natural – just imagine the adrenaline that courses through your body when you see a spider or snake (if you happen to be afraid of these for-the-most-part harmless creatures). You get a spike of chemical response and, well, think about it for a moment. It typically dissipates after a couple of minutes and you become able to laugh at yourself or maybe take an Instagram picture, post it and move on with your day.

Unless you have a phobia of snakes or spiders, there is no behavior patterning in your body to re-trigger the response. It moves you into action – like running away.

When we move into talking about fear in a more personal way (e.g. fear of the future, fear of losing a parent, fear of speaking in public, fear of giving up our comfort strategies like eating or drinking), we relate to these a little differently.

These fears have stories and patterns and behaviors attached to them, so when fear strikes, our patterning typically allows for the fear to keep getting re-triggered over and over and over again. This basically means that, for many of us, the whole idea that fear lasts 1.5 minutes seems like a made up unicorn fairy story, until I have now presented you with some facts.

I don't know about you, and I am no scientist by any means, but looking at fear in this way allowed me to see my *role* in perpetuating it. Some of you may know what I mean. When my partner looks at me and says, "Why can't you just let it go!" and I am in the claws of whatever is gripping me, I literally feel as though I cannot.

Fear + Resisting = Suffering.

You become locked in resisting the fear, getting re-triggered over and over again. The more we try to control the fear (instead of sitting with it and letting it run its course) the more we identify with it at a core level.

Do you feel where this is leading?

It is like bellying up at the *Bar of Fear* and doing shot after shot of whatever your poison is. Yes. You are choosing it at this point. It's like waking up with a hangover. When I lose myself to the grip of fear, I wake up the next day holding my head mumbling, "I am way too old to be doing things like this to myself."

Understanding a little bit of the science behind fear has helped me to grasp my role in it. Understanding my role in it has helped me get behind creating and seeking out resources and tools to support me in what Tara Brach calls "attending and befriending" it.

Become besties with your fear.

We don't need one million strategies to deal with ourselves. We need one or two – maybe three. When we start trying to do more than that, we do nothing more than distracting ourselves from the core issue with yet another strategy. And what I am going to share may or may not resonate with you.

If it does, great! If not, then – like I said – there are a million strategies out there. Just pick one and then write a blog about it.

Find a still spot. Finding your still spot is like having absolute faith that there is a sandbar exactly your size out in the ocean of fear. You may not be able to see it or feel it yet, but taking that first step towards finding your still spot *is* knowing that it is there.

When we access our still spot, it allows us to numb the fear for just enough time – even if it is only a few seconds – to step back, assess the situation, slow down the sympathetic nervous system and anchor in the parasympathetic nervous system.

I would like to preface the actual techniques in saying that they are nothing you don't already know how to do. Perhaps you already do it. What good would it do any of us if these techniques were hard and difficult to learn? Dealing with our fear is hard enough. Sometimes we just make things more difficult than they really are.

First, you must realize that fear is present. Fear is here. Don't be scared.

Still Spots…

- Grounding – begin to feel your feet on the earth. Feel your sitting bones on the chair.
- Breathe – slow, deep and full.
- Touch in – place a hand over the heart or perhaps over your navel.
- Use a loving kind message – say to yourself: May I be safe, May I be peaceful.

Keep moving your thoughts to an anchor. The reality is that you will probably not be able to stay anchored in a still spot for very long at first.

One second? Half a second? One inhale… May I be… and maybe you won't even get the rest of the statement out before you are back in the grip and patterning of fear. That is ok.

Don't give up. Just keep going back to one of your still spots, trusting and knowing that your sandbar is there. Be determined. Even just 30 seconds of this work can help to dramatically interrupt a life pattern and open a doorway to freedom.

"The whole of spiritual life is to meet our edge and soften."

~ Chogyam Trungpa Rinpoche

(Again and again and again and again.)

No one said this would be easy. As we continue on our collective journey, let us together know that we are all doing this work, supporting one another in the name of inner freedom and in pursuit of inner revolution.

I used to distract myself by making things harder than they were. I used to want a quick fix answer. The truth is that there is only one answer – *we* are the ones who seem to forget it and show up again and again with the same question.

Johnny Cash: Life, Love and Magic of Being Your Badass Self.

By Chantele Theroux

> *"Sometimes I am two people. Johnny is the nice one. Cash causes all the trouble. They fight."*
>
> *~ Johnny Cash*

For as much of a progressively independent, stand-alone hellcat-in-heels as I can be, I'm the first to admit that I'm a sucker for old-fashioned flair and finesse in life, and in love.

Part natural-born talent or studied subtle art, believe me boys, it's all sexy. It's the hold-the-door-open, pull-my-chair-out, offering-your-coat-kinda man. You can't buy that kind of charm, and charisma doesn't come bottled or on tap.

You're tearing apart your dirt bike by day and enjoying dinner with your grandma by night. Your rugged edges frame that wildly kind and considerate heart of yours, and we love you for it.

I'm not talking about launching ourselves back into a revivalist regression of gender stereotypes. From the royale femme fatale to the manliest man among men, we all seek to satiate that natural craving for a delicious balance of feminine strut and masculine swagger. It's the yin and the yang of it, Baby, and we're a limited edition of both.

While we *oppose*, there doesn't have to be *conflict or competition*. It's a hearty dose of resonant convergence where strength in *doing* meets the goodness of *being*. Rocking your very own, real balance is what makes *anyone sexy*, especially the Man in Black.

Johnny Cash was a full on outlaw-country badass blessed with a locomotive voice so strong it busted through prison walls. He epitomized grandeur in complexity and the exquisite contradiction of soft and beautiful strength, expressed through the songs, stories, scars, triumphs and trials of his very real, remarkable life.

Six classic ways to live and love a little more like the one and only Man in Black:

1. Be compassion. Compel with charm and sincerity. For over 20 years, Johnny Cash performed free prison concerts for inmates in the US, and even once in Sweden. 'The Johnny Cash Show' also provided a forum for social issues that ranged from the war in Vietnam to prison reform to the rights of Native Americans in the 1960s.

He helped build bridges of commonality by propelling unpopular opinion and often unmarketable ideas into the mainstream. He also passionately supported SOS Children's Villages, an international child charity that provides long-term care for orphans and children in need.

2. Define devotion. This love and life isn't all happily ever after. It's sometimes wrought with disappointment and near disastrous, total train wreck tragedy. For as bulletproof as a heart can become, most can still bleed and cause a bloody massacre. To those who have totally unraveled, full on fucking lost it or have met the rock-bottom versions of yourselves, I salute you, and welcome you to our club.

After you've been blinded by the full and colorfully real expression of the human spectrum, life seems different. You start to realize that beauty isn't always pretty, that not much in life is black and white, and that the only real guarantee in any fairy tale is that one day it will end.

Believe me ladies, if you lose your shoe(s) at midnight, chances are you're walking home barefoot. Please try your best to keep them both on your feet. Mr. Cash said (when asked about June), "she loves me in spite of everything, in spite of myself. She has saved my life more than once."

He and his first wife, Vivian Liberto, wrote over 10,000 pages of love letters to each other during the time he was stationed in Germany and he proposed marriage, *over the phone*. Because sometimes when you know what you want, you do what needs to be done to make it happen.

Johnny Cash battled alcohol abuse and drug addiction most of his adult life, burned down over 500 acres of a national forest, and affairs were one of the main reasons for the breakdown of his first marriage. He wasn't a saint, but never claimed to be.

"You build on failure. You use it as a stepping-stone. Close the door on the past. You don't try to forget the mistakes, but you don't dwell on it. You don't let it have any of your energy, or any of your time, or any of your space."

~ Johnny Cash

In 1970, he also played a free concert at LaFayette's High Scholl football stadium along with other country artists. It attracted 12,000 people (amazing, considering the town's population was about 8,500) and raised over $75,000 for their athletic association.

3. Simple is Sexy. Scars don't hurt either. Depth doesn't have to be complicated. Scars show the world you've risked it, came out wounded, *but landed on your feet...eventually, and somehow.* Wear all of them with pride.

4. Stir. Merle Haggard (another iconic country music Hall-of-Famer) credits Johnny Cash with giving him the inspiration to launch a music career after prison recording an impressive 38 #1 hits on the country charts. At age 11, Haggard's mother turned him over to the juvenile authorities as "incorrigible." By the age of 20 he was sentenced to 15 years in San Quentin. In 1958, Johnny Cash played that now legendary concert that helped steer his path to becoming a country music legend in his own right. The world has too many limitations as it is – let it be a motivating force.

5. Rage. With the night. Against the dying of what's light. Be fearless, and please find a cause beyond how much literal cash you carry, the ride you roll in, or style you rock. He famously said,

"I wore black because I liked it. I still do, and wearing it still means something to me. It's still my symbol of rebellion – against a stagnant status quo, against our hypocritical houses of God, against people whose minds are closed to others' ideas."

In addition to being a music legend, Johnny Cash was also a best-selling novelist and an artist. He showed the world that your greatest gifts are what you can give back to it.

Rage and be a rebel with a cause, anyone worthy of 1-4 will love you for it.

6. Respectfully Yours. Given and earned, esteem is one of the best gifts on earth.

Bob Dylan described to Rolling Stone Magazine that Johnny Cash used his gifts *"to express all the various lost causes of the human soul."* Muhammad Ali was also a big Johnny Cash fan.

Johnny Cash also covered hundreds of other artists' songs over the span of his career, always gave credit where credit was due, yet made them his own. Trent Reznor described hearing Johnny Cash's cover of his Nine Inch Nails song, *Hurt,* to Rolling Stone Magazine:

> *"We were in the studio, getting ready to work – and I popped it in, by the end I was really on the verge of tears. I'm working with Zach de la Rocha, and I told him to take a look. At the end of it, there was just dead silence. There was, like, this moist clearing of our throats and then, 'Uh, okay, let's get some coffee.'"*

About to celebrate what would have been Johnny Cash's 82nd birthday, take it from him, *"be thrilled to death with life,"* and remember that the fastest way to anyone's heart is staying true to yours.

The Epidemic of Being Stuck.

By Jeannie Page

As I see it, there is an epidemic occurring in our society; it is an epidemic of people being terrified to be alone and as a result remaining stuck in the wrong relationships.

Sadly, I see examples of this around me on a daily basis. And unfortunately I see far more examples of that than of the opposite. Should it be any surprise, then, that 50% of marriages end in divorce? It isn't to me.

One of the benefits to growing older is that as you experience (and learn) more, and as you observe more, you are (hopefully) much more clearly able to see when a relationship is right… and when it is wrong.

If the 20s were the decade of friends getting married, the 30s have proven to be the decade of friends getting divorced. I think it was around the age of 35 when I noticed that what had once been the "summer wedding season" had instead turned into the "summer divorce season." And all of the couples that I saw in my 20s and thought to myself "those two are so wrong for each other!" those couples have in my 30s ended up divorced: almost without fail.

Conversely, I'm sure we've all seen the couples that when you look at them, you think to yourself "Yes, that is how love is supposed to look!" and it is just so obvious that the pair are so in love; they show mutual respect, admiration, and affection; and they show it over years, regardless of the passage of time. Such couples reveal such a beautiful, powerful energetic connection, and they complement each other so well, truly embodying the spirit of yin and yang.

They are simply a joy and an inspiration to be around. I am grateful that growing up I had a friend whose parents exemplified this for me, even after 25 years of marriage. So even from a young age, I knew what love could look like. And today I am so grateful to have even a small handful of such couples in my life, for they remind me over and over again of the kind of love that I want in my life and why I choose to not settle for any less than that.

And I am by no means under the illusion that a relationship should be easy all the time, nor am I espousing that. I am the first to know that love can be messy and that it takes real work to keep a relationship intact.

But what I can say, from experience and from keen observation, is that the right relationship should be much easier than the wrong one. And if the relationship is a constant uphill battle, a constant struggle, then it's not the right one. We can choose to have something better, more easeful.

Unfortunately, for every one of the couples that exemplify what love can be, I have known twice as many couples who exemplify the opposite of that. I have known the couples who fight all the time and who you just dread to be around. I have known the couples where it's just so obvious to an outside observer that one of the people is in love, but not the other. I have known the couples where the woman is so desperate to get married and make babies, that she ignores all of the signs that scream that he is not the proverbial "one."

I have known the couples that break up and get back together, over and over again (Oh wait, that was me!). I have known the couples where one partner wants to have kids and the other does not, and they stay together for years, one partner clinging onto hope that the other will change their mind.

I have known the couples that are simply tolerating each other, out of some sort of misguided sense of obligation, rather than showing or feeling anything resembling love. I have known couples where the man only got married because of pressure (or even an ultimatum) from the woman.

I have been in the weddings where you are biting your tongue as the bride walks down the aisle, because you just know with every fiber of your being that they are making a mistake (incidentally I've been in three such weddings, and all have ended happily in divorce). I have even known multiple couples who themselves admit that they knew it was a mistake, but they walked down the aisle anyway.

I have seen people engaged in extramarital affairs and in circumstances that are far too "complicated" to be "right," people who are clinging to the unhealthiest of situations in a desperate attempt to find happiness.

And when I speak of such couples, I do so with deep empathy and understanding, for I too have lived through my own version of the "wrong" relationship.

And I know that these souls are on the same powerful journey of growth and learning on which I reluctantly found myself (that is if they are open to such growth and learning). I spent years with the wrong person, trying to convince myself that it was right. I have always said that one of the cruelest aspects of life is that we have the ability to fall in love with the wrong person.

Frankly, it's brutal and there are few things more painful than star-crossed lovers. And I know how difficult, how painful, and how seemingly "impossible" it can be to extricate ourselves from the wrong relationships; I know all too well how paralyzed we can become, how stuck we can get. I know the feeling of having the constant pit in your stomach and of your head trying to rationalize that it's caused by something else, when deep down in your heart, you know the real reason but don't want to admit it.

I have also learned that love is not enough, and that of equal importance are timing and compatibility. You can love someone with every fiber of your being, with every breath of air in your body, but if it's not right, if they are not the right match for you, it won't matter. Of this I personally know all too well.

So why is it that so many people stay together for all the wrong reasons? Why are people so afraid to be alone? Fear. Society. Expectations. As I've observed people and relationships over the years, it has become clear that so many people are terrified of being alone; terrified of ending up alone, and of dying alone.

I once shared this fear, so it is one I relate to and understand well. And as I already said, I understand how it feels to be stuck with the wrong person, and in the wrong relationship, for all of the wrong reasons. I have been there and I am fortunate that my partner had the guts to release me from it, as I'm not sure I ever would have had the courage on my own; for I too was living in fear.

Society tells us that we are meant to follow a very specific formula for life: college, career, love, marriage, and babies… only in that order!

We do not even realize how brainwashed we have been as a society. And what society teaches us, our friends and families only reinforce. Everyone has an opinion about what we should be doing. When we see our friends getting married and having kids, we feel even more pressure to be doing the same. If we do not follow that formula, our parents disapprove, people think there is something wrong with us.

We all have the aunt who asks, "So when are you going to get married?" There is so much pressure to conform, to fulfill the expectations of society.

I spent the first half of my 30s gripped in sadness and despair, because I too felt that I had to fulfill that formula, and it just wasn't working out for me. I found myself 32 (and then 33, 34, 35…), single, and childless and that had never been the plan. I should have had three kids by that age. For all of my life I had planned to get married and raise a family. And I am such a passionate, openhearted woman with so much love to give; how could I not be finding a beautiful soul to complement my heart?

Well, if life has taught me one thing, it's that the most difficult times are the most valuable and that by walking through each one of them, there are invaluable lessons to learn. I had to walk through an extremely dark time of loneliness, of being completely on my own, for years, before I could come to understand the importance and value of being happy on my own. It was only by walking through my own darkness that I was able to find the light, and in doing so I realized that the light comes from within. The true joy, the absolute bliss is only to be found within us, never outside of us.

And if there's one universal truth, it's this: Before you can ever be happy with someone else, you must first be happy with yourself.

And I have not only made full peace with the fact that I am now 38, single, and childless, but I have fully embraced it and the truth is that I have never lived more happily, more vibrantly, more fulfilled. I love my life and there is nothing missing. I now could care less about having children (If you'd told me 10 years ago that I'd be saying that now, I'd have thought you were crazy!) Does this mean I am cynical and do not believe that true love exists? Not at all.

I have the gift of having experienced it with my own heart, so I know it's out there. And if I happen to find it, well great, because that would just be the cherry on top of an already wonderful life. But I know it's not necessary for my happiness. I know I already am, and will continue to be, happy and fulfilled no matter what comes into my life.

The moment we release the expectation that we can only complete ourselves with another, the moment we can release the idea that we have to adhere to society's mold, is the moment we find freedom. And in freedom, we can find true happiness.

I suspect that many of my friends might pity me for being alone, for not yet having had the "fortune" of getting married and having children. But what they may not realize is that I choose to be single. I could easily have been in relationships over the years, but I knew they would be with the wrong person, and I have no interest in getting myself embroiled in something wrong, when instead I can be keeping myself open for something right.

And I'm happy to say that I have absolutely learned the valuable lesson that it is far better to be single than to be with the wrong person.

So, yes, some people may feel sorry for me that I am alone. But the irony of that is that when I look around me and observe so many unhappy, dissatisfied relationships and I see so many people who are stuck, all I can think to myself is, "Thank God I'm single!"

10 Kick-ass Ways to Remember Who You Are.

By Kristoffer Carter

Have you ever hit snooze on your 6 a.m. run alarm, pulled up the blankets, and then beat the living crap out of yourself for not springing out of bed? Me neither.

The marathoner forgets he can run. The artist forgets they can paint. The songwriter forgets she can write. The CEO forgets he can lead. Stella loses her groove.

Most of us have figured out by this point that life is an endless cycle of remembering and forgetting. We remember our power, gifts, and higher identities, and then we promptly forget them. Sometimes we spend months or years in the limbo of forgetfulness, disconnected and oblivious to our value to the world around us.

Often those we love, or an epic test of our will can snap us back into remembering. Maybe we even jump up a couple levels. But the buzz never lasts forever. We get overwhelmed by the growth and self-care needed to sustain our knowing, and then, dammit...We've slipped our own minds again.

It's okay. You're not bipolar. You're human. It's how we do. For this reason, I have an orange 3×5 card taped above the exit in my office. Scrawled on it in Sharpie is: remember who you are.

The world around us powered by sleepless technology and clever marketers barrages us with negative attention hooks. They hammer our pain points then politely offer to hold our wallet while we writhe in self-loathing. Because once we remember ourselves, we are complete, and need a lot less material gratification.

Once you start getting away from your routine of self-care exercise, spiritual practice, healthy eating, or diet, you become vulnerable. Your once-impervious bubble of self-realization gets punctured, and you slump around like a deflated little balloon.

After I ran my first marathon, I literally forgot that I ever ran 26.2 miles, let alone 5. I thought I had been tasered by *Men In Black*. Getting back on the saddle after my healing, my runs were impossible. I was determined to prove that I didn't only run the distance to appease my ego (or other equally crazy BS). So each morning the run alarm would beep, and I'd suck my thumb like a forgetful little baby-man. It's kind of entertaining how insane this was. Then the voices would start in on me…

"You've never really been a runner. That was a fluke."

Even though these inner critics reeked of bullshit and onions, it was up to me to rebuild my own inertia. I'd lace up, and start my slow train a-rollin'. I called this 'outrunning the demons.' Four miles in, and those bitches couldn't touch me.

I'm not athletic? Mile 5, mile 6.
I don't finish what I start? Mile 7, mile 8.
I don't expect to see you at mile 26, Judge Judy. Mile 9.

Ten miles later, I was laying on our front lawn, watching the sky breathe and swell from the center of this massive blue and white marble. My kids were laughing and jumping all over me.

In these small, personal triumphs, we are literally reminding ourselves who we really are and what we're capable of…

1. Write it out. Journaling about your strengths and current passions is huge. If you were going to move to a new city, or go job-hunting, you'd work it out on paper. Why then should it feel corny to write down your dreams, dog? Put quill to parchment, Shakespeare. Send me a copy. I'll hold your words like a scroll, and read them back to you in a ridiculous British accent.

2. Talk to yourself in your mirror, or while you're running. Passers-by on the trails near my house think I'm schizophrenic. I use incantations while I run to remind myself of my personal philosophy: "I joyfully expect everything to work out. I use my creativity to inspire and entertain others. I consciously pursue excellence. And that's what I do, every damn day." If you say that to yourself a good 5 to 20,000 times, you just might start believing it at some point.

3. Ask leading questions to the people who love you. Although you may seem like a droopy-drawers baby if you need reassurance all the time, it's healthy to ask others what they like or love about you. I always lead with: "Gayle (my wife), aside from my monster pecs and bulbous glutes, what else do you love about me?" Seriously, whenever Gayle reminds me who I am, (relative to the scared little punk she started dating 16 years ago), it bolsters my E'rythang. The people who bare witness to our journeys are the most capable of reminding us how far we've come. Ask. If the reply is silence, or "Nothing, really" find new people.

4. Print and collect any positive feedback about you that rocked your world, or made you want to cry. Hang it in a corner of your private space. Reread it from time to time. Call the people who took the time and thank them again for reminding you who you are. I remind people what they've done for me years after they took a few minutes to send a nice note.

5. Schedule time to do the things you're good at. Knit a blanket and send it to your friend's new baby. Visit Guitar Center and shut that shit down with your bass grooves. Sing "Panama" at the karaoke bar while employing each of Diamond Dave's ridiculous karate kicks. Demonstrate who you are, on blast. And do it with zero apologies.

6. Employ technology. Set up meeting reminders to pop up randomly throughout the year with ridiculous subject headings: Mandatory Family Dance Party! Solo Wii Tournament! You Survived Q2 Party! Pegasus-Wrangling! (Be sure to grant access to everyone on your staff, so they can see what your Big Days consist of.)

Humbly request some recommendations on LinkedIn. Offer to return the favor. Collect the friggin' truth about yourself, as seen through the eyes of your colleagues.

7. Cut and paste. Cut out lines from "Raving Fan" emails and tape them inside your journals.

8. Make time to lay in silence each evening before bed. Inventory all of the great stuff that happened today, and set an intention for how you want to feel when you wake up. If you had a crappy day, don't fall asleep until you find at least 3 great things that happened. They can be small, but they are there. I'm guessing that you may have even had something to do with them.

9. Photograph yourself doing something ridiculous and text it to somebody you care about. Ask for constructive feedback. I snapped a pic of myself eating mashed bananas from a plastic spoon while wearing our infant son's bib that reads: This is What Handsome Looks Like. I sent it to random coworkers and asked them if they had any thoughts. The responses were amazing -- especially the radio silence.

10. If all else fails, call your parents. This is a delicate one, because depending on their level of crazy you may need to put on your haz-mat filter. Reminisce about an epic vacation. Thank them for being patient with you. Sincerely thank them for having a hand in making you a fulfilled person.

I Need You to Know Something.

By Jessica Hesser

My heart aches lately, but after thinking about it for a while, I'm pretty certain it's not just for me. My heart is aching for all of us, for this beating, throbbing collection of human hearts.

My friends, we are at a critical and precious point in time and I think there is a mass need for healing and love on this sweet planet right now.

I feel, then, I must tell you something, and it's very important, so although we might not have met yet, (and may never), I need you to believe me when I tell you this.

I need you to know how loved you are, how tremendously loved you are. I need you to understand how much the very universe from which you were born is madly, deeply and truly in love with you. I need you to understand that in all ways you are perfect, magnificent and divine.

> *"Your task is not to seek for Love, but merely to seek and find all the barriers within yourself that you have built against it"*
>
> *~ Rumi*

I know it doesn't always feel like this. I know that sometimes you think you are not good enough, that you would be better if this or that were different. I know you think there are times you have failed, or that maybe you are failing right now.

I know that sometimes your chest gets so tight, the air so heavy with the weight of regret and worry and shame that you think you cannot possibly go on.

I know you think you have done things that can't be undone and that there are parts of you that are bad, selfish or unclean. I know there are things about yourself that you don't like and sometimes secretly hate.

I know there is a loneliness that can take hold, a loneliness so big that it stretches to the edges of eternity and pushes on your heart so hard you shake in fear that it will never end. I know at times you have hurt so badly that the pain has dropped you to your knees.

Sometimes the layers of life can pile up so high that it seems impenetrable and you start to forget your true self, to mistake the experience of who you are. But that is not who you are, my friend.

"Your problem is you're ... too busy holding onto your unworthiness."

~ *Ram Dass*

Let me tell you what I see when I look at you. In you, I see the infinite. I see the very seeds of life itself. I see universes being born into existence. I see the mother of all that is. I see the wind that blows the mountains into form. I see the awesome and endless enormity of the sea. I see the fierceness of the mighty sun. I see the graceful allure of a silver, siren moon in a cobalt sky.

I see the roots of history, the old blood and the new blood, fresh and vital. I see the ancient stories, and the ones not yet written. I see the kind of hope that can only be found on the breath of angels. I see the unbearable sweetness of a baby's touch and the soft warmth of its skin.

I see endless, passionate, consuming love. I see gentleness. I see deep, deep joy. I see the courage of a warrior's heart. I see the endurance of one who is loved to the depths of the being. I see all the things you sometimes forget about yourself.

"You are very powerful, provided you know how powerful you are."

~ *Yogi Bhajan*

All the things that you are create an amazing, intricate and unique expression of life. All that you are is exactly as it should be. The idea that you are somehow not good enough is a lie, so let go of the judgments you hold for yourself.

Know that, at all times, you are doing exactly what you should and being precisely who you should be. Life is unfolding exactly as it should. Everything is happening for your awakening and for your highest good, even when you can't see it. Your path is supremely designed and if you find the faith to follow it, it will always lead you back to love.

So soften, my friend. Move closer to the heart. Trust that all is well and give yourself permission to be exactly who you are and to celebrate the light that you have brought onto this earth. Fill your life with love and joy and beauty and know that you deserve these things always.

You are never alone, you are held at all times in the arms of love. When everything starts to feel heavy and hard, it is only because you have forgotten your inherent radiance. You have forgotten the awe-invoking brilliance of your soul. You have forgotten that this remarkable life has been given to you for your own delight, born from your breath, and bathed in your godliness.

If you could catch even a glimpse of what I see, of the stunning power and exquisite perfection that dwells within you, you would never be the same.

When you see who you are, you will know the love that the universe has for you and you will love yourself in equal measure and, really, this is the most important thing you can learn to do.

There is unequivocal magic created when you find the grace to truly embrace and love who you are. It transforms your life and the lives of those around you.

"To love yourself right now, just as you are, is to give yourself heaven. Don't wait until you die. If you wait, you die now. If you love, you live now."

~ Alan Cohen

Offer yourself kindness, forgiveness and acceptance and you will automatically and naturally offer this to others and then, my friend, the world (and you) will have the love and the healing that it needs so much right now.

If you feel sad, broken, lonely, wrong, unworthy or not good enough in any way, I need you to know that you are loved. There is nothing that you have ever done or that has been done to you that can take away from the perfect wholeness of your being, nothing that can diminish your greatness or the love that the universe has for you.

I need you to know how loved you are, how tremendously loved you are.

A Beacon of Light for the Dark Days.

By Jenn Grosso

Some days we wake up forgetting all about our magnificence. Some days, we feel enveloped in a cloud of shit and every step forward gets us further down that slippery slope of self-loathing and destructive thoughts.

Those days are hard. It seems like the more you think about it, the more you feed into those doubts and the more you bring yourself down. Slip.

These kinds of days can absolutely paralyze me. Everything seems to be happening on the other side of this grey fog and I feel like I am miles away from everyone else. I am stuck in darkness while the rest of the world is dancing in light. Slip.

However, I have discovered a beacon of light that was in my back pocket all along. A tonic of sorts for the mind, heart and soul, that can, even in the darkest of days, comfort and sooth me. It helps bring my bruised sorry-ass self back into the light and brush away the grey fog that was limiting my view, polluting my perspective.

My beacon of light is the fact that we are not small and never alone. We are made of the same stuff as the moon and stars, as the incomprehensible entirety of the Universe that is all us.

> *"The first peace, which is the most important, is that which comes within the souls of people when they realize their relationship, their oneness with the Universe and all its powers, and when they realize that at the center of the Universe dwells the Great Spirit, and that its center is really everywhere, it is within each of us."*
>
> *~ Black Elk*

Everything is already inside us, everything that we seek. Even the whole universe is within each of us. To me, there is no more comforting and grounding knowledge than this.

"Recognize that the very molecules that make up your body, the atoms that construct the molecules, are traceable to the crucibles that were once the centers of high mass stars that exploded their chemically rich guts into the galaxy, enriching pristine gas clouds with the chemistry of life. So that we are all connected to each other biologically, to the earth chemically and to the rest of the universe atomically. That's kinda cool! That makes me smile and I actually feel quite large at the end of that. It's not that we are better than the universe; we are part of the universe. We are in the universe and the universe is in us."

~ Neil deGrasse Tyson

I mean how astonishingly amazing is this! When I contemplate the vastness of the universe, yet how we are all still connected to all of it, it greatly humbles me. How can I be so hard on myself with this knowledge? I can't.

I hope that in your dark days you can reach into your back pocket and hold this knowledge in your heart, in your mind and soul, and be comforted as well. It will not eliminate these days completely, it has not for me.

However, when I remind myself of these simple yet huge facts, I cannot help but be in awe. I can only do my very best to put aside my personal beefs with myself and the trivial day-to-day ego bullshit and surrender, at the amplitude of it all, at our shared magnificence.

80% of Success is Showing Up.

By Matthew Foor

> *"A real decision is measured by the fact that you've taken a new action. If there's no action, you haven't truly decided."*
>
> *~ Tony Robbins*

You could write a book about the whole concept of showing up, probably twenty books…

Something good can happen if you just do something, go somewhere, call somebody, or say quit your job and buy a one-way ticket to a tropical island (like I did three months ago). The point is: showing up.

So what is it that drives you? Is it desire? Is it emotion? And what does or could make a difference in the quality of your life? Perhaps all you need to do to figure any of it out is to start showing up. Showing up is an invitation to explore your desires, your calling and to discover whatever truly motivates you in your life.

Why are people afraid to 'show up'?

From my own terms, fear and psychological bullshit are the things that tend to keep people away, and my guess is that it's the same for a lot of people. And in addition to fear and the mental obstacles, we place ourselves in all of these little boxes that prevent us from trying or doing new things.

I also think we spend too much time with people who tell us 'we can't,' so we end up believing that we can't and then we don't even try. Being open about your dreams can inspire others people to do the same, but my best advice when it comes to sharing your ambitions is to listen to Kenny Rogers (as not everyone can handle someone else showing up to life):

> *"You got to know when to hold 'em, know when to fold 'em, Know when to walk away and know when to run."*

Everybody has the power to try. Most of us just stop ourselves too soon. This is something I definitely want to get better at. The possibilities are endless if you think about it.

What happens when you give in and decide to 'show up'?

At the end of the day, nothing really matters, and I mean this in the most positive way possible. When you actually do what you want to do, you typically find out that it's not that big of a deal. Sure, your problems follow you everywhere and you have to deal with them, but you sort of find out that your dreams aren't that hard to achieve.

The point: we just have to do what you have to do. What I mean by this is doing what we have the desire to do. When we do this, there is all the potential in the world.

Your ideas and expectations.

Chances are, no one is going to knock on your door and tell you what you need to do or what your desires are, so the best encouragement I could ever tell someone is to just start doing things.

Show up, experiment and try things out. Try to follow the clues. Make the smallest amount of effort every day, even if you don't have the money, resources, or whatever it is you think you need.

Work with what you have. Work with what is right in front of you – today. Right now. And remember, even after you live out your desires, you still have to do something after that.

You have to keep going. It's never ending. You can make a lot of amazing things happen in your life and still not experience 100% bliss. Once you get to a certain place, you realize you still have to do the inner work all the time, every day and every single second.

Perfection is a fish you can't catch and even if you did catch it, perhaps you'd find out that you didn't want it. That's not what this life is all about.

"80% of success is just showing up."

~ Woody Allen

How to Talk to Someone with Cancer.

By Caitlin Marcoux

Here's the thing: people living with cancer are a complicated bunch, and we know this about ourselves.

Our senses have been rubbed raw by diagnostic testing and medical evaluations. We've been graded, staged and given projected survival rates. We've seen the fragility of our lives held up before our own faces, and we've come away from our treatments feeling vulnerable in a way we've never felt before. We cling to our independence, but know we're dependent on others for healing and help.

Cancer survivors know better than most how fleeting life can be. The very nature of our disease has thrown us into a world off-balance. Not only are our bodies working overtime to halt the production of alien-like rapidly mutating cells, they are struggling to process the toxic poisons we voluntarily ingest to cure ourselves. The very treatments we implement to make us healthy make us sick. We walk a fine, contradictory line on a daily, weekly or monthly basis.

We are emotionally taxed and psychically drained: we live with a foreboding and heavy awareness of risk. We are almost painfully aware that each day we have is precious.

While certainly there are many silver linings, we remember wistfully what our lives were like before cancer, before the silver linings needed to be pointed out. We navigate the remainder of our days knowing that we will never again feel the pre-cancerous freedom we may have taken for granted.

> *"Toleration is the greatest gift of the mind; it requires the same effort of the brain that takes to balance oneself on a bicycle."*
>
> *~ Helen Keller*

We know it's a tall order, and that our needs are inconsistent, but we really appreciate your patience as we figure out exactly what we need. We want you to be sympathetic, but we don't want your pity. We want you to look us in the eye, but please don't stare. We'd like it if you could meet us where we are, not judge us for where you think we should be. We want you to reassure us that we are capable and brave, but don't blow smoke up our asses; being the authority on ourselves, we know we've looked better, felt better, or seemed more grounded.

We'd like it if you lent us a compliment or even two, but for heaven's sake, please don't go overboard. Sure, Bald is Beautiful, but given the choice, most of us liked ourselves just fine with hair.

How can you love us? Let me count the ways.

We still want to be *loved*, and by that I mean *made love to*. Those of us with breast cancer and facing mastectomy could be on the brink of losing the very largest symbols of our sexuality and femininity. If in the face of buzz-kill cancer, we can muster up enough energy to jump in the sack, please do whatever you can to rise to the occasion.

We might complain all day long about not feeling pretty, but at night we'd like to be pursued as if we were the most beautiful women you've ever seen. We might ask you to turn off the light, just go with the flow.

Shower us with empathy.

Compassion is a prized commodity amongst our kind. It's better that chocolate, red wine, or our anti-nausea medication. A single empathetic commiseration that indeed things can suck may be more appreciated than any other grand gesture of affection you can bestow upon us. It'll certainly go over better than the knee-jerk condolences you might be tempted to offer up.

The truth is, no matter how above it we may project ourselves to be, we are embarrassed by our vanity. Even those of us who walk a path spiritually devoted to cultivating an awareness deeper than the skin, know real and intense discomfort when our physical identity starts to fall apart.

We may attempt to take control of our hair loss by cutting it short, or completely shaving it off. We may throw ourselves a Boob Voyage party before a mastectomy, or parade around with our newly bald head held high, *but* we are actively engaged in the most difficult task of accepting that we are completely and utterly out of control.

This week I'm grappling with something I find simply humiliating. As if it weren't bad enough that my hair has fallen out only in patches, to add insult to injury, I now have something called folliculitis, a bacterial infection of the hair follicles, not only on my scalp, but also in the soft downy follicles on my neck and all the way down the small of my back. It is nearly impossible to feel sexy when touching your own head gives you the heebie-jeebies.

For all the cancer patients out there who have experienced this particular itchy, hot, and unflattering torture, I bow to you. It takes a formidable person to rock this particular look without tears. And to those of you who, like me, have wanted to hide far from society in the seclusion of your own homes, or at the very least under a hat, I feel you. I know the last thing in the world you want to hear is how beautiful you look, when you feel like shit.

Let's get real. We know that you know we are strong, but don't you know we don't always feel that way? Do you know how hard it is for us to be brave when our hair is falling out and our bones are itching? Do you know there are days when we don't feel graceful, moments when we don't act graceful, and times when we fail to live up to our own graceful expectations? It is hard for us to feel empowered with an ice pack on our head, a heating pad on our knees, dry red eyes, and rashes lashed across our skin. Sometimes we feel bad.

We don't envy you: those of you who run into us at the grocery store or the coffee shop on one of our bad days. We know it's awkward to hear us panicking on our cellphones with our mothers, or crying to our husbands. But please don't walk away and pretend that you didn't hear. Chances are, we need your help in a moment like that, but might be too proud to ask for it.

Forget attempting to offer up some gratitude platitude (we are more grateful than most for the chance to keep living), just give us a silent squeeze. One hand on the shoulder is worth a million well-crafted aphorisms. Most likely, we will hug you back with all our strength, perceived or projected.

We want you to see us. To see our strength and our vulnerability. To feel our pain and to know the depths of our gratitude. Ask us sincerely how it is, and we will tell you the truth.

"There is no difficulty that enough love will not conquer; no disease that enough love will not heal; no door that enough love

will not open; no gulf that enough love will not bridge; no wall that enough love will not throw down; no sin that enough love will not redeem..."

~ *Emmet Fox*

Here are a few more things to keep in mind when talking to someone with cancer:

1. If you know about our disease, address it immediately. Chances are, we already know you had dinner with a friend of a friend the night before last and they told you all about it, so get it off your chest. Waiting for us to tell you how we are puts us in the awkward role of feeling like we're complaining; usually things could be better, but if you're curious about how we feel, just ask.

2. If you're not prepared for some detailed response to your inquiry, just don't ask. We may need to vent about some gnarly side effect, and most of them are kind of yucky. Be prepared to listen. Your shoulder to cry on might be the biggest boon we get all day.

3. Please refrain, if possible, from telling us a story about your friends and relatives who died of cancer. Just like a pregnant woman gearing up to deliver her baby, it's important that we surround ourselves with stories of success, and not those of fatality. If you haven't experienced cancer firsthand, it is normal to want to relate in any way possible, but for our sakes, think twice before sharing a story with a bad ending.

4. Unsolicited advice might be great, but it's still unsolicited. You might just have the most miraculous out-of-the-box alternative therapy that you're dying to put to the test, but please, unless we've asked, soften your enthusiasm. No one takes their diagnosis more seriously than the patients themselves. Most cancer survivors I know have thought long and hard about their treatment plans. They've often consulted their nearest and dearest, and have got second and third opinions. And by the time we are in active treatment, we have a pretty solid plan of attack in place.

5. Empathy, empathy, empathy. Plain and simple, cancer sucks. If anyone wants to talk about how it's a gift, leave that to the patient to offer up.

6. Shower us with love. According to the mother of Western yoga, Judith Lasater, all emotions stem from the two most basic emotions: Fear and Love. We, cancer patients, are confronting our fears in a full frontal attack. Showering us with love is like helping us stock up our arsenals; it helps us prepare for battle.

7. Lighten Up. The more you can make us laugh, the better. This is not to say we don't appreciate you taking our challenges seriously, but let's face it, laughter is the best medicine. If you can find a way to make us giggle, we will love you forever.

I am lucky enough to have some of the best and silliest girlfriends in the world. When three of them came to visit me last month, we took over the infusion room at the Nantucket Cottage Hospital. When Gretchen, my infusion nurse, slipped out to go to the lab, the girls promptly took over and we turned Cancerland into Clubland.

8. Touch us. Cancer is not contagious. We can't give it to you. What we can give you is the chance to heal our aching hearts.

Many of us just want to be held.

7 Traits of Magical People.

By Carolyn Elliott

1. You know you're magic.

This is the big one. In their heart of hearts, everyone is magic. But most folks just don't know it. It's very sad, and it's not their fault. They've had the awareness beaten out of them one way or another. Our society in general is very anti-magic.

Magic people always have a mission. And part of that mission is to help folks still stuck in the clay (that's my catchy way of saying "folks still stuck in naive materialism and unaware of their innate magic-ness") understand that magic is real and within them, too. So basically, if you know you're magic, you're ahead of the game.

2. Synchronicities happen for you – a lot.

And they tend to speed up when you spend a lot of time on meditation, art, ritual, intentional movement or prayer. Sometimes these synchronicities are just cute or silly, but often they're life changing and dramatic. The biggest synchronous thing that can happen to a magic person is to meet another magic person. Or a whole enclave of them. It's thrilling. It's overwhelming. It's love.

When lots of synchronicities are going on, I like to say "the jewel net is moving." Why? Because we're all jewels in an infinitely connected web of silken joy. And sometimes the net shifts and folds in on itself and we run smack into a whole bunch of other jewels. *And it's great.*

3. You're sensitive to seasons and lunar cycles.

The more magic you are (and remember, being magic is mainly a matter of… knowing that you're magic!) the more the energies of light and the two big cosmic lamps in our region (the sun and moon) affect your business. You might find that you can't sleep on full moon nights (all that energy, so ramped up!) and that you go through epic mythopoetic cycles of emotional birth and death as spring turns to summer turns to fall turns to winter.

4. You have very vivid dreams.

Magic people have at least partially developed aetheric bodies. This means, at the very least, that one or more of their chakras (Rudolf Steiner liked to call them "lotus flowers") are open and active. Maybe you're a magic person with a giant, pulsing, highly empathic heart chakra. Or maybe your third eye is open and you have an easy time seeing the visionary fluid dance of all things.

At the highly developed end of the spectrum, magic people have fully-formed aetheric bodies that can freely navigate the astral planes. But having your aetheric sense perceptions open, even a little bit, means that you can see more vividly in the nighttime dream world than others can. So, you got that goin' for you. *Which is nice.*

5. When you fall in love, it's psychedelic.

Forget a loaf of bread, a jug of wine and thou. When a magic person falls in love (very probably with another magic person), it's more like a sheet of acid, a gallon of mushroom tea and thou. And I'm not saying that actual drugs are involved. I'm saying that the intensity of dopamine and oxytocin rushes, in magic brains, tends to produce more than just sexy-cozy-attachment.

They tend to also unleash psychic perception (you can read your lover's thoughts – not just "I was thinking of you!" "I knew you were thinking of me, baby. 'Cause I was thinking of you!"), encounters with your lover in the night time dream world, ecstatic sex that ruptures the boundaries of your identity, and other fun stuff. Also, be careful with all that. It can get hairy if your lover happens to be one of those not-really-very-stable-or-sane magic people. Of which there are quite a few. Magic people fall in love and it's all like, *whoah.*

6. You have an abundance of prana.

Or creative energy. Or genius, or whatever you want to call it. Wilhelm Reich called it "orgone." Kant called it "Geist." Emerson called it "Soul." Mezmer called it "animal magnetism." It's sexual energy which transmutes into different feeling-tones when centered in different chakras and channels in the body.

In other words – even though it's sexual energy, your abundant prana doesn't necessarily feel "sexy" (although it probably does in spring and summer). It might just feel buzz-y or space-y or urgently creative. You get seized with the need to write that poem, plan that ritual, record that song, make those spicy ginger fudge brownies. It's implacable. Also, no matter what you look like, folks tell you that you're "hot." And they mean it. You are. You radiate the light and heat of the cosmos. You're a star, you magic darling!

7. You love to spread the magic around.

Your chief motive for making art, cooking great food, tending your garden, whatever – isn't to be rich or famous. *Though that could be cool.* If you're magic, your biggest motive is to spread the magic around, because you just can't stand not doing it. The magic is so fun, so beautiful, so warm, so true.

This means that it drives you a little crazy when you can totally see the magic in someone, and they can't see it in themselves. It drives you maybe even crazier when you can totally see the magic in the world, and the world at large seems to not tenderly care for and appreciate its own magic.

So, you put effort everyday into doing stuff that increases the sum-total of magic and wonder and joy and love and delight in the world. You turn up the volume on everything gorgeous so it can't be ignored.

In conclusion,

You're magic and I am too, and I love you.

The Path Less Traveled.

By Anja Bergh

"The path less traveled is less traveled for a reason – it requires courage to march to the beat of a different drum. Sometimes it can be a lonely trek – because very few will understand why you don't walk the popular well-trodden path like everybody else. But you know you can't. Your heart won't let you. You must be true to yourself. And your regrets will be few. For at the end of your life you will look back at your short journey and with a satisfied smile, quietly acknowledging that it could never have been any other way."

~ Christian Cabanilla

Dear Christian,

You wrote to me: "Goddammit woman! Congratulations on escaping the trap of the city." I had just moved off the main streets of the city grid and into an area where you aren't really allowed to live year round. I don't know why I'm writing ''not really allowed'', because the law clearly articulates, No! No living year round. Anyway, there I was, living year round, breaking rules and laws, taking life in my own hands.

(To this I was congratulated and sent an electronic high-five!)

Goddammit woman…

Dearest Christian,

I don't know if it was you or I that missed our Skype hang out a couple of weeks ago, it doesn't matter. I looked for you and you weren't there. You looked for me and I wasn't there. And now… now you are not breathing. I just found out. You got out-powered by Mother Nature. I just found out. You merged into the snow masses you loved so much.

You are not breathing.

From deep in my belly there is a roaring of sadness, waves, deep longing, and the tears… the tears… The tears have not yet been cried on the outside. I am around people, and I don't want to be comforted. They don't know you. So I am grieving deeper still. Not letting them out. They might come later, the tears. But for now they stop inside, leaving my eyes glossy.

I remember your lips on mine my love. And even though it's been 14 years, I can still feel your chest resting on mine, lifting and sinking, breathing together. I don't want any memories to float out on the energy I carry of you. I don't want them to leave the tissue of my body. I remember it wonderful, the kissing. The loving.

We were so young then. I saw you and you saw me, and by just watching you move through that crowded bar, I knew I had no chance of avoiding sharing paths and beds with you. As I think back, I feel warm hands holding mine, but dearest Christian, I don't know if they are yours, if the skin I'm feeling against mine is someone else's, or if it's you I am near. Well, it doesn't matter, because once I held yours. And I know you wanted to share your life with me.

I wanted to share it with you too, but you know, I wasn't as brave as you back then! So we shared life with others and I hope you loved a lot my dear! Goddammit, I hope there was so much love in your life! I know you loved what you did, your path. But I also hope there were women you poured all that sweetness over and all that hot passion and love you had in your heart! In a way I have shared my life with you from a distance. I have walked with you. I have always been proud of us and of our lives. I always thought you did the right thing, not coming back for me. Even I could hear the strong beating of your heart – into the wilderness!

"You won't make it," you said during my last chance to talk to you. "Try me!" I responded and smiled. But you were right, I didn't make it to where I was going, I stayed longer in your presence, taking my chance to twirl with your spirit and gave you deep access to my heart.

Please rest there, Chris! Don't leave me when you dissemble. Leave a twinkle of your bright light here. If you can – maybe it's against the rules.

"The path less traveled is less traveled for a reason – it requires courage to march to the beat of a different drum."

12 days they say. 12 days till the soul moves on. I found out late. So I only have tonight left. When I get back home, I will take out my guitar and play my favorite chord for your journey. A-minor. I don't know your favorite, so all I can offer is mine.

You were so brave. Making the choices you did. Flying your heli around the peaks of Alaska. I bet you saw so much beauty! Even if I wasn't brave back then my love, not like you. I am now. And there is no way I'm going to back down from my path, even though it is very lonely there at times.

Christian moved to Alaska just a few weeks after we met. That was his plan and dream and he was sticking to it. I don't remember if I was asked to go along with him. Did you ask me, beautiful? I bet your mother might have been happier if I had! Her phone card bills were out-of-the-roof expensive! If I ever have the great honor of having children, I will remember this when they fall in love and cost me mad cash. Rest assured, I will happily empty my pockets for love!

Dear Christian,

Your passing comes as a big, lit up, determined message! To get out of fear and into life. From the outsiders looking in, my life might look like one of great courage and direction. But for me… You see for me, I am standing in line, waiting. For someone, for something, to take my hand and lead me, and I have been standing here now on the edge of this cliff, dropping all my weight down to the earth below. Giving it back to where it can dissemble and give life to something else.

I am watching it go, tumble and dance, like you tumbled and danced down the mountain just a few days ago. And now I have very little left. Very little pride. I don't know anything anymore. I don't have many things left, but still I have too much. I feel life closer when I have little. I feel everything closer.

Did you have a lot of things, Chris? I know you owned your direction.

"But you know you can't. Your heart won't let you. You must be true to yourself. And your regrets will be few."

It is so true. And so damn wise, Christian! The heart, le cour, is always in full courage! And the voice is strong, isn't it? It's just that most often it gets suppressed.

You know my sweet, I have been writing a piece for quite some time now. But the words didn't feel true as I read them. I couldn't get to what it was I wanted to get to. I could only write old truths. No new was coming because there was still fear. I was holding back again, afraid of losing something, someone. But here it goes, fear wall getting torn down. Fear only serves as a barrier to joy and clear sight. Sometimes it helps me to avoid falling into holes in the road, but mostly, it just limits me.

You know, my prayers for some time now have been sung to a goddess called Kali. She cuts the false faces off with her sword. Granting you clear sight. At least that is how I see it. There are many takes on it. "Be careful with praying to Kali," my friends have said, "She's fierce."

But you see – I have been taking the soft approach for a long time. And I needed to be fierce. I am in no way insinuating that your death has anything to do with my singing Kali's name. No, no, that singing or praying, or intention making, call it what you like, were to the parts of myself who know the clarity of life. Asking them to inform the parts of me that are afraid. What I am saying though, is that your exit has been the slap in the face I needed to realize the urgency of my own longing. It astonishes me that you sung that song so young! Goddammit, you should have told me back then! Maybe you tried.

I long for nature too, like you.

"I have to leave," my inner voice started saying about a year ago. "I have to learn new. I'm stuck. I don't like to be stuck. Something is not right, this is not how I want to live my life." So I stopped all regular activity. I stopped having an apartment. I stopped teaching my classes. I stopped moving in the same way. I stopped putting things off. I stopped thinking I know who I am. I stopped trying to prove anything to anyone.

I didn't stop breathing.

Dear Christian,

You stopped breathing. And it makes me shiver with sadness. Cause I'm still here and I am breathing! And I'm crying on the inside. I am on my way home and I don't care anymore what people think. I stopped caring… I stopped caring about the surface. So I walk through the airport with my bags, with my bright green boots on. And when kind eyes meet mine, I smile, because that's the gift of breathing – getting to smile to kind eyes, or kind stars in the night sky. I stopped caring about the surface.

I started caring about the source of the surface.

> *"For at the end of your life you will look back at your short journey and with a satisfied smile, quietly acknowledge that it could never have been any other way."*

I am breathing so I should breathe! I am a loving being so I should love! I am a free spirit so I should roam! I may not always be the most convenient person to be around, but I shouldn't compromise clarity. I know the next step or two, it's enough to trust and lead myself on.

Onward to find what my heart says its yes to. What I want to live now is the experiment. There is so much content to our bodies and breath. We are capable of way more than we can conceive, and it is never-ending. Every step we take on our life path leads to another, like a solid chain of consequences.

Goddammit Woman…

I don't know where consciousness goes when the heart stops pumping blood through our bodies. Now you know dear Christian. I don't know, but I am quite sure it transforms into something else, dissolving back to what it was before if focused itself into the form of our bodies and identities. "We are all stardust," the modern wise men say. So that's why I'll play for the stars tonight my love.

I hope you hear my good-bye song! I will keep singing to you my dear, all days will be lived a little fuller because of you. I do love you, very much.

Safe travels loved one… and there he goes. Gone.

Will Power – The James Bond of the Mind.

By Chantelle Jahara Pinto

He's totally insane; can't put two sentences together. Evil; then sweet and generous. Power-hungry; then puts Mother Teresa to shame. He knows the answers to the world's problems, but forgets himself under pressure.

So who is this guy? I want you to meet my MiND. A resident of me; more like a squatter really. Be warned, he tends to laugh in extremely inappropriate moments, but if you stick around, he says he's going to solve the Middle East crisis after I get back from my run.

I'm not the only one who owns a Ruprecht or Jack Sparrow up there.

Obviously I don't know your mind in particular, but judging by the way people behave in this world, we all seem to have a lethal buffoon in our head running around with scissors. He's the cause of our suffering – but only all of it; a trickster, plain and simple.

I told him to sit down and shut up, once. It was late, after being suckered into an evening with Ethiopian rap singers whom I had never met before. Ended up in a bad part of town; watched them make more hallucinogenic mushroom pancakes than I had ever seen (my previous count being zero). It dawned on me that this wasn't going to be my life unless the dumb-ass upstairs handed over the reigns, and he wasn't going to do that nicely.

That definitive realisation happened in the last moments of darkness before the sun switched on, so I began to meditate. I didn't know at the time that this was the A-bomb for my narcissist MiND, and I had just pressed the disproportionately large red button.

It took just moments for him to respond. You might imagine that he's not one for subtlety. First, MiND registered my meditation as an act of aggression, and an attempted assassination (as defined by The Geneva Convention). Then, he gathered his arsenal and declared war.

His weapons were surprisingly more intelligent than I expected of a squatting one-eyed pirate ass. I espied no less than three varieties of ballistic responses to my assault:

Weapon 1: Sleep.

My attack: Resolve to get up early every day and meditate. Stitch my awareness to my spiritual self. Learn the purpose of my existence.

Counter Attack: Says, Oh yeah?! Well, try and do that if I make you crazy tired every time you close your eyes!

Weapon 2: Headache.

My attack: Push through the tiredness and pursue my daily meditation and yoga practice. Learn from great texts and people I consider wise.

Counter Attack: Says, Well, try to do that with this Muther Farking headache you're about to get out of Flooking nowhere!...And watch out for my phantom nausea ray! KA-BAM!

Weapon 3: Emotion.

My attack: Increase determination. Do not fall for any phantom physical discomfort. Be present with every moment. See those around me as people trying to do their best, even if their best is to be ignorant and abusive.

Counter Attack: Says, Time to make you insanely sensitive. You'll have no choice but to misinterpret innocently intended words and go fricking ninja-ballistic on everybody!

This was a particularly deadly weapon. But wouldn't you believe it, it turned out I had the WMD the whole time. What is it?!! you ask. The name is Will... Will Power.

Kryptonite for my fatuous one-eyed pirate, and for anybody's half-cocked captains of Maya. Military training always asserts that you've got to know your weapon inside and out before you wield such power in combat, so I memorized the instructions that detailed the nature of this beast. It went like this:

1. Once you engage this weapon, pass the cross hairs over your target. Always follow through to the end until you've blasted the bastard good and thorough.

Field example: You decide to stop eating junk food and begin a healthier regime. Engage Will Power. When in doubt, keep firing. If you fall for your MiND's counter-attacks, such as frequent memories of the delicious junk food taste, Will Power will disengage.

2. When you misuse this weapon, it becomes less effective. MiND will assimilate your strategy. In the event that you have misused Will Power repeatedly, and today is, say, your 612th attempt at adding yoga to your busy schedule, you will need to re-spawn your weapon.

To do this, you have got to stand your ground just one time against MiND's attacks. Will Power's force will resurge, and together, you shall reign supreme once again.

3. Self-Discipline fuels Will Power. Beware of alcohol consumption, over-eating and over-sleeping. While not an immediate liability, when indulged in regularly, Will Power will lose its mojo (to use the official term). Silence is where you will discover Will Power's lair. Visit often.

You are now armed and dangerous. Remember, with great power, comes great responsibility.

Our Sexy Sacral.

By Cassandra Alls

You are a moving tower of energy. No matter what your stature, there are seven major energy centers or *chakras* floating in our body. They run from our crown or head down to the base of our spine or root *chakra*. Our hands and feet are also strong energy centers.

The term and theory of *chakras* is rooted in ancient Hindu and Buddhist traditions. The *chakras* correspond to vital points in the physical body but are generally understood as being part of the ethereal body.

We are energy. When all our power cords are pumping out good mojo, we feel good, we look good, and we are pleasant to be around.

The sacral *chakra* swims with all of the emotions, giving and receiving desire, pleasure, sexual and passionate love, change, movement, assimilation of new ideas, health, family and tolerance. When it is in balance, everything flows, and you work in harmony and creatively with others.

The power center of the sacral *chakra* , the sacral plexus, resides about two inches below the beautiful belly button. It associates with the color orange, and its element is water. The organs and glands corresponding to this area are the ovaries, testicles, prostate, genitals, spleen, womb and bladder. The functions of this energy center are for procreation, assimilation of food, physical force, vitality and sexuality.

If the sacral *chakra* is out of balance, you may have symptoms in the physical area or the associated organs or glands. An overindulgence in food or sex, possible sexual difficulties, confusion, depression, jealously, envy, desire to possess, impotence, and uterine or bladder problems are all symptoms of this imbalance.

You know those gut feelings you may get from time to time? Well, they arise from the sacral plexus. It's the place where we either suppress our emotions or allow them to flow, tune into our gut instincts about situations and people, and unleash or shut down our sexual and creative energy forces.

Many have sacral *chakra* imbalances due to family, cultural and societal conditioning. Some people have been raised to let their emotions run wild, while others have been programed to believe that it's not *cool* to show emotion or share and honor one's feelings.

Some have learned to live in their heads, and not trusting their gut instincts, while others have their intuition turned on so high that they pick up emotions and energy from everyone around them. Other imbalances may be from current health conditions as well as sexual abuse that can block the energy flow.

This sexual energy center is not just about sex (not that there is anything wrong with that). It's a vital energy force that enlivens the body in every way, and can be harnessed for living life to the fullest with passion and purpose.

When we balance this second *chakra*, we feel comfortable expressing our own emotions. We trust our intuition, but don't use it to sift through everyone else's experiences, and we allow our sexual energy to flow, adding vitality and life force to our body.

To balance your *chakras* and your body as a whole, it is important to eat well (nutrient-dense foods), drink water, herbal teas, and a rainbow of fruits and vegetables. Orange foods are specifically suggested for the sacral *chakra*.

Exercise, like yoga, is recommended, and so is a meditation with your hands on your lower abdomen, while visualizing the color orange. You may also enjoy using essential oils such as Rose, Sandalwood or Ylang-Ylang for aromatherapy – either create a massage oil or put a few drops in your bath.

It's all about balance and going with the beautiful energetic flow of life.

Are you turned on?

Discovering Your Archetype: Are You a Princess or a Queen?

By Osmara Vindel

Swiss Psychotherapist, Carl Jung, was fascinated by the study of archetypes as collectively transmissible patterns of being that are present in individual psyches and in what Jung called the 'Collective Unconscious.'

Essentially, archetypes are the embodiment of collective personality traits and personas we all share. They're like the timeless characters we've seen on stage throughout history. Like a Halloween costume, we take on these traits as part of our identities without even knowing it.

Role playing is at the heart of the archetypical energies that have pervaded history. These roles of 'personalities' can be very useful in understanding ourselves and why we do what we do and why we are how we are; they are also very beneficial when learning how to understand others.

Here are a few "traditional" archetypes:

The Warrior
The Seductress
The Mystic
The Nurturer
The Trickster
The Victim
The Mother
The Addict
The Wounded Child

I believe we each have our own specific blend of archetypical traits and ways of being, and we also have access to each archetype over the course of our lives. For example, we have all (at one time or another) embodied the seductress, nurturer, victim, addict, etc. even though we may, at our core, be predominantly a warrior/mystic/wounded child blend.

I want to focus on two main archetypes now: the *Princess* and the *Queen*. Why? Because as modern-day women we are affected by the energies of these two very much. In my own quest for self-awareness and healing I have come face to face with both of these archetypes as I teeter back and forth from one to the other.

Accepting and understanding how I embody these energies is helping me heal what is screaming to be healed within so I may become the highest, most potent version of myself. (And isn't that what we were all born to do here?)

When we work with the power of archetypes we are better able to see our own patterns and stories. My hunch is that in one way or another, at some point in time you've exhibited any range of qualities pertaining to these two archetypes.

My goal here is to help you become aware of how you embody both the Princess and the Queen in your life. I want to help you uncover your blind spots and shed clarity on what is asking to be healed within you; I want you to reclaim your power by utilizing and working with the power of these archetypes.

The Princess.

The Princess energy has long pervaded our childhood psyche through fairy tales and Disney movies such as Sleeping Beauty and Rapunzel. It has pervaded our popular culture by labeling gals that come across as entitled or spoiled "a princess."

What does the princess archetype symbolize in us modern women? How does the Princess inside us manifest in our lives? When does she come out?

Princess energy can be characterized by the following traits:

- Dependent and needy... "Damsel in distress" awaiting her Knight in shining armor to arrive.
- Handles others and situations with an air of entitlement (*"I was born into this, therefore I deserve it."*) and may come across as "spoiled."

- Self-centered or self-absorbed… very much interested in how events affect her, often without regard or consideration for those around her.
- Diva-like tendencies and demanding energy.
- Bratty, whiny, and full of complaints.
- Oftentimes lacks gratitude and appreciation.
- Wants to be taken care of more than she wants to take care of others.
- Highly materialistically/superficially focused.
- Seems to have a lack of attention span for anything non-superficial, such as service and contribution.
- Wants (and demands) she be admired and stroked.
- Troubled or wounded in some way. (Though not always.)

Although the Princess inside us can be bratty, conniving, self-absorbed, and entitled, she can also be fun, vibrant, wondrous, and noble. Think of the endearing Princesses we adored as little girls: Cinderella, Snow White, and Ariel (Little Mermaid)… they were each gracious, beautiful, and even humble.

The thing I want you to remember is that we are in a dualistic reality, so each archetype possesses its light and dark side. As with everything, there are two sides of the coin. When you approach each trait from this perspective, even the ones we deem "negative" have actually served us in a positive light.

The question is: Is your Inner Princess aiding you in creating what you want? Or is the embodiment of this energy actually keeping you stuck, perpetuating the same patterns without expansion or growth?

The Queen.

Although the norm is that Princesses grow up to be Queens (the natural progression), it is not necessarily so when it comes to archetypes. Many times, the Princess stays stuck as the Princess for life.

How does a Princess become a Queen? When she desires to become the master of her domain more than she desires to live "the life."

A Regal Queen oozes a dignified, magnificent energy to her, which makes her a powerful magnetic force to be reckoned with. A Queen is more intrinsically driven as opposed to extrinsically driven. She values internal goals as opposed to the external ones (even though the external ones surround her very existence.)

Intrinsic Goals: Contribution, self-actualization, harmonious relationships, connection, community, compassion.

Extrinsic Goals: Recognition, admiration, status, fame, pleasure, material goods (money), physical beauty enhancement.

The following is a mix of light and dark traits that make up the Queenspace:

- Light side: The Regal Queen who is dignified, striking, awe-inspiring, brilliant, genius.
- Dark side: The Ice Queen who is numb, vengeful, envious, angry, control-freak, manipulative.
- Has authority and exercises it with discernment.
- Knows her limits and how far her authority takes her; consciously creates and follows right boundaries.
- Has a strong sense of duty and responsibility for the power bestowed upon her, especially when others form part of her domain.
- Somewhat isolated – cannot be accessible to all those who desire to be in her presence all of the time. (Few are the people who can relate to her high place of power.)
- Humble, yet, majestic.
- Powerful – not because of her "crown" but because that's just innately who she is.
- Possesses a deep confidence and wisdom, not because of her external value but because of who she is within.
- Strategic thinker and doer.
- Adored and admired by those who see her inner light; envied and judged by those who are uncomfortable with her inner light.

Like me, you too probably teeter between both these powerful archetypes. That's totally okay; both have much to teach us. Both are integral parts of our ultimate Becoming.

Summon forth your Queen. Feed her and nurture her daily so she can lead you to your highest achievements and contributions to this world.

You are worthy.

Nothing's Gonna Change Your World.

By Riikka Rajamaki

> *"Meditation hasn't got a damn thing to do with anything, 'cause all it has to do with is nothing. Nothingness. Okay? It doesn't develop the mind, it dissolves the mind. Self-improvement? Forget it, baby. It erases the self. Throws the ego out on its big brittle ass. What good is it? Good for nothing. Excellent for nothing. Yes, Lord, but when you get down to nothing, you get down to ultimate reality. It's then and exactly then that you're sensing the true nature of the universe, you're linked up with the Absolute, son, and unless you're content with blowing smoke up your butt all your life, there's the only place to be."*

~ Bobby Case

Meditation is a risky business. When you become really good at it, you may end up risking all your previous hard work and reputation. You drop your titles, your trainings, your need to prove you have been there and done that.

Why? Because when you get real with yourself, you get real with the world. All veils melt away and all that remains is only this: Space. No more here and there, just this. Nakedness. Nowhere to hide because there is nothing to hide. Nothing to prove because there is nothing to prove. Nowhere to go because there is nowhere to go, really. Just here.

Past and future disappear before they even enter the horizon. You try to grasp and it all slips away. You try to hold on to someone but they are gone. You try to manipulate something and it comes back and hits you right on your face. You want something so badly that it makes you throw up. And there you are, cleaning up the mess of your wanting.

Because you forgot that what you are wanting is only a future reflection of your current vibrational state.

Please do not go woo-woo on me.

It simply means that there is nothing out there in the world that cannot belong to you, but in order to have it, you need to match it, my love. You need to get out of your mind. You cannot give it form too soon, and you cannot define it too much. Pretend that you already have what you want, and find an energetic twin, or a version of that. It can show up as a color, a symbol or pure feeling tone. (Energy does not speak English.)

Once you get what it is, then be it. Step into it, embody it, and surround yourself with it. Dance with it. But please, I beg you, do not try to control it, manipulate it or make it yours too soon. Trust your powers. Only hold on to your intention of what you want, and as for the rest: drop it. Let it go.

Stop whining about things you do not have, because dear heart, you are being heard. It is already on its way. Do not ask for something and then change your mind.

Receive, baby. Open your arms and let yourself have it. All the way. To the deepest, softest, juiciest and ecstatic corner of your inner temple, open the door, for God's sake. Make some tea. Sit down and ask: can I pour you some, too?

We resist the present moment because there is not much that is happening in the present moment. It drives our mind nuts, because our mind wants to solve problems, and figure shit out. Thank God for that. But it gets tricky only if we think there is always something to figure out – kind of like if you were to think that you need to lie down under your car all day long, waiting and watching if something goes wrong, before you can go for a ride.

Let me get this clear: I am not talking about existential nihilistic nothing that sees life with no meaning, no purpose, and no point. I am not talking about a transparency a la Jean Baudrillard that has become borderline depressing, too dull and indifferent to leave any room for the divine presence to occupy the emptiness:

"The apocalypse is finished, today it is the precession of the neutral, of forms of the neutral and of indifference...all that remains, is the fascination for desertlike and indifferent forms, for the very operation ‘ of the system that annihilates us. Now, fascination (in contrast to seduction, which was attached to appearances, and to dialectical reason, which was attached to meaning) is a nihilistic passion par excellence, it is the passion

proper to the mode of disappearance. We are fascinated by all forms of disappearance, of our disappearance. Melancholic and fascinated, such is our general situation in an era of involuntary transparency.

~ Jean Baudrillard, Simulacra and Simulation, "On Nihilism," trans. 1995

I am talking about the kind of nothing where we go to discover our meaning, our true potential and reason for being. I am talking about the ultimate freedom from suffering, and from everything that we are not.

How do we do nothing in the culture that is full of everything? How do we access nothing in a society that worships bigger, better and faster? How do we stay still when we are surrounded by chaos? How do we replace indifference with neutrality? How do we learn to love without conditions when most of our agreements are built on conditions? How do we remain in the state of wonder without being swallowed by curiosity?

How can we become so passionate about God's love that your lover needs to knock on God's door before entering your Heart?

Right now, close your eyes, and find out how many thoughts, concepts and beliefs – yours or other people's – are shooting across your mind like you had built a freeway inside your head, available to host anybody and anything? How many? 10? 50? 1000?

Nothing is not about sitting around being useless, but being in full action, while being a host only to the guidance you receive directly from your own divine and authentic core. It is about being so empty that whenever something arises, you know it is something original, something uniquely you, something that is fully aligned with your magnificence. You have a filter system in your mind that recognizes what is yours and what is not.

And this takes practice. Yes, practice.

"I saw the angel in the marble and carved until I set him free"

~ Michelangelo

Just like David, you already have it all inside you. There is nothing out there that will fill your sense of lack. It is the chipping away of anything that is not you that will set you free.

But it is often that freedom itself that scares the shit out of us. So we keep resisting the one thing that could give us what we so desperately want.

May this guided meditation give you a glimpse of your own Nothing. Use it to hold onto your Nothing – because "it is the silence between the notes that makes the music; it is the space between the bars that holds the tiger." (Old Saying)

> *"But, if you have nothing at all to create, then perhaps you create yourself."*
>
> *~ Carl Jung*

Sitting, doing nothing, creating nothing.

Feeling useless, an outsider, a failure.

Been there.

Keep holding the tension between doing and not doing, dear one.

Somewhere between the two, a star is being born.

Abandon the Flock — 9 Tips for Unleashing the Human Within.

By Christian Ryd Hoegsberg

A wise woman once told me, "You live in a city of sheep, a country of followers." I didn't think much about it at the time. I live in a larger city in the so-called westernized part of Europe — a decent place to live by most people's standards. Education is free. So is healthcare. Unemployment is relatively low. So is crime. Why reproach my neighbors, or myself, for defending and following without question a system that makes this standard of living possible?

Nevertheless, a seed was planted in me.

I began to notice how people, myself included, would slip into defense mode, when the system that we had accepted and selected by election, our system, was questioned. But if every challenge of the system, be that of social norms or national legislation, is met with an automatic search for the best defense, instead of a search for the truth in the challenge, if every critique of the spoken and unspoken rules of society is beaten to the ground before it has the time to sink into people's consciousness, then who's going to notice the flaws? And there are always flaws. *In every system. In every matrix.*

Time and time again, the wise woman's words would echo in my mind. *City of sheep. Country of followers.*

In this globalized world, inspiration is available from all corners of the planet. We communicate with and influence people on the other side of the world almost as easily as with our neighbor. At the same time we grow in numbers and are drawn toward big cities. As we live increasingly close together both in the urban sense and through means of electronic communication, we risk sacrificing part of our individuality to consciously or unconsciously fit in with the pack.

Maybe that is what this wise woman meant. That overwhelming means with which we are able to influence each other makes it too easy for us to form a unified set of norms turning us into sheep, mindlessly following the same blueprint of life. That it requires intelligent resistance and willpower to pause, gather information and evaluate it, before deciding whether to adopt the goals and beliefs of our neighbors. But isn't that exactly what makes us human? This big brain of ours that is always the focus point when we need to point out what separates us humans from the rest of the animal kingdom?

9 tips for unleashing the human within:

1. Cherish your own individuality. There are many forces in modern society urging you to make life decisions that go against your inner wishes, pulling you in the direction of perceived safety and comfort away from objects of fear. You will be a happier person as well as a better son, daughter, sister, brother, wife, husband, girlfriend, boyfriend, dad, mom or friend, if you make sure that the outcome of these decisions are speaking to your own authentic desires.

2. Encourage the individuality of others (and they just might do the same to you). Avoid telling people what to be, but never stop asking into who they are. We are all different. It's only natural if we choose different directions.

3. Surround yourself with people of different beliefs. It might be more challenging to have friends that often disagree with you, but you'll learn something from it and they will learn something from you – even if you don't end up discovering common ground.

4. Make a living doing something you love. Don't let yourself be fooled into thinking that it's necessary for you to spend most of your waking hours doing something you dislike. Create a living that makes you want to get out of bed in the morning. It will make you more content. Your peers might not agree with your decision, but in the end, your joy will inspire them.

5. Seek out nature. The air is fresher there. The colors will please your eyes. It will clear your mind and offer you perspective. It will remind you how silly our norms and conventions can be.

6. Avoid being a victim of your own cause. Few things are as prone to instigate fruitless arguments as when we jump at little things and take them out of context to champion our own favorite cause, distancing us from the chance of understanding the original point that was made.

7. Nurture your creativity. Creativity has more than 6 billion faces. You don't have to take up painting or writing. Whatever sparks your creativity may not be easy to find. The matrix you live in (be it real or not) is designed to keep you safe and to keep you giving back to it, but it is not designed for you to give back through creative expression (in some ways creativity even represents opposition and competition to the matrix). Nevertheless, it is possible to use your creativity to give something back. You just have to make the effort of finding out how best to do so. Every living, thinking person has creative potential.

8. Move your body. We know that exercise keeps you healthy and even energizes you, but like being in nature it also liberates your mind. It takes you out of the zombie state and — when you're done exercising — leaves you with the energy and overview to make better decisions in other aspects of your life.

9. Take chances. To create something is to take a chance. It leaves you open for judgment. You don't have to take every chance you get, but be sure not to let them all pass by. There are no safe decisions. All decisions are a matter of life. Your life.

Whatever path you may choose, try to forget your fears and fill your mind with hope. Hope is powerful and hope is dangerous, but it can take you places. Fear is also powerful and fear is also dangerous, but it will keep you where you are.

So choose your path now while your mind is full of hope. The past is gone and the future is futile. The present is the only available time for action – the only available time to shed the woolen coat of the sheep and make use of the intelligent and creative mind of the human.

> *"I have heard what the talkers were talking, the talk of the beginning and the end, but I do not talk of the beginning or the end. There was never any more inception than there is now, nor any more youth or age than there is now; and will never be any more perfection than there is now, nor any more heaven or hell than there is now."*

> *~ Walt Whitman*

Shattered Reflections and Shifting Perceptions.

By Jim Fry

Have you been told, "I love u" … yet found it was actually conditional?

I find this quote the truest reflection of love, where we release the past, release expectations and allow the space for each other to be perfectly imperfectly ourselves…

> *"The beginning of love is the will to let those we love be perfectly themselves, the resolution not to twist them to fit our own image. If in loving them we do not love what they are, but only their potential likeness to ourselves, then we do not love them: we only love the reflection of ourselves we find in them."*
>
> *~ Thomas Merton*

when we look within
and find ourselves within our abyss
habitually withdrawing from deepest recognitions
as we tell ourselves, & each other, stories & myths

yet as we dive, even further
propelled by both surrender & courage
juxtaposed into a synergy fueled by our very souls

there is nowhere to hide
from the intensity of our truths
as we recognize the deep hypnotic trances
by which we've allowed ourselves to be entrained
while we engage in relations, with each & all, entertained

unmasked and without shelter
we feel our abraded hearts & minds
from lifetimes of skirmishes within ourselves
always, we have the potential to transform

as we remember & return to states
of consciousness fueled by intent
as we embrace & create
in love, with magick*
with magick*
in love

magi
imagine
imagination
transformation
transform
form

Blessed Be Your Longing. Your Endless Ache. Your Sharp Crystal Shatter. Your Sea Glass Heart.

By Jeanette LeBlanc

Blessed be the long, slow slide into desire. The swift plunging wound to the heart. The bleeding out onto the kitchen floor.

Blessed be the fierce of want and the howl of despair and the swan dive of surrender. Blessed be the indignation of right and the never more naked of wrong. Blessed be your strong smooth body and your roadmap of scars and brittle bones that give way under the weight of lives unlived.

Blessed be the unmet passion, the relentless boredom, the absolute certainty of regret.

Blessed be the sweet laughter. The hard fuck. The bitter fight. The soft of impossible forgiveness. Blessed be the restless seeker. The relentless urgency. The unanswered call. Blessed be the giving up. The hope unraveled. The void at the end. The clenched fists and the desperate grasping and the way it all slides away when the time comes.

Blessed be your trembling breath and your strong knees. Blessed be your siren song and your briny tears and your frantic prayer. Blessed be your violin body, your electric hipbone, your staircase ribs.

Blessed be your slaughtered dreams and your cynical projection. Blessed be your fire of initiation and your ritual of comfort. Blessed be your secret shame. Blessed be your whispered confession. Blessed be your primal roar.

Blessed be the rejection. The hollowed out, disregarded heart. Blessed be the end of the rope, the absence of expectation, the way it all gives way eventually.

Blessed be the blood and guts and gore of it all. Blessed be the emptiness of lust and the brutal havoc of love and the way peace grows in between cracks in cement.

Blessed be the dirty street corner hustle and the pretty surface of things and where they meet in the most sacred center. Blessed be the harsh divinity. The winged flight. The salt skin. The symphony of lust.

Blessed be the holy and the worship. Blessed be the sacred mother. Blessed be the faithless edges. Blessed be the ritual of liturgy and agnostic faith. Blessed be the profane and the provocation. Blessed be the solitary pilgrimage and the long journey home. Blessed be the one who contains herself. Blessed be the truth that demands reckoning and the goodbye that wrenches long held secrets from behind closed lips.

Blessed be the sucker punch bruises. Blessed be smooth slide of sun behind the mountains. Blessed be the wise desert and the pounding sea. Blessed be the sweet swell of words. The silent spaces between bodies. The ragged sigh of breath on bone.

Blessed be the poet and the poem and the one between them who has no words of her own. Blessed be the plagiarism, the thievery, the rash disregard for origin, the gratitude for the beginning of things. Blessed be our free fall into destiny. Our slow burn. Our consuming fire.

Blessed be the breaking and becoming. Blessed be the ugly. Blessed be the sweet sin. Blessed be the rage. Blessed be the grace.

Blessed be. Blessed be. Blessed be.

In the end, all words are just another way to say Amen.

10 Tips to Keep an Open Heart from Breaking Every Day.

By Tanya Lee Markul & Laurana Wong

"How do you keep an open heart from breaking every day?" she whispered sweetly from inside the cardboard box labeled Lost & Found that was sitting on my doorstep.

It was dark out, I could not see inside, but the peculiarity of that gentle voice emanating from within those four walls felt warm and familiar.

Her warmth radiated out from inside her little shelter. She needed me. (I couldn't tell if I were dreaming or not.)

I reached my hands slowly inside and felt for, for whatever was connected to that voice. That angelic sound, it was like the gentlest, saddest stroke of a harp combined with the sweet note of a chime hanging in heaven that sang when invited by even the softest wind.

My fingers reached slowly in to find two warm pockets between her naked under arms and the delicate sides of her ribcage. I lifted her up as gently as I could.

As I held her, she kept her eyes closed and her head on my shoulder. She felt like a warm, soft pillow in my arms. She was weightless and she contorted right into the fibers of my being without any force, without even a hint of resistance.

As I walked her inside, she whispered, "I've been feeling fragile lately." Funny enough, I had noticed the sticker on the lid of her box that read, *Fragile Handle With Care.*

I am a little lost. I am a little found. I stand looking at myself inside the box hidden, broken, hurt and scared. I peer out at myself standing outside of the box aware, grounded, not fearful, and steady. We are one.

As much as I am angry, hurt and heart-broken, I am also strong, courageous, forgiving and open to love, and… I am (we are) fragile, so please, handle with care.

How do you keep an open heart from breaking every day? Here are ten tips from within and outside the box:

1. Remember that you are a lantern, a flashlight, a watchtower in the dark. There is no need to react (ever) with fear or anger. You have the courage to reach inside the box. You have the courage to be held.

2. Care for yourself. An open heart may suffer because you have moved it into dangerous territory. Not every situation requires your sacrifice. Certain types of giving move you too far from center.

3. Remember the Universal laws of compassion. Be and react with pure honesty but also non-violently and with a heart overflowing with forgiveness like our friend Gandhi, 'be the change you want to see in the world' add a sprinkle of that guy Jesus, 'forgive them for they know not what they do.'

4. Sing and dance every day.

5. Open up your heart to love beyond your imagination. Make it a daily practice. Go beyond surface-level, default poisons (greed, anger, fear, delusion and yes, even ignorant bliss).

6. Love Life itself, and all the experiences it contains. The pains, the cruelties, the joys and triumphs. They are all part of being alive. To love means loving indiscriminately. To love deeply means to expand.

7. Move past the masterful illusory of the mind and its magnificent abilities to distract you from the present moment. Instead of living in a constant parallel universe of the angry past and the worried future, spend more time right here and now.

8. Realize that some people aren't equipped to receive the full force of your love. To send it to them may throw their world into chaos. Love these people gently, with your understanding instead of your passion. And know that there are always people who receive you, in full.

9. Don't be attached to outcomes, or try to control or force them either. Being the best you that you can be, sincerely, compassionately, creatively, is doing your part. You don't need to do more than that. Let the reaction of the people around you be spontaneous, mysterious, magical and something that is intuitively gained. (We can't force anyone to love us or to feel love.)

10. Accept that sometimes your heart's just gonna break. It's okay to let it.

30 Questions to Ask Yourself Before You Die.

By Andréa Balt

> *"Rather than money, than fame, than love…give me truth."*
>
> *~ Thoreau*

I woke up this morning and my life clock marked 30. My first sleep-deprived idea was to pack a small suitcase, get on the first train, move to another country, change my name, change my hair color (or get plastic surgery if needed), and start from scratch. When I don't know how to deal with life, I hide sometimes. And others, I fight it.

By now, I'm good at both: fighting and disappearing. I'm old enough to be acquainted with life's darkest and most elevated places, and young enough to take more. But there's no merit to either, fighting or flying, if they don't come as a result of one's deepest truth. When fueled by fear (a.k.a. lies we've been forced to believe before our reason kicked in) both responses are cowardly, both are equally wrong.

A true warrior doesn't feel forced to do either, but moves through and with and for life, like water.

So after I washed my face and considered the costs of running and those of fighting, I decided to do neither and have some juice instead. And I started contemplating a third alternative.

We are a constant process, an event, we're change.

Our life is the house, the rest are just projections, shadows of the greater structure: even our deepest thoughts, beliefs, you, me and everything and everyone we've ever known, are subject to interpretation. All our constructions of reality, all the words and ideas we use to understand the world are fragile and temporary, they are a medium, they're not the end, but just another way to understand the journey of Us.

As such, our smaller houses, our temporary homes can only be made of cards. And the I-don't-know is the most powerful ground you could lay your house of cards on. Because it allows you to adapt to any unexpected changes and even to pick up those cards when the smallest, sudden movement, brings down any of your structures.

Loving the questions means to love yourself. You are the biggest question mark the world (your world) has ever known.

I'm embarrassed about what different alien species might think of us from outer space. You know, if they actually watched Human Reality TV on their Martian screens:

"I don't get this dramatic species, Rango," says a green-skinned, 2.5 meter tall, half-lizard, half-nymph, flying-lady with robot voice and snake orange eyes. "They go to the bloodiest ends to come up with the most elaborate answers about life, yet they forgot the most basic, liberating act their 5-year olds still practice: the simple art of asking. The wonder, Rango, they have lost the wonder. They love to talk about life, as if this could somehow excuse them from living it." Rango nods and snorts green cosmic powder.

So here is an exercise we can do together: a tweak to your usual bucket list. Some 30 questions you and I should ask ourselves (hopefully) before we die. Grab your journal. Turn this into a self-inquiry practice. You'll be surprised at all the subterranean world that comes out of you. And it might just save your life by bringing it into the *right* perspective: ahem…yours.

There is no truth other than your truth – as long as you exist. Somebody else's won't do. And you know how most doors are opened? Not by struggling to find the right keys. All you have to do is knock.

Today, 30 years after "I" started happening, I'd like to re-evaluate the meaning of life and knock on doors I don't have a key for. Maybe my higher self will open and we will sit and chat, and in between one aha and another, we'll have a sip of truth that feels like home.

Warning: You may have already answered or are in the process of answering some of these questions. If so, a bit of repetition will only help you get clearer with yourself. If not, they should be in our elementary school curriculum. But most of us get to 30, 40, 60… or even spend our entire lives as strangers to ourselves. So shall we get re-introduced?

1. How much have you loved? Count the people. Add it up. When it comes to love, I've always felt in red numbers. I've been so focused on the minuses – all of them based on the not-enoughness, the virus most of us suffer from, the glass half-empty, the "but" – the "won't" – the "can't" – the "don't" – the "what if."

So if you're in red numbers too, let's put the ball back in our court. How much have *you* loved? Have you loved even when it hurts, when you can't, when you shouldn't, when you wouldn't, when you didn't – just because love is a verb, not a noun, and it's the hardest, most beautiful gift of life? If so, you're richer than you feel.

2. What do you love doing that you aren't doing? Furthermore, how could you get paid for doing what you love? Let's brainstorm. It's your right to be alive every second of the day. You're not supposed to spend eight hours a day in chains and the remaining four getting high on mental and physical distraction in order to cope with the depression of not doing what you should, what you really want, what you need to be doing.

3. What person or type of person would you choose as a life companion? A witness to your life? Forget the shoulds / the can'ts / the won'ts / the impossibles. Who would you love and who would love you back if you could have a say in it? Because see, your say in this makes all the difference. When you say your dreams out loud, you turn on the engine. It's like this whole unlived, abundant life is waiting to come rushing out of you and in wishing it – out loud – you open the gates and give it permission to happen.

4. Where do you want to live? Are you happy with your life where you are? Could you be happier somewhere else? It's true that you can be home wherever you are. But it's also true that some places are more in tune with the kind of life that comes bursting out of you. There's nothing more inspiring and motivating than good company and an environment that reflect and support your mission.

5. What do you want to accomplish? And most importantly, why – what's your motivation? Be unrealistic. Life itself is unrealistic. Your very existence is as random, impossible and unrealistic as it gets. Only unrealistic people accomplish extraordinary things.

6. What do you want to be remembered by? Write it down. This is the man / the woman who _____. Take your time.

7. What kind of life would make you jealous? And why? If you could start over, what would your life look like, right now? (psst…you can – but shh, don't let your doubts in on this yet – they're gonna ruin everything).

8. What adventures do you want to have? Can you list five? Adventures aren't just for children – or maybe the 10-year old in us never dies. And it's that inner child that really loves and lives life for what it is: the greatest adventure in the universe.

9. If you had to add something to humanity, what would your contribution be? List at least one. The world doesn't owe you. You owe the world. The good news is that whatever the answer to this question, you'll enjoy doing it. Your mission is encrypted in your blueprint.

10. What are your ghosts? Your unspoken demons? The stuff you keep in your closet under a lock? What are you most deeply afraid of? Say it out loud. Get real with yourself. It's how you conquer them.

11. What are your favorite memories? Can you picture four or five instances in your childhood you are fond of? Do you see a river running through them? What's that river, that common denominator, the deepest statement about you and life that lies at the core of them? There is usually only one – or two life-altering statements that come up when you dig.

Get to the bottom of it. How can you live from that same belief now? How can you transform your current experiences so they begin with that same idea – that fueled your most cherished childhood memories?

12. Who do you love the most? What 10 people would you put on a lifeboat in case of a universal tsunami / asteroid / zombie attack or any other *realistic* end of the world? Make a list. You can have a million friends on Facebook, but at the end of the day, you're lucky if you can find 10 people you would die for and who would die for you. Email them as soon as you can. Remind them that if the world ends tomorrow, they'd be on your lifeboat.

Truth is…you never know if the world will end tomorrow. At least for you. And human beings are the most forgetful animals. Do you eat, drink and sleep every day? Then love everyday too.

13. What worries you the most? Why? Worry comes from fear. And most fear is imaginary. Fear of the Thing is not the Thing itself. Learn to distinguish one from the other. It's as simple as asking Why.

So what are you worried about? List even the most trivial worries, they're a projection of a deeper fear. And if any of these worries came true, do you think you could survive? And if the answer is No, then all the more reason to enjoy the world before it ends (and not worry about dead *or dying* ends).

14. What type of people inspire you and make you come alive? What people – at this point in your life – add to the truest equation of You? Reach out to them, get closer, "touch" them, spend time with them, be around them…Aliveness is the one virus you always need to catch.

15. What type of people bring you down and make you hate yourself? Break up with them. Today. It's not rejection, it's just selection. Life is short. You can't invest your love in people who don't want it and who use it to deplete you.

Love is the most elevated, beautiful transaction between two creatures. But it's still a transaction. The whole of nature is transaction: a give and take.

When one is missing, the cycle is interrupted, the fire swallows all the oxygen and you burn out. We each have a choice – to give and to take love – and whether we are aware of it or not, we choose the people we give to and take from. You are responsible for your heart's investments.

16. Who are your mentors? What have they taught you? Can you make a list? If you know them personally, thank them? Writers, thinkers, teachers, people who've shown you the way at some point, and the beautiful mystery of life made sense in their hands. Inspiration is contagious. It fuels you up.

You owe them a mention on your lips and in your heart; and you must pay it forward and become a way-shower to someone else.

17. What is your cosmic elevator pitch? Not your job description, not your professional bio, not your resume, not your About page. But if you got in an elevator on a spaceship that tours the galaxy and you could say anything you wanted about yourself, what would you tell your elevator mates?

In short, who are you – raw, unedited, wild, ordinary and extraordinary you? What does it come down to? And why? (Always, that goddamn solid why).

18. What issues can you help with? We're in trouble as a planet, as a species, as a global community, and as individuals. It's not a choice, actually. If you want to live here, you need to pay the toll of helping out, or your so-called-living won't be more than a selfish idea of living.

Interdependence is the new Independence. In order to make it real, you have to help clean up the mess others have made. Don't worry, so will others help clean yours. It's how it goes with humans. They mirror each other, for better or worse.

19. How can you express yourself creatively? Starting with the belief that we are all creative animals by nature, what's your medium? Don't think about profit, think only of how you can recycle your demons and become a channel for truth.

Art (any kind) speaks directly to the heart. It doesn't go through reason. They are two parallel languages. You need to speak Art if you want to understand Heart. So pick a medium and start practicing.

20. How do you manage your time? What works for you? If you're a mess, how can you get it together? Can you make a schedule, write down your routine (to help you stick to it), come up with a productivity manifesto of some sort?

21. What makes you come alive? What ignites you? What makes you forget time, and space, and love, and food and water and even why – if taken to extreme? As Charles Bukowski put it, "Find out what you love and let it kill you." (Or resurrect you.)

22. What are your most painful memories? Are you still replaying them in your mind and using them as an excuse to fuel your fear of getting hurt again? Do you think they might be keeping you from trusting your heart again?

23. If you were to leave the world today, what's your manifesto? What would you tell your children if you were forced to abandon them unexpectedly? Tell them now (even if you don't have children). You do actually, we're all inextricably interconnected to each other – in ways beyond our wildest imagination, and every child born on this planet is also a bit yours.

24. Why do you eat the way you eat and the things you eat? What do you think you should you eat that you're not eating – and why? What can you put in your body that gives you pleasure and also respects and nourish it? If you don't know, can you find out? Google it, read books, take a nutrition course, a cooking class, an online support program, hire a health counselor, do whatever it takes to get to know your body's needs and then give it what it's really asking for.

Your cells are made from the very food you eat. What you eat is the most important physiological aspect of your aliveness. You can't honor life through your work, mission, relationships (you name it), if you don't eat what gives you life.

25. What ignites your brain? What turns your light bulb on? Can you add more of that to your everyday? Get smarter? Train your brain? Evolve? Don't waste your precious time on meaningless entertainment that numbs your mind and makes you smaller. It's later than you think.

26. What physical exercise makes you sweat it like you mean it and enjoy both, the process and the afterward feeling? If you're not currently practicing it, can you read more about it, surround yourself with people who practice it, sign up for a class, do whatever will motivate you to practice it?

27. What does your body need in order to function at its best? Can you make a list of what makes you feel healthiest and function optimally and try to practice it every day? If you're not sure, start experimenting. Your 100% is just a little higher than your 80% but it makes a lifetime impact.

28. What feeds your spirit? What gives you goosebumps? What makes you fall down to your knees in awe (and weep)? Is it god? Religion? The universe? Science? Starry nights? Philosophy? Nature? Music? Art? It has to be higher than a person (than you), and surpass your understanding. There is no awe without mystery.

29. What are you proud of so far? What have you accomplished? Don't compare yourself to others. There will always be someone who's done "more" and some who's done "less." But what can you, at this point in your life (your circumstances, your reality), give yourself a hug for? Do it.

30. Fast-forward to your epitaph. What does it say? As a place-holder, let's paraphrase Jack Kerouac:

"They lived and loved and asked, blessed and adventured...and they weren't sorry."

Question 31 (I don't like even numbers): What is the meaning of life?

To sit and have a drink with life, and ask her things, and hear your own heart (usually ignored) echo your larger-than-life answers in your chest? To realize that you're rich solely because you have a universe inside you that you can reach at any given moment – a world that will shrink and expand on your command? Yes. That.

There is no meaning outside of You that won't take Your deepest, greatest truth in consideration. Fuck money, fame or *love* if they don't come as a result of your life-driving truth – they are the roof to your inner house, and to add a roof you must first discover, understand and create that house. And if you don't know where to start building, just ask.

Life is an endless flow of questions – meaning is always in the making and it is constantly being created as we speak. The ultimate meaning of life then, is the One that creates meaning: the traveler (not the journey), the subject (not its objects, ideas, circumstances, possessions), the lover (not the love), the way-seer (not the way), the warrior (not the battle)...

You.

An Additional Thank You

To all the creative and talented rebelles who made this past year what it was: extraordinary.

These artists, alchemists, healers, poets and creativists have also contributed with a creative footprint on Rebelle Society's fertile ground and have a treasured place in our hearts…

Adebayo Akomolafe, Anna Ingham, Aparna Khanolkar, April Norris, Atreyee Gupta, B Willing James, Bartholomeus Nicolaas Engelbertus, Beth Gillespie, Birgitte Gorm Hansen, Bob Weisenberg, Brandon Snell, Dana Damara, Edith Lazenby, Eric Vogt, Eva Hermogenes, Franz Andrini, Genevieve DuBois, Gerald Saluti, Hilary Lindsay, James Abro, James Clear, Jamie Glowacki, Javed Hassan, Jaycee Gossett, John McAndrew, Julie Garcia, Katarina Silva, Katie Gutierrez, Kris Oster, Lauren Foster, Lone Morch, Magdalena Larsson, Mamaste, Margaret Ward, Marilyn Harding, Mary Ann Cherry, Mary Long, Marylisa DeDomenicis, Melanie Imhoff, Melissa Rubin, Michelle Alva, Mushk Hoor, Naganath, Nanna Wagner Nielsen, Niki Driscoll, Peter Yates, Rachelle Smith Stokes, Rebecca Butler, Ruby Bernardo, Seth Newfeld, Sheila Jaillet, Shawnee Thornton, Shayne Laughter, Silvi Alcivar, Susanna Harwood Rubin, Sze Huei Yek, Tabatha Kirke, Tet Gallardo, Tom Grasso, Tori Elfstrom, Yulady Saluti, Zoe Quiney …and last, but never least, to the talented Robert Sturman, artist & photographer and long-time Rebelle friend & supporter.

***

If you'd like to join the creative rebellion as a guest writer or a columnist, please check out our publishing guidelines on RebelleSociety.com and send us your submission to: create@rebellesociety.com.

About the Authors

Alison Nappi believes that mental health crises are opportunities to become aware of our own natures. She coaches writers finding their prolific voices. Connect: writewithspirit.com.

Andréa Balt is Co-Founder of rebellesociety.com & rebellewellness.com. She is also a writer, creativity curator & wellness alchemist. Connect: andreabalt.com, Facebook, Twitter @andreabalt & Instagram @creativerehab.

Amber Shumake is a writer, yogi, teacher, student, miracle hunter, fear stalker & royal illuminator. Connect: ambershumake.com, Facebook, Twitter & Instagram @ambershumake.

Anja Bergh is a yoga-teacher, community space-holder, writer & lover of great natural beauty! Snowflakes make her smile. Connect: yogabuddhi.se.

Anjana Love Dixon *at a glance is ethereal. In our world she is a writer, musician, artist, actress, universe maker & dream catcher. Connect: theanjananetwork.net.*

Anna Mattinger *is scrambling sideways on a pilgrimage to nowhere in particular, aiming to sample everything until she's done. Connect: debonairdirtbag.blogspot.com & debonairdirtbag@gmail.com.*

Braja Sorensen *is an author (Lost & Found in India, 2013), writer for several magazines worldwide & soon to be crowned Queen of India (no, really). Connect: brajasorensen.com.*

Caitlin Marcoux *is a mother, yoga teacher, writer, breast cancer survivor & creator of Strong Girls Yoga. Connect: caitlinmarcoux.net & Instagram @caitlinmarcoux.*

Cameron Shayne *is a guru killer, primate provocateur, literary warrior & yoga liberator. Connect: cameronshayne.com & budokon.com.*

Carolyn Elliott, *PhD, is a sought-after creativity & desire coach for magical people. She's the celebrated author of Awaken Your Genius: A Seven-Step Path to Freeing Your Creativity & Manifesting You Dreams. Connect: awesomeyourlife.com.*

Carolyn Riker *is a writer & teacher. She's working on her first children's book. Connect: Facebook @carolynriker.*

Cassandra Alls *is an organic goddess, soldier of love, healer, plant based foodie, activist, writer, rebel & spiritual junkie. Connect: about.me/holisticdiva.*

Catherine Ghosh is an artist, mother & bhakti yogini since 1986. Co-Founder of The Secret Yoga Institute & Women's Spiritual Poetry. Connect: secretyoga.com & Facebook @thesecretyoga.

Chantele Theroux is a writer, rolling with it to rock her own balance. Get down & dirty with her in life's beautiful mess. Connect: chanteletheroux.com.

Chantelle Jahara Pinto is an Australian writer living in Rio de Janeiro. Her passion lies in the pursuit of higher dimensions of health & spiritual evolution. Connect: yogaleaks.com.

Chris Grosso is the author of Indie Spiritualist: A No Bullshit Exploration of Spirituality. Connect: theindiespiritualist.com, Facebook, Twitter @XchrisGrossoX & YouTube @ drawingstatic.

Christian Ryd Hoegsberg is the CFO & Business Manager for rebellesociety.com. He is also a writer, sports enthusiast, lover & in pursuit to reveal his true creative potential. Connect: Facebook @christianrydhoegsberg & christian@rebellesociety.com.

Elise Museles is an attorney turned eating psychology & nutrition expert, Founder of Kale & Chocolate & creator of The Good Enough Quiz. A self-proclaimed "recovering perfectionist," she shows women how to loosen the reins, bend the rules, and experience true satisfaction. Connect: kaleandchocolate.com, Facebook & Twitter: @kaleandchocolate.

Hannah Coakley is a learner, an explorer, a loyal friend & a relentless optimist. Connect: hannah.coakley@gmail.com.

Jeanette LeBlanc is a writer, photographer & inspirationalist. She teaches one-on-one coaching, online classes & in-person intensives. Connect: peacelovefree.com.

Jeannie Page is an inspirational writer & yogi striving to create positive change in the world. Connect: jeanniepage.com & Twitter @jeannienpage.

Jenn Grosso is an artist & writer who plays host to the fleeting dance of shadows & light. Connect: perilsoftheliving.com, Facebook @perilsoftheliving, Instagram & Twitter @jenn_grosso.

Jessica Durivage-Kerridge is a new mama, teacher, speaker & head guru in charge at whereismyguru.com. Connect: jessica@whereismyguru.com, Facebook & Twitter @whereismyguru.

Jessica Hesser nurtures healing & creates a sacred space for people to experience their own Divinity through her writing, yoga & shamanic energy healing work. Connect: mantrasandmiracles.com, Facebook @personaltrainernaples & jessicahessertrainer@gmail.com.

Jim Fry *is a gypsy scribe & Rebelle, seeking to parlay words with ultimate magick, to narrate & reflect, our stories.*

Kirk Hensler *likes to write stories that will make you cry, train ballet, box, & boss people around. Connect: kaleandcigarettes.com, Facebook, Twitter & Instagram @kirkhensler.*

Kris Carter *is a Kriyaban yogi, Father of 3, & writer & speaker on Inspired Business. Grab his free multimedia manifesto "The Framework" at thisepiclife.com.*

Kristi Stout *is a loving and deep spiritualist, inquisitive adventurer & die-hard dreamer. She writes on many formats. Connect: kristilstout.com, thequestofheart.com, Facebook @KristiLStout & kristi@rebellesociety.com.*

Laurana Wong *is best, taken hot. She might destroy your world, when all she meant to do was to love you. Connect: lauranawong.com.*

Long Distance Love Bombs *are trying to make the world better than it was yesterday. Connect: bloglongdistancelovebombs.com, Facebook @longdistancelovebombs & Pinterest @ LDLBLDLB.*

Macaile Hutt *is a lover of life, excavator of beauty, spelunker of hearts, weaver of dreams into inspirational flights of literary delight. Connect: takeyourheart.com*

Matthew Foor *is a professor of Party Science at the University of Party Hard, (in Outer Space). He is a world-traveler, renowned smoothie mixologist & inappropriate humor enthusiast. Connect: via smoke-signal & ESP.*

Melissa Smith *is a mother, writer, 500 E-RYT, founder of Grace Yoga and Grace Yoga Retreats currently with one foot in Texas and the other in Kuala Lumpur teaching yoga therapy, Thai yoga massage, and AcroYoga. Connect: melissasmithyoga.com.*

Osmara Vindel *is Founder of The Butterfly Club, author of The Unleashing & a transformational thought leader. Connect: butterflyclubtribe.com, osmara.com & Facebook @osmara.vindel.*

Patricia Biesen *is a health coach, blogger & visual artist. Connect: patriciabiesen.com, Facebook & Twitter @patriciabiesen.*

Patrick Linder *is an award-winning novelist & regular contributor to rebellesociety.com. His Seattle-based mystery Ghost Music is available at Amazon & Barnes & Noble. Connect: patricklinderbooks.com.*

Ramanjit Garewal *is a Yogi, writer, troublemaker, lover & spiritual healer. Connect: ramanjitg@yahoo.co.in, Facebook & Twitter @ramanjitgarewal.*

Rasmus Hammarberg *is a poet, a writer, a believer in creativity & peace. Connect: thenakedandthetrue.tumblr.com, Facebook @rasmus.hammarberg & Twitter @mrrhammarberg.*

Richard LaRosa *is a writer, actor, bodyworker & fervent Shakespeare enthusiast. He has been writing for rebellesociety.com since August 2012. (Photo © Victoria Trujillo deMontrond shutterp&emonium.net.)*

Riikka Rajamaki *is a lover, certified Spirit Coach®, masseuse & Founder of The Daily Nothing. Connect: riikkarajamaki.com & Facebook @thedailynothing.*

Sarah Voldeng *is a writer, mother & lover with a rebel heart. She is a nutritionist & Founder of absolutelynutrition.com.*

Saran Kaur *is a channel, healer, spiritual counselor & Kundalini Yoga teacher. She teaches & works internationally with spiritual communication & empowerment technologies. Connect: sarankaur.com, YouTube @piasaranpreetkaur, Facebook @sarankaurcom & saran@sarankaur.com.*

Skip Maselli *is a shape shifter, reposeful executive, belletristic writer, quixotic father, vagabond gnostic, & a drunkard at the tavern door. Connect: phosphorimental.blogspot.com, Facebook & Twitter @proseplay.*

Shasta Townsend *is a storyteller, wild card & lover of life, She teaches the power of true connection as a catalyst to innate wholeness & happiness. Connect: shastatownsend.com.*

Shavawn M. Berry *lives to write. A portfolio of her work is available at shavawnberry.contently.com. Connect: Facebook @shavawnmidoriberry & Twitter @shavawnb.*

Simone Datzberger *researches, writes about peace building, development & various other topics that prey on her mind. She loves yoga & socializes around the world.*

SR Atchley *is a writer, artist & dreamer. She also works behind the scenes as a talent recruiter for rebellesociety.com.*

Tanya Lee Markul *is Co-Founder of rebellesociety.com & rebellewellness.com. Devoted yoga student & teacher, writer, creativist, wellness alchemist & love warrior. Connect: tanya@rebellesociety.com, Facebook & Twitter @tanyamarkul.*

Thomas Lloyd Qualls *is a writer, novelist, videographer, bike rider, painter, foot massager, & sometimes salvager of lives. Connect: tlqonline.com.*

Tracy Wisneski *is managing editor at rebellesociety.com. She is also a dream weaver, a freelance writer, editor & social media specialist. Connect: Facebook @tracy.wisneski.*

Victoria Erickson *is based in Austin, TX. Victoria leads creative writing workshops & is a holistic esthetician, massage therapist & reiki practitioner. Connect: victoriaerickson.com, Facebook @VLE1031 & Pinterest @victorialynn756.*

Valerie Gangas *Valerie Gangas is a meditator, speaker, author, spiritual rebel & life coach. She invites you to step out of your existing patterns & start experiencing the miracles that life has to offer. Take a journey within with Wonderlust Living at valeriegangas.com. Connect: Facebook & Twitter @valeriegangas.*

Zofia Cartlidge *is an adventurer, writer & yogi. Her favorite things are words, open skies & leaps of faith. Connect: wordsbybabybird.com.*

Made in the USA
San Bernardino, CA
09 December 2015